Insects of Newfoundland & Labrador

STOUTS, MILLERS, & FORKY-TAILS

CHAPMAN | DIXON | PARSONS | WHITNEY

Library and Archives Canada Cataloguing in Publication

Chapman, Tom, author

Stouts, millers, and forky-tails : insects of Newfoundland and Labrador / Tom Chapman, Peggy Dixon, Carolyn Parsons, Hugh Whitney.

Includes bibliographical references and index.
ISBN 978-1-927099-95-7 (softcover)

1. Insects--Newfoundland and Labrador--Identification. I. Dixon, Peggy, author II. Parsons, Carolyn, author III. Whitney, Hugh, author IV. Title.

QL476.3.N6C53 2018   595.709718   C2018-900155-0

© 2019 Tom Chapman, Peggy Dixon, Carolyn Parsons, Hugh Whitney

Design and layout: Tanya Montini
Editor: Stephanie Porter
Copy editor: Iona Bulgin
Printed in Canada

Excerpts from this publication may be reproduced under licence from Access Copyright, or with the express written permission of Boulder Publications Ltd., or as permitted by law. All rights are otherwise reserved and no part of this publication may be reproduced, stored in a retrieval system, or transmitted in any form or by any means, electronic, mechanical, photocopying, scanning, recording, or otherwise, except as specifically authorized.

We acknowledge the financial support of the Government of Newfoundland and Labrador through the Department of Tourism, Culture, Industry and Innovation.

We acknowledge the financial support for our publishing program by the Government of Canada and the Department of Canadian Heritage through the Canada Book Fund.

Insects of Newfoundland & Labrador

STOUTS, MILLERS, & FORKY-TAILS

CHAPMAN | DIXON | PARSONS | WHITNEY

BOULDER
BOOKS

CONTENTS

Preface 6

Introduction 12

How to Use This Book 20

The Insects:
    Hymenoptera: Ants, Bees, and Wasps 28

    Diptera: Flies 76

    Siphonaptera: Fleas 108

    Coleoptera: Beetles 110

    Neuroptera: Lacewings 154

    Trichoptera: Caddisflies 156

    Lepidoptera: Butterflies and Moths 158

    Hemiptera: True Bugs 240

    Thysanoptera: Thrips 256

    Psocodea: Lice 260

    Orthoptera: Crickets and Grasshoppers 266

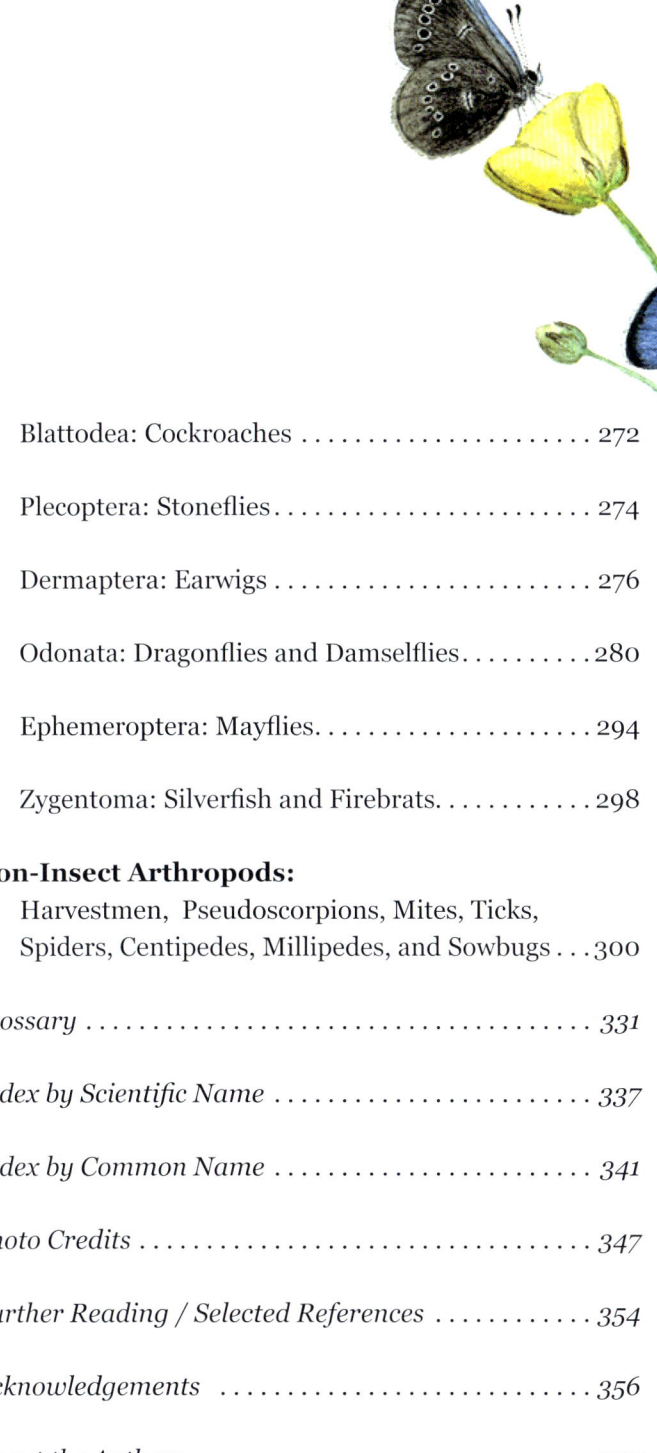

    Blattodea: Cockroaches 272

    Plecoptera: Stoneflies 274

    Dermaptera: Earwigs 276

    Odonata: Dragonflies and Damselflies 280

    Ephemeroptera: Mayflies 294

    Zygentoma: Silverfish and Firebrats 298

Non-Insect Arthropods:
    Harvestmen, Pseudoscorpions, Mites, Ticks,
    Spiders, Centipedes, Millipedes, and Sowbugs . . . 300

Glossary *331*

Index by Scientific Name *337*

Index by Common Name *341*

Photo Credits *347*

Further Reading / Selected References *354*

Acknowledgements *356*

About the Authors *357*

PREFACE

> *[T]he species richness of insects is so great that, to a near approximation, all organisms can be considered to be insects.*
> —P.J. Gullan and P.S. Cranston,
> *The Insects: An Outline of Entomology*

Approximately 1 million species of insects have been described to date. Are there only 1 million on the planet? No way. In 250 years of cumulative effort we have fallen far short of a complete inventory. One extrapolation puts the total number of species as high as 80 million, while others put it at a more moderate 4 to 6 million. These creatures occupy the most hostile conditions on our planet, from the hottest to the coldest, the wettest to the driest, and the tops of the mountains to the margins of the oceans.

To document each insect species on the planet is probably beyond human efforts. In my own research, focused narrowly on the gall-inducing thrips of Australia, I have (with the help of colleagues) gone to the effort of describing a new species, only to never find it again in many years of trying. I have also applied molecular genetic tools, again in collaboration, in studies of these insects and discovered putative new species cascading out ahead of me.

We are too few and insects and other arthropods are too many (and sometimes too secretive) for us to know them all well, but the effort to shed light on some of this species richness is essential to an understanding of life on earth and the protection of human health and industry:

- Insects are models for studying physiological, behavioural, ecological, and evolutionary phenomena. Studying insect biology has sharpened our understanding of general biological principles.
- Insects play significant roles in the functioning of almost all terrestrial and freshwater ecosystems. Learning more about insects is essential to safeguarding these ecosystems for the health and economic benefits that a healthy environment accrues to all.
- Insects can also inflict immense harm on humans and other animals as vectors of disease. Learning about disease-transmitting species has and will alleviate potential sources of suffering.
- Insects are destructive. Better understanding them is necessary to prevent and prepare for the damage they can inflict on our industrial activities. The costs that insects such as the eastern spruce budworm, cabbage maggot, and salmon lice inflict on the Newfoundland and Labrador economy alone are in the millions.
- Insects are essential to our food security. Many of our crops rely on their pollination services; additionally, they can produce food (honey) or be food. Cricket flour is easily ordered from Canadian sources, and one of our entrepreneurial citizens is bound to start culturing crickets here soon for us to eat.

It is impossible to ignore insects, the most dominant animal group on the planet, in pursuit of an understanding of life on earth.

The biological origins of Newfoundland and Labrador ecosystems are complex. Due to glaciation, life has restarted in the region more than once—most recently, the province, scraped of its life-giving soil, re-emerged from under ice about 7,000 years ago. Colonization re-established the boreal forest biome (including biological communities such as bogs, heaths, and barrens), but with an impoverished flora and fauna compared to mainland North America. The arrival of people from North America and Europe brought accidental and intentional introductions of plants and animals which, along with human-induced extirpations or extinctions, altered the province's ecosystems.

The post-glacial movement of insects and other arthropods into Newfoundland and Labrador primarily came from North American populations on the winds or aided by people. Insects hitchhiked along with Europeans landing on the shores over the last 500 years (and the decades-long visit by the Norse about 1,000 years ago). Consequently, the arthropod fauna (assumed to be true specifically for the Insecta) of Newfoundland and Labrador is the most Europeanized in North America. With the modern speed and scope of human movements and trade, as well as the impacts of climate change, assessing the diversity of insects in Newfoundland is a moving target.

Much of that flux in insect diversity goes unnoticed. Assessments of insect diversity in Newfoundland and Labrador have been episodic and incomplete. The first formal documentation or study of Newfoundland and Labrador insects occurred in 1766. Joseph Banks and his friend Constantine Phipps (both born into affluence) arranged passage from Great Britain to Newfoundland and Labrador aboard the fishery protection vessel HMS *Niger*. This vessel was captained by another friend, Sir Thomas Adams, who was sympathetic to Banks and Phipps's goal: to reveal the natural history of the region, a mystery to scientists of the day. Their collections of plants and birds were extensive, but they also collected fish and invertebrates. Banks's notes refer to all invertebrate specimens as insects; later evaluation indicates that there were at minimum 12 species of insects. A few of these have not been seen in Newfoundland or Labrador since, but the majority are still abundant—see Banks's illustration of the sawfly *Trichiosoma arcticum* (page 9). In addition, while in St. John's, Adams introduced Banks to the famous Captain

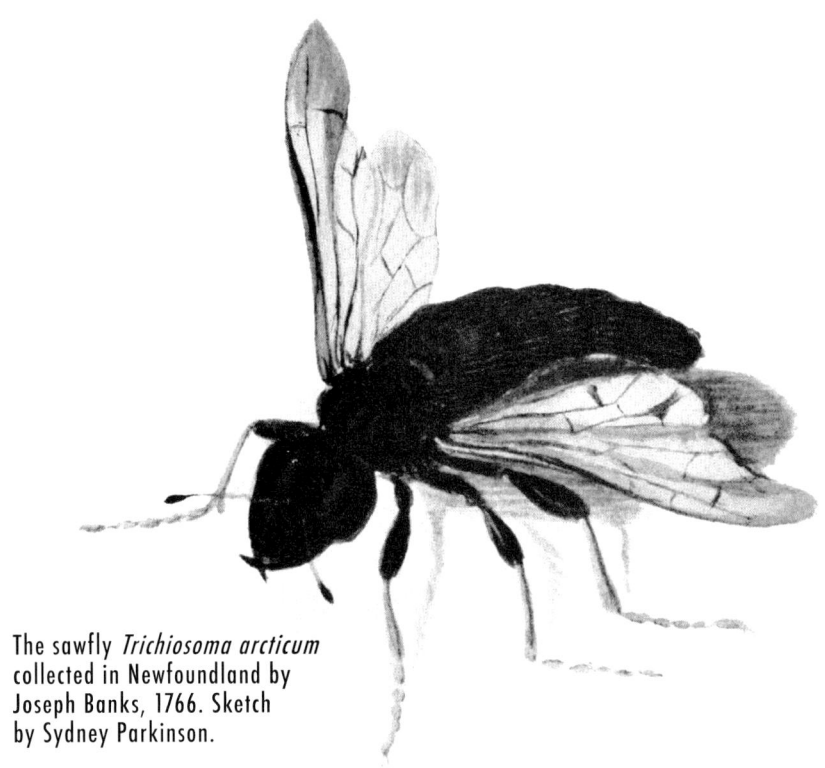

The sawfly *Trichiosoma arcticum* collected in Newfoundland by Joseph Banks, 1766. Sketch by Sydney Parkinson.

James Cook. Banks's efforts in Newfoundland must have impressed the captain—Banks went on to join Cook as a naturalist on a circumnavigation of the earth (1768–71), and Banks's work on that voyage made him famous.

Less than 100 years later, another Englishman contributed to our understanding of the diversity of insects in Newfoundland, although the affluence that enabled Banks and Phipps to follow their adventurous whims were not the circumstances that brought Philip Henry Gosse from England to Carbonear in June 1827. Gosse's father was an itinerant miniature portraitist, but he was absent from the family for long periods of time and provided them scant monetary support. Instead, it was Gosse's mother, working as a lady's maid, who paid the bills and scrimped for Gosse's education. Even so, Gosse had to quit school at 15, and at 17 he was sent to Carbonear to work as a clerk—not what he dreamed of doing with his life. During his spare time, Gosse studied entomology and scoured the local landscape for insects.

Having also mastered the skills to paint in miniature, Gosse beautifully illustrated a book of his Carbonear collection, the never-published *Entomologia Terrae Novae* (the source of the colour illustrations on this page and throughout the introduction), which now resides in the Canadian Museum of Nature in Ottawa. For Gosse, like Banks, Newfoundland was the start of something grand. Gosse went on to become the foremost natural history author of his time. Some argue that he invented saltwater aquaria—all agree that he popularized the hobby. Many Victorian families vacationing by the sea would have packed one of Gosse's books detailing the variety of living organisms encountered in the intertidal zone of the English shores.

For the past century or so, Newfoundland and Labrador has had entomological expertise in residence—some of whom you will be introduced to in this book. Memorial University and provincial and federal government agencies have, at least in part, allowed a focus on the insects and other arthropods of our region. Even so, it is impossible to feature all living insect species of Newfoundland and Labrador in these pages. The species we know about are too many for one field guide. We have focused on species that reflect the expertise of the four authors (a retired provincial veterinarian, two applied entomologists, and a professor of entomology), as well as those most likely to be encountered by Newfoundlanders and Labradorians at home and outdoors. On the other hand, we have expanded our scope to include some other creepy-crawlies that are not technically insects (see *What Is an Insect?*, page 12).

On these pages we'll introduce you to many of the smallest and most fascinating animals living in our province. In some cases, you have already met them—and we know this in part because you brought them to our attention. You delivered your curiosities to us, sometimes in sandwich bags, disposable coffee cups, pill bottles, jam jars, and, in one case, a rum bottle. You wanted answers to your questions about the impact of these animals on your health or property. And, in many cases you just wondered what you had found. This book is for the people of Newfoundland and Labrador who are fascinated by the diversity of life that surrounds them.

You have inspired us. Have fun with this book, and do continue to make your discoveries known to us.

> ***And we carry home as prizes***
> ***Funny bugs, of handy sizes,***
> ***Just to give the day a scientific tone.***
> —Charles Edward Carryl,
> *Robinson Crusoe's Story*

Tom Chapman

INTRODUCTION

APPROACH TO THIS BOOK

Stouts, Millers, and Forky-Tails is intended to present the facts known about many of the insects and other arthropods Newfoundlanders and Labradorians routinely encounter at home (including on ourselves and our pets), in the garden, in the community, or in the wilderness. We hope also to show the beauty and complexity of this element of our natural world and how these creatures affect our lives, language, and culture, both in the present and the past.

WHAT IS AN INSECT?

To the public, *insect*, *fly*, and *bug* are often used interchangeably for any small creeping, crawling, or flying creature, whether a pest in the garden, an annoyance in the woods, or a flittering thing of wonder. But to an entomologist, these words have specific meanings. *Arthropod*, if you recognize the term at all, may be a word that you saw once on a high school biology exam but has since lost its meaning. Insects are arthropods, but so are crustaceans (lobsters, crabs, shrimp, and sowbugs), arachnids (spiders, ticks, and mites), myriapods (centipedes and millipedes), and the extinct trilobites. An arthropod is a member of the Animal Kingdom that has jointed legs (*arthron*, jointed; *pod*, foot), an exoskeleton, and a segmented body.

Insects, the primary subject of this book—and the domain of study of entomologists—are members of the class Insecta, within the subphylum Hexapoda. As well as having the jointed legs and exoskeleton of all arthropods, insects have three body segments (head, thorax, and abdomen), at least one pair of antennae, compound and simple eyes, wings, and six jointed legs (*hexa*, six). The words *insect* and *entomology* derive from Latin (*insectum*) and Greek (*entomon*), meaning *cut into segments*. Nature, however, assures us that all rules will have exceptions, and even though by definition insects have wings and six legs, there are many wingless insects (including fleas and lice) and not every insect has six obvious legs. Some butterflies, for example, use only four legs to walk; the third pair is vestigial, tucked up by their heads.

Zebra jumper spider.

Painted lady butterfly (page 224).

Fourteen-spotted lady beetle (page 141).

A *fly* refers to an insect of the order Diptera, having but one pair of wings (*di*, two, and *ptera*, wings). Common examples include the house fly, fruit fly, and stout (deer fly). The second pair of wings is reduced to structures called halteres that provide information to flies about body orientation and position during flight.

Strictly speaking, *bugs* belong to another insect order, Hemiptera (true bugs). That alone will not clear up all confusion—for example, we use the term "ladybug" for insects that are actually beetles. A sowbug (also known as a carpenter or pill bug) is not a bug, or even an insect—it's a crustacean.

ARTHROPOD CLASSIFICATION

All named living organisms are classified taxonomically, according to shared evolutionary history and, thus, shared characteristics. As mentioned above, all animals belong to the same kingdom—Animalia. Under that large umbrella, animals are divided into phyla (plural of phylum). Within a phylum, the organisms are generally subdivided into class, then order, family, genus, and species. In reality, and for the specialist, not all creatures will be so neatly categorized—additional levels of organization include subphyla (as shown below), supergroups, superorders, and suborders. Taxonomy continues to be subject to lively debate and revision as discoveries and connections are made, particularly with advances in molecular and genetic research.

The chart below shows the commonly accepted system for arthropod classification. Only the groups to be discussed in this book are shown—but a fraction of the organisms classified as arthropods.

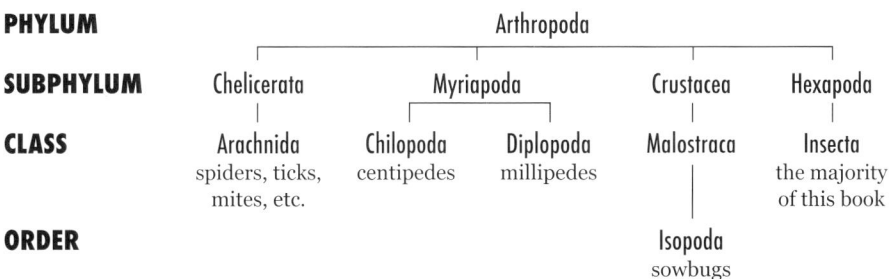

LIMITATIONS OF THIS BOOK

The number of species of insects and other arthropods in this province is unknown. Research tends to focus on species that are of direct interest to humans because they are garden pests (such as aphids) or because they cause economic damage to industries such as agriculture (carrot rust fly, diamondback moth), forestry (spruce budworm), or aquaculture (gill lice). Arthropods may also be of interest because they are considered a nuisance or spread disease (ticks and mosquitoes), have economic value (lobsters, crabs, and shrimp), or are things of beauty or of cultural significance (butterflies, dragonflies, and some beetles).

Research also tends to focus on the geographic areas in which people live and work, or which are at least accessible. As a result, vast areas of Newfoundland and Labrador, where unknown species may exist, are virtually unstudied. It is safe to say, however, that the total number of arthropod species in Newfoundland and Labrador is easily in the tens of thousands, if not quite a bit more.

By limitations of space alone, this book bypasses most of the fascinating world of crustaceans, including sea-dwelling lobsters, crabs, shrimp, sandhoppers, and barnacles and the shrimplike scuds (*Gammarus* spp.) of tidal pools. The common sowbug is the only crustacean profiled. The book only discusses extant species—and so the extinct trilobites, visible in many fossil beds across the province, are left for other publications.

Trilobite fossils. Trilobites belong to an extinct subphylum of arthropod.

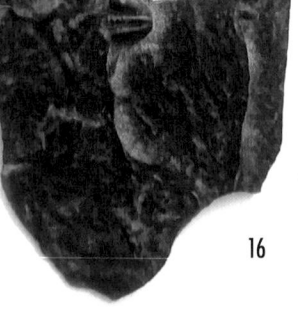

The authors of this book have chosen to profile just over 300 species—most of which are insects—considered the most common, interesting, or valuable in Newfoundland and Labrador.

Descriptions given in this book are written in a non-technical manner to help you identify insects and other arthropods without the aid of microscopes or dissection. Sometimes, it is relatively easy to identify a species in the field; other times, you may only be able to identify an individual to order, family, or genus.

THE ARTHROPOD BODY PLAN

As previously stated, arthropods have segmented bodies, an exoskeleton, and jointed legs. Below are two sample body plans by way of introduction to some of the terminology you'll encounter throughout this book.

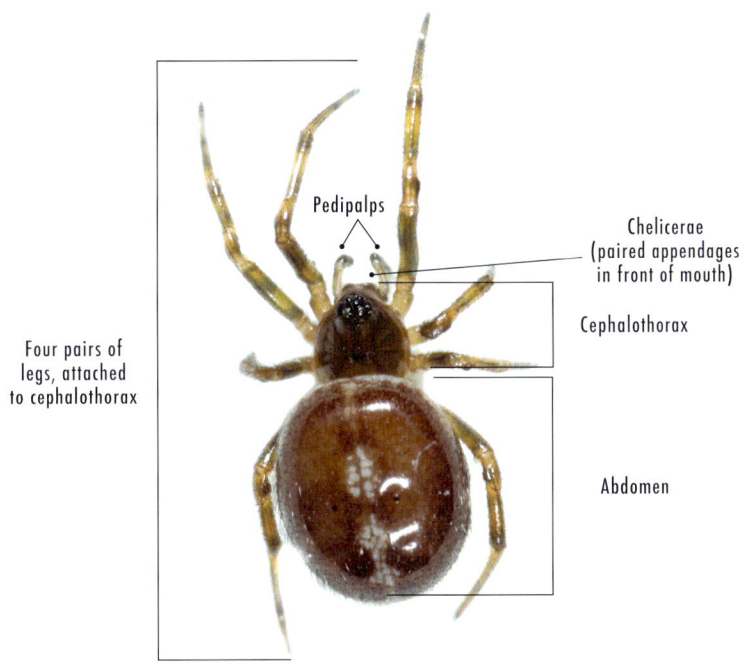

Red-belted bumble bee (page 51) colony. This species exhibits notable colour variation; this is the black form.

GENERAL LIFE CYCLE OF ARTHROPODS

Arthropod reproduction and development vary greatly and specifics will be described, where appropriate, within the main sections of this book. In general, arthropods are either male or female and reproduce sexually. Asexual reproduction does occur occasionally among arthropods—for example, female water fleas (which are actually crustaceans and of no relation to fleas) may produce viable eggs without requiring fertilization. In the complex social world of the honey bee, the queen is the only reproducing female—male drones are the result of unfertilized eggs; and female bees, fertilized eggs. Other species, including some midges and aphids, can alternate between sexual and asexual reproduction as external conditions demand.

Fertilized eggs are usually laid outside the female. In many species, eggs hatch into wormlike young—maggots, caterpillars, or grubs—that eventually undergo complete metamorphosis into a fly, butterfly, beetle, or other winged adult. In other species, including grasshoppers and true bugs, the young resemble the adult form and are said to undergo incomplete metamorphosis.

The mottled stink bug (page 252) undergoes incomplete metamorphosis—the young resemble the adult stage.

The mourning cloak butterfly (page 219) undergoes complete metamorphosis.

HOW TO USE THIS BOOK

In *Stouts, Millers, and Forky-Tails,* insects and non-insect arthropods are organized first by order (see Arthropod classification, page 15). The insect orders covered in this book are arranged roughly in reverse evolutionary order—the groups that appeared on the planet most recently are first (the Hymenoptera: ants, bees, and wasps); the more primitive, toward the end. The final section, Non-Insect Arthropods, is a catch-all that includes selected arachnids, crustaceans, and myriapods.

Within the orders, insects are arranged alphabetically by common name, with some exceptions, to ensure that closely related species appear side by side. Scientific (Latin) names are also listed, as well as other common names—including traditional Newfoundland and Labrador names for various insects, some of which are carry-overs from British terms.

Many insects and non-insect arthropods are identified to species. Where that is not possible or useful—many species cannot be distinguished easily outside the laboratory—the insects are described to order, family, or genus level.

The first step in identifying an insect or non-insect arthropod is to determine its order. A generalized body shape is shown below for each order, as well as examples and a brief description that may help you determine to which group your specimen belongs.

Use the colour bars and icons at the top of each page to help you find the correct section for your insect.

HYMENOPTERA Ants, bees, wasps

The forewings of ants, bees, and wasps are attached to the hindwings through a series of hooklets. Wings are membranous; body shapes are variable, but generally elongate with a constricted waist. Some species live in social colonies.

DIPTERA True flies, including house flies, fruit flies, mosquitoes, and deer flies (stouts)

True flies have only one pair of wings (*di-*, two). The hindwings have evolved into club-shaped structures (halteres) that detect the fly's body movements in flight, assisting in balance, steering, and stabilization. Antennae and body shape are variable.

SIPHONAPTERA Fleas

Fleas are wingless, with tough, laterally (sideways) flattened bodies. A prominent proboscis extends from their mouth, with which they pierce their host's skin and take a blood meal. The front two pairs of legs are short and stout; hind legs are modified for leaping.

COLEOPTERA Beetles, including ground beetles and lady beetles

Beetles have two sets of wings, with the front set hardened into wing cases (*koleos-*, sheath), called elytra, that must be raised to allow the second set of wings to function. Many beetles are compact and highly armoured, with variously modified legs—some with claws or hooks or other adhesive structures. Antennae usually have fewer than 12 segments.

NEUROPTERA Lacewings

Lacewings have long, slender bodies, large eyes, long multi-segmented delicate antennae, and the namesake lacy wings. No abdominal cerci ("tails").

TRICHOPTERA Caddisflies

Caddisflies have long, slender bodies and antennae and four similar-sized hair-covered (sometimes scale-covered) wings. The wings are held tent-like over the body when the caddisfly is at rest. Generally, caddisflies are beige, brown, or black, often with irregular dark wing markings.

LEPIDOPTERA Butterflies, moths

Butterflies and moths have four scale-covered wings (*lepidos-*, scales) which are often, but not always, brightly coloured. In general, butterflies are day-fliers, while most moths are likely seen at night. Butterfly antennae are clubbed; moth antennae are not. Most butterflies and moths have a long, sucking proboscis, which is coiled at rest.

HEMIPTERA True bugs, including aphids, bed bugs, and water striders

True bugs have variable body size and shape; variable antennae. The forewings of true bugs are thicker at the base than at the tip. In many cases, the forewings are hardened, giving the appearance of a half wing (*hemi-*, half; *-ptera*, wings). Mouthparts are usually modified to a sucking tube or rostrum.

THYSANOPTERA Thrips

Thrips are brown to black, small (1 to 3 millimetres long), and slender. Wings are narrow and fringed. They are usually found on plants.

PSOCODEA Lice

The parasitic lice are wingless, with short, stout legs for clinging, short antennae, sucking or piercing mouthparts, and a flattened body. Most book lice are wingless; bark lice may have membranous wings, long, threadlike antennae, and long legs.

ORTHOPTERA Crickets, grasshoppers

Crickets and grasshoppers have long, enlarged hind legs for jumping. They also have prominent compound eyes, multi-segmented antennae, and a pair of short cerci on the abdomen. Forewings are often narrow, short, and leathery. Hindwings, when present, are veined, transparent, and pleated beneath the forewings.

BLATTODEA Cockroaches

Cockroaches have flattened oval-shaped bodies with small heads partially obscured by a distinctive shieldlike pronotum, and spiny long legs which enable fast running. Antennae are long and multi-segmented. Forewings are hardened, called tegmina; hindwings are larger and membranous.

PLECOPTERA Stoneflies

Adult stoneflies are long and narrow with four membranous wings, which sit flat on the body when the insect is at rest. Antennae are long and threadlike. Stoneflies have two distinctive long cerci at the end of the abdomen.

DERMAPTERA Earwigs

Shiny and leathery in appearance, earwigs have prominent cerci (a forked tail), threadlike antennae, and a long, slightly flattened body. Earwigs have wings—toughened forewings and larger, fan-shaped hindwings—but rarely fly.

ODONATA Dragonflies, damselflies

Dragonflies and damselflies are day-fliers with large bulging eyes, short bristlelike antennae, jewel-like colours, long slender bodies, and agile flight. The two pairs of transparent net-veined wings are roughly equal in size. The dragonfly is typically larger than the damselfly, with its wings projecting straight out from its body when at rest. The damselfly holds its wings more parallel to the body when at rest.

EPHEMEROPTERA Mayflies

Delicate in appearance with a slender, elongate body, adult mayflies are extremely short-lived (*ephemeros-*, lasting for only a day), and are usually seen near fresh water. They have large, heavily veined triangular forewings and much smaller, round hindwings. Mayflies also have two or three long, hairlike cerci at the end of the abdomen.

ZYGENTOMA Silverfish, firebrats

Fast-moving and wingless, silverfish have carrot-shaped bodies. Silverfish are silvery in colour; firebrats are generally mottled grey or brown. Both are found in dark areas of homes and other buildings.

NON-INSECT ARTHROPODS

The **Arachnida** have eight jointed legs and include spiders, ticks, mites, harvestmen, and pseudoscorpions. The many-legged elongate **Myriapoda** include centipedes and millipedes. **Crustacea**, including the sowbug, have a segmented exoskeleton, jointed limbs, and two pairs of antennae.

HABITAT ICONS

To help with specimen identification, icons representing the *most likely* habitat for each insect or other arthropod appear with each entry. Seven icons are used:

People/pets: These are the insects and other arthropods most often found on you, your pet, or other animals: ticks, mites, fleas, lice, and others.

Home: Houses and other buildings are home to a range of insects and other arthropods, including house flies, larder beetles, earwigs, spiders, cockroaches, silverfish, sowbugs, and pseudoscorpions.

 Garden: This includes flower gardens, lawns, ornamental trees, vegetable gardens, woodpiles, rock walls, and other natural or artificial structures.

 Community: This includes a variety of natural and man-made habitats such as introduced tree species and large parks and other urban areas.

 Wilderness: This broad habitat area includes bogs, fens, and forests—the areas relatively untouched by humans but where you might be hiking, camping, boating, hunting, or fishing.

 Water: Many insects and other arthropods are primarily aquatic and found in some or all life stages in or on rivers, streams, ponds, and other water bodies.

 Agriculture: This habitat includes large farm fields, barns, greenhouses, and crop storage areas.

River Jewelwing Damselfly, atypical form; the outer third of its wing is not black. See typical form on page 293. The white marks on each wing (pterostigma) indicate that this River Jewelwing is a female.

Long-lipped tiger beetle (see page 128).

SAMPLE PAGE

Bar colour and icon indicate insect order (see pages 21-24).

Water striders.

WATER STRIDERS
Family Gerridae
Pond Skaters, Water Doctors

These slender, dark-coloured insects are commonly observed resting on or running across the surface of slow-flowing or still water, where they live. Their long middle and back legs splay out and help water striders literally walk on water. The feet and underside of the body are covered with water-repellant hairs which help them stay afloat.

Some species of water striders gather in groups and scatter when disturbed. In any single population of water striders, some adults have wings, others do not.

The short front legs are used to grab prey, often small dead or drowning insects on the water surface or just underneath the surface. Because the middle and back legs are long and the front legs are short, water striders appear at first glance to have just four legs. Nymphs resemble the adults in appearance, except they are smaller and wingless. Adults and nymphs live in water.

Twenty-two species of water striders are known in Canada, with four from Labrador and five from Newfoundland.

- Size: 2-25 mm body length
- Habitat detail: on the surfaces of temporary or permanent fresh-water ponds and slow-moving areas of streams, some marine species
- Distribution: worldwide

Common name.
Scientific (Latin) name.
Other common names.

Icons indicate the habitat in which the species or group is most often found (see pages 24-25).

Fact box for at-a-glance information on size range, habitat details, and distribution.

Make sure to look at the size range—many of the beautiful pictures in the book are close-ups and may give you a false sense of the actual size.

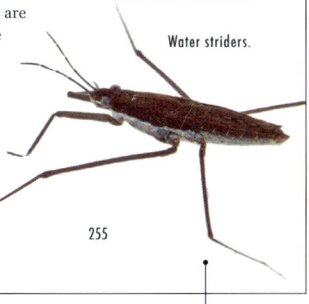

Water striders.

255

Photos to aid in species recognition.

HYMENOPTERA: ANTS·BEES·WASPS

Lemon cuckoo bee on goldenrod.

Sweat bee on a strawberry flower.

Icy ants.

Face of a cellophane bee.

Rhyssa persuasoria (see page 74).

Potter or mason wasp.

HYMENOPTERA
ANTS, BEES, AND WASPS

The Hymenoptera is a diverse order of insects including bees, wasps, ants, horntails, and sawflies. As an order, they are distinguished by their forewings being attached to their hindwings through a series of hooklets (*hamuli*) and by the membranous appearance of these wings. This has led to two different explanations for their name: one, that the wings are membranous (Greek *hymen* means membrane); two, the Greek god of marriage is *Hymen*, indicating that the wings are joined together as in marriage.

Hymenopterans have segmented antennae. Females generally have a specialized ovipositor at the anterior end of the abdomen for depositing eggs in hard-to-access areas; often this ovipositor is modified into a stinger. The larvae vary widely but are often wormlike—some even legless—and will undergo complete metamorphosis.

ANTS

Family Formicidae
Emmets

About 140 million years ago ants and wasps evolved from a common ancestor, and then ants evolved sociality around 40 million years after that. Not surprising, then, with 100 million years of diversification, ant sociality is quite complex. More than 12,000 ant species exist worldwide, all of which are social.*

Sociality does not mean that ants are agreeable or friendly, as anyone who has suffered the nips (from powerful mandibles) and stings (many species have stingers and venom) of a group of ants protecting its territory knows. Sociality refers to cooperation among a group of organisms. In the case of ants, not all individuals in a colony are involved in reproduction; those that do not reproduce commit themselves to altruistic tasks.

Depending on the species, an ant colony can have one to many hundred mated queens. As queens can store sperm, in many cases for years, kings are either absent from the colony or present in very small numbers, and do no work.

Queens can choose the sex of their offspring. A queen's first eggs develop into wingless female workers, which are the toilers of the colony. Worker ants nurse immatures, forage for food, and defend the colony. The number of workers in a colony can range from dozens to millions. Workers are often smaller than the queens; there is a loose correlation between the size of the queen and how many eggs she produces in a lifetime. The workers too may dramatically differ in shape from the queens.

Periodically or seasonally, queens shift from producing workers to producing winged kings and queens. These sexuals, called alates, hang out in the colony, waiting for the right time to take off en masse on a nuptial flight. After the nuptial flight, the kings die and the queens break off their own wings and begin the building of a nest.

As little research has been done on the ants of Newfoundland and Labrador, the total diversity present remains unknown. Four representative species are profiled here: two that have been studied, at least in a preliminary way; the third, because it is a slave maker; and the fourth, the flying carpenter ants, a seasonal topic among Newfoundlanders on talk radio most years.

---

* If you are a quibbler: some ants are actually social parasites (and therefore technically not social), but even these parasites evolved from social ancestors.

CARPENTER ANTS

***Camponotus herculeanus,
Camponotus pennsylvanicus***

- Size: workers 5–12 mm body length
- Habitat detail: nest in rotten wood, as well as in man-made or natural cavities such as wall spaces and under rock
- Distribution: Canada and US

Of more than 1,000 species of carpenter ants, the black (*Camponotus pennsylvanicus*) and the red (*Camponotus herculeanus*) carpenter ants are the most frequently encountered in Newfoundland and Labrador. They are the largest ants recorded in the province. The black carpenter ant is brownish black all over and likely to be found in buildings, with colonies headed by a single queen overseeing a workforce of up to 10,000 individuals. The red carpenter ant, also brownish black, but with a reddish upper body, may have multiple queens.

Carpenter ant.

Carpenter ants bite but they do not sting. They are not as destructive as many think, but their presence is a symptom of water damage to wooden structures. Both red and black species excavate nests in rotten wood. Their heads house the large muscles that extend into and articulate the mandibles, giving these ants their considerable strength. Neither species eats the wood; they deposit what they excavate outside the nest entrance—a telltale sign of an ant infestation.

Carpenter ants forage alone and at night. They look for juice from plants or dead insects or, if they are in a house or cabin, for sweet human food. When they find what they seek, they return to the nest and tell the others, using a chemical signal to mark a trail to the food source.

Carpenter ants tend aphids (page 242). Aphid diets contain so much water and sugar that they excrete out the excess, called honeydew. This is a favourite food of the carpenter ant, and they will aggressively protect the aphids that produce it. Alates leave on nuptial flights from late spring to mid-summer, usually triggered by heat and humidity.

Red carpenter ants can survive temperatures to -40°C.

 Human and ant muscle fibres exhibit similar strength. The famous feats of strength by ants are a consequence of their small size in relation to the cross-sectional area of their muscles relative to that in humans.

European fire ant.

EUROPEAN FIRE ANT

Myrmica rubra

- Size: workers 4-5 mm body length
- Habitat detail: moist, lightly shaded soil
- Distribution: recorded on the Avalon Peninsula and west coast of Newfoundland

These tiny and most often red-coloured ants deliver a big sting, usually accompanied by a welt and pain that may last an hour or more. Anyone with an allergy will have it even worse. Watch household pets: these ants sting them too. Although European fire ant stings are obvious, their nests are not. They are known to nest under wood or rock and often their nests are associated with plant roots.

European fire ants have many queens per colony, and colonies can extend to more than one nest; worker numbers range from 1,000s to 10,000s.

Native to Europe and Asia, European fire ants are found in Washington state, British Columbia, and eastern Canada, including Newfoundland. The movement of soil may best explain the expansion of this ant's range. Historically, this happened via the ballast of ships; in more modern times, the root balls of horticultural plants are often responsible.

 Barry Hicks (College of the North Atlantic) was the first to formally note the presence of this ant in Newfoundland and Labrador. Hicks, along with Brettney Pilgrim and Dawn Marshall (both of Memorial University), assembled a DNA sequence data set that suggests that fire ants were introduced to the province multiple times. The first could have happened centuries ago, via vessels from Dorset, England, taking part in the historic cod fishery. A connection between Newfoundland's fire ants and those in the state of Maine also appears to exist. Hicks and colleagues suggest that the US Air Force may be responsible for that, as it is the genetic sequence of ants collected near Fort Pepperrell that supports the connection.

ICY ANT

Formica glacialis

Icy ants are black, smaller than carpenter ants, and difficult to identify to species. They are part of a group of very similar looking ants referred to as the *Formica fusca* group, of which a few members have overlapping distributions and behaviours in Newfoundland and Labrador. They do not have stingers, but they do bite, although it can barely be felt. These ground-dwelling ants are recognized as ecosystem engineers: they play a critical function in Newfoundland and Labrador's terrestrial environment in soil processes, seed dispersal, and energy flow through ecosystems. They eat a variety of food, including honeydew (aphid excretions), plant seeds, and small arthropods.

- Size: workers 4–8 mm body length
- Habitat detail: areas with high groundwater
- Distribution: formerly glaciated areas from Saskatchewan to Newfoundland and Labrador

Icy ant.

Focusing on the icy ant, Holly Caravan (Memorial University) successfully used DNA sequence data to identify colonies to species. As little is known about the natural history of this ant, Caravan went to White Hills on the north edge of St. John's with a camp stove, several kilograms of wax, and a shovel. To capture all the ants in a nest, she poured melted wax into the nest, let it set, and then dug it all up. By re-melting the wax, she was able to extract, count, and measure the ants. The largest colony size Caravan found was greater than 80,000 workers and a few hundred queens. Using an approximation of the energy needs of an ant, this colony would consume about 1.6 kilograms of food a day, which is more than half of what an average person eats and drinks.

Icy ant.

RUDDY SLAVE-MAKING ANT
Formica rubicunda

The front body of this ant is light red, the back black, and the legs brownish. Their nests are small and topped with gravel or debris. The nests and ants are found in the same areas that one might choose to pick blueberries or picnic along the East Coast Trail: a rocky opening in the forest. The pain from the sting of this ant is short-lived, but you will want to quickly move on. If you linger, you might notice two species foraging together, because *Formica rubicunda* is a slave maker.

Ruddy slave-making ant.

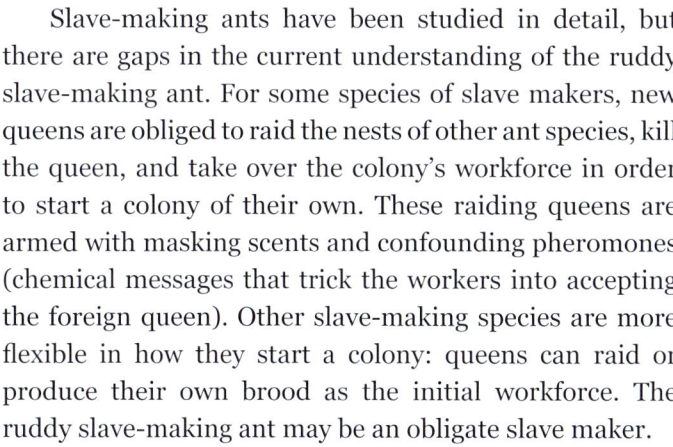

Ruddy slave-making ant.

- Size: workers 5.5–6.5 mm body length
- Habitat detail: rocky and dry areas
- Distribution: Mexico, US, and most Canadian provinces

Slave-making ants have been studied in detail, but there are gaps in the current understanding of the ruddy slave-making ant. For some species of slave makers, new queens are obliged to raid the nests of other ant species, kill the queen, and take over the colony's workforce in order to start a colony of their own. These raiding queens are armed with masking scents and confounding pheromones (chemical messages that trick the workers into accepting the foreign queen). Other slave-making species are more flexible in how they start a colony: queens can raid or produce their own brood as the initial workforce. The ruddy slave-making ant may be an obligate slave maker.

It is known that, as the colony of the ruddy slave-making ant grows, its workers raid neighbouring *Formica* species colonies (e.g., the icy ant). These raids are all-out battles and, if successful, the raiding ants carry the pupae of the losing colony away. Some of these pupae are used as food; some, raised as slaves.

Leafcutter bee.

Yellow-banded bumble bee.

BEES

Families Andrenidae, Apidae, Colletidae, Halictidae, and Megachilidae

The word *bee* conjures up images of honey bees and bumble bees. This is not surprising given our long association with honey bees for honey and wax and the conspicuous nature of the fuzzy, loudly buzzing bumble bees.

The bee was the symbol of the Greek goddess Artemis. Humans have been interacting with bees for at least 7,000 years, with the first evidence of bee "keeping" dating to 2400 BC. The European honey bee, *Apis mellifera*, may be the most well known, but in fact nearly 20,000 species of bees in seven recognized families are recorded worldwide. In Canada, just fewer than 1,000 species are known; in Newfoundland and Labrador, approximately 84 species of bees in five families have been recorded.

Most people are familiar with the social lifestyle of the honey bee. Each hive has an egg-laying queen that is completely reliant on her colony of workers. Colonies can be made up of thousands of bees, with workers splitting nest-making and reproductive responsibilities. The workers also have the ability to communicate with one another.

This social lifestyle, however, is more of an exception in the bee world rather than a general rule.

The majority of bee species are solitary—they do not live in colonies or hives and do not have a queen. The female mother bee is nest finder and maker, and pollen and nectar collector, and she never meets her offspring. These solitary bees live for less than a year and are usually active for a short period during the summer. A typical life cycle of the solitary bee begins in the spring, when individuals, both male and female (males emerge before females), emerge from the nest, and mate. The female bee then searches for a suitable nesting site, and begins building her nest. Nest design varies considerably in the bee world, from tubelike holes in trees or the ground to elaborate nests dug in the ground with multiple tunnels and cavities. In general, the mother bee collects pollen and nectar and makes a pollen ball in a single cavity or brood chamber (called provisioning) on which she lays an egg. She seals off the brood chamber and moves on to the next cavity. The eggs hatch and larvae

Leafcutter bee nest in a log.

Bees are differentiated from all other Hymenoptera by the presence of branched hairs. Many bees also have unbranched hairs.

Bee bodies are designed for pollen collecting and carrying. In addition to branched hairs (page 39), bees are electrostatically charged, which aids in the attachment of negatively charged pollen grains. This ligated furrow bee, a species not present in Newfoundland and Labrador, demonstrates how effective these traits can be for a pollinator.

feed on the provided pollen ball, eventually pupating before emerging the next spring.

Five bee families are found in Newfoundland and Labrador: Andrenidae, Apidae, Colletidae, Halictidae, and Megachilidae. Each is described below, as are some of the more conspicuous bee genera and species.

Andrenid bee scopa on hind leg.

> Scopa (pl. scopae): Most bees have scopae, groupings of specialized branched hairs which are used to store pollen. Pollen grains are held in the spaces between the hairs. The presence and location of these masses of dense hairs help identify the family to which a bee belongs. Not all bees have scopae—bumble bees and honey bees, for example, have specialized structures called corbiculae to carry pollen, and some kleptoparasitic bees have no scopae at all.

MINING BEES

Family Andrenidae

Mining bees (family Andrenidae) are some of the first bees to fly in the spring and can often be seen sunning themselves on leaves, warming up before foraging. The largest family of bees in North America, they show great variation in size. *Perdita minima*, for example, measures less than 2 millimetres in length, but most are 10 to 15 millimetres in length, dark coloured, and lightly fuzzy. Mining bees are mostly ground

Male *Andrena* sp. resting on a flower.

nesters. Their choice of nesting material will vary by species—some prefer sand, others clay, and some dig just about anywhere. These bees are solitary but can often be found in nesting aggregations where multiple nest entrances are located in the same general area. Some species even share nest entrances but have separate chambers for their brood off the main tunnel.

Most bees in this family have two grooves below each antenna, which can be used to distinguish them from other bees, as most have only one. In Newfoundland and Labrador this family is represented by approximately 15 species, all in the genus *Andrena*.

Mining bee nest entrance.

- Size: 9–13 mm body length
- Habitat detail: boreal and transition zones where willow bloom
- Distribution: Holarctic, found in Newfoundland and Labrador

Clarke's Mining Bee
Andrena clarkella

Clarke's mining bee is one of the first bees to emerge in the spring, as they forage almost exclusively on early blooming willow. Females are bulky bees that can be identified by brown-orange hairs on the thorax which match the colour of the scopae. They also have distinct black hairs on the face and yellow-orange hind tibia. Most of the hairs on the males are golden, with black hairs on the side of the face.

Male Clarke's mining bee emerging from its ground nest.

^ Female Clarke's mining bee; the colour of its thorax matches that of its hind leg scopa.

Wilke's mining bee.

Wilke's Mining Bee
Andrena wilkella
Flat-Faced Mining Bee

Wilke's mining bee is found early in the spring. Females have yellow hind tibiae and a primarily hairless abdomen, although the last segments have narrow fringes of white hairs along the hind margins. This species' cold hardiness makes it an important pollinator of many of Newfoundland and Labrador's native berries, including blueberries and cranberries.

Wilke's mining bee foraging on red clover.

The Wilke's mining bee is thought to have been introduced into North America from Europe as nests in ships' ballast. Specimens have been collected in Newfoundland and Labrador foraging on a large number of plant species, including clovers, brambles, blueberry, rose, and goldenrod.

- Size: 9–12 mm body length
- Habitat detail: nests in sparse vegetation, old meadows, sandy paths, and dry roadbeds
- Distribution: Holarctic; found in Newfoundland, not recorded from Labrador

BUMBLE BEES, EUROPEAN HONEY BEES, NOMAD BEES
Family Apidae

Apidae is a diverse family that contains some of the most recognizable bee species. In Newfoundland and Labrador, it includes the eusocial honey bees and bumble bees as well as kleptoparasitic bees in the genus *Nomada*.

In season, honey bees and bumble bees can be readily spotted flying with balls of pollen on their hind legs, most likely heading back to the hive or nest to provision young larvae. They collect pollen, moisten it with nectar, and store it in a structure called a corbicula or pollen basket, unique to bees of this family.

Fully loaded bumble bee corbicula, or pollen basket.

The corbicula is a shiny cavity located on the hind legs and is surrounded by a fringe of hairs which helps keep the pollen ball in place. Honey bees bring their loot back to the perennial hive, which survives and functions year-round, whereas overwintered queen bumble bees build a new nest and colony each spring.

Bumble Bees
Bombus spp.
Dumbledores

Bumble bees get their name from their bumbling flight and the humming sound they make as they buzz from flower to flower collecting pollen and nectar. About 45 species of *Bombus* are recorded in Canada, with 13 found on the island of Newfoundland and 15 in Labrador.

Because of their fuzziness and their ability to contract flight muscles to warm themselves, bumble bees are active at lower temperatures than most bees and are important early spring and cool climate pollinators. Bumble bees are truly social in that they have a queen and worker bees. A mated queen emerges in the spring to search for a nest site, often in the ground in an abandoned rodent hole. Once a suitable space is found she will forage for pollen and nectar to start her colony. When the nest is sufficiently filled with pollen, she lays her eggs on the pollen mass and incubates them by covering them with her abdomen. The first emerging daughters build additional nest cells and provide their sisters with pollen and nectar, at which time the queen has sole responsibility for egg laying. Colonies build over the summer, reaching maximum numbers of 50 to a few hundred individuals. At the end of the season the original queen produces male offspring, followed by new queens, which leave the nest to find mates. After mating, the males

Male bumble bees do not maintain the nest but spend late summer and fall nights sleeping on flowers.

Tricoloured bumble bee, with labelled body parts. The abdominal segments, or terga, are numbered from 1 to 6 and are used to describe bumble bee coloration.

die and each mated queen settles in to overwinter in a small nest underground, usually just big enough for her.

Common names are often associated with the colour patterns of the hair or pile on the abdominal segments. Some of the more common or unique bumble bees in the province are described. The descriptions are of females; identification of males requires inspection of genitalia.

 **Queen's choice:** The queen bee, who only mates once in the fall, stores enough sperm for her entire life and has the ability to determine the sex of her offspring. As she lays her egg, she can choose if it will be male or female. In order to produce a female, she releases some of the stored sperm as she lays her egg. To produce males, she does not release sperm. This system is called haplodiploidy and is the same for all bees.

 **Buzz pollination:** Bumble bees are effective buzz pollinators, which involves the bee rapidly contracting its flight muscles to produce strong vibrations that expel pollen from inside a flower's anther. Many plants, including several economically important plants such as tomato, bell pepper, cranberry, and blueberry, are more efficiently pollinated if visited by buzz pollinators.

Half-black bumble bee worker.

Half-Black Bumble Bee
Bombus vagans

- Size: workers 11–14 mm body length; queens 17–21 mm
- Habitat detail: urban parks and gardens, forests, and wetlands
- Distribution: wide distribution in North America, including Labrador; *B. vagans bolsteri* only found on the island of Newfoundland

The half-black bumble bee is just that—half black. The anterior (head, thorax, and first two segments of the abdomen) of the body is predominantly yellow; the rest of the body is black. The recognized subspecies *Bombus vagans bolsteri*, found only on the island of Newfoundland, varies slightly from this and tends to have an intermixing of black hairs near the head on the thorax and a darker band of black hairs between the wings. Many have yellow hairs on the tip of the abdomen.

Half-black bumble bees' nests are usually aboveground. In the field this species is easily confused with the similar-looking *Bombus sandersoni* and can only be distinguished by measuring the length of the cheeks under a microscope. Workers and queens have been recorded foraging on red clover, thistle, and meadowsweet.

Lemon Cuckoo Bumble Bee
Bombus citrinus

The lemon cuckoo bumble bee is a parasitic species. It usually has yellow pile on most of the thorax. If a black spot is present on the upperside of the thorax, it does not usually form a band between the wings. Abdominal segments can vary in coloration: in some, only segments 4 and 5 are predominantly black; in others, segments 1 to 5 are all black.

Lemon cuckoo bumble bees do not have corbiculae, as they do not collect pollen to raise their young. When it is time to lay eggs, females enter the nests of their hosts and kill or subdue the queen. Through pheromones or physical force, they enslave the workers to feed her and her developing young. The lemon cuckoo bumble bee has been recorded as a kleptoparasite of the half-black bumble bee (*B. vagans*). Before taking over a nest, the adults can be seen retrieving nectar from different plants, including thistles, goldenrods, and asters.

- Size: 18–22 mm body length
- Habitat detail: forest edges, seen in urban areas
- Distribution: eastern North America, not recorded from Labrador

Kleptoparasites are animals that steal food or prey from another animal. Cuckoo bees are kleptoparasitic bees that lay their eggs in cells that have been built and provisioned by a bee of another species. Although detrimental to that individual, the presence of lemon cuckoo bumble bees can be used as an indicator of a balanced, functioning ecosystem. More than 15 species of kleptoparasitic bees have been recorded in the province, of which the lemon cuckoo bumble bee is just one.

Lemon cuckoo bumble bee collecting nectar.

- Size: workers 13-15 mm body length; queens 18-22 mm
- Habitat detail: woodlands, nests underground
- Distribution: common in Newfoundland and present in Labrador

Northern Amber Bumble Bee
Bombus borealis

The northern amber bumble bee is one of the last of the queens to emerge from hibernation in the spring. It can be identified by its large size and amber pile. The northern amber bumble bee has a long face with white hairs between the eyes and a band of black hairs that extends down the sides of the thorax, between the wings. This bee has been recorded collecting pollen and nectar from raspberry, clovers, vetches, lupins, and other flowers. It nests underground and is usually seen in woodlands, but also in gardens and urban settings in both Newfoundland and Labrador.

Northern amber bumble bee; note its white facial hairs.

Northern amber bumble bee.

Red-Belted Bumble Bee
Bombus rufocinctus

The red-belted bumble bee has two primary colour forms: a red form and a black form. This is highly variable, however, and colour variations can occur in individuals of the same colony. The easiest way to identify the red-belted bumble bee is to note the shape of the black area on the upperside of the thorax. In most species, it is either a spot or a rectangular shape; in the red-belted bumble bee, it is oval.

This species forages on a wide range of plants, including clovers, vetch, and sunflowers. The red form, on first glance, is similar to the tricoloured bumble bee, *Bombus ternarius*; however, the red-belted bumble bee lacks the distinct black V found on the thorax of the tricoloured bumble bee. This red-belted bumble bee, native to North America, has recently been recorded in Newfoundland. Look for it in wooded areas and in open sites such as meadows, urban gardens, and parks. It often nests above-ground or at soil surface.

- Size: workers 11–12.5 mm body length; queens 16–18 mm
- Habitat detail: urban parks and gardens, forests
- Distribution: North America, not recorded from Labrador

Male red-belted bumble bee (black form).

Red-belted bumble bee worker (red form).

Tricoloured bumble bee, with the distinct V of black hair splitting the yellow hair of the thorax.

Tricoloured bumble bee nectaring on clover.

Tricoloured Bumble Bee
Bombus ternarius

- Size: workers 8-13 mm body length; queens 17-19 mm
- Habitat detail: open woodlands and meadows
- Distribution: North America; occurs in Newfoundland and Labrador

The tricoloured bumble bee is named for its yellow, orange, and black coloration. It has a distinct black V on the thorax between the wings, abdominal segments 2 and 3 are entirely red, and the last two abdominal segments have black pile. This bee's short, even pile gives it a clean-cut appearance, compared to some of the shaggier or fuzzier bumble bees. The top of the head has a mixture of black and yellow hairs.

Tricoloured bumble bees have been recorded foraging on a variety of plants, including raspberry, blackberry, blueberry, goldenrod, rhodora, Labrador tea, dandelion, and clover. They are seen in open woodlands and meadows and often nest underground. This species can be confused with lookalike *B. sylvicola*, which has small amounts of yellow pile on the sides of abdominal segments 5 and 6, and *B. rufocinctus* red form (see distinction under *rufocinctus*).

Yellow-banded bumble bee.

Yellow-Banded Bumble Bee
Bombus terricola

Yellow-banded bumble bees are one of the first bumble bees to emerge and forage in the spring. To identify this bee, look for the black pile on the sides of the thorax and the head as well as on abdominal segments 1 and 4 through 6. Segments 2 and 3 are most often yellow, forming the yellow band.

This bee was once one of the most common bumble bee species within its range of northeastern North America. Although still relatively abundant in Newfoundland, in certain parts of its range the population has declined and in 2015 was listed as of Special Concern by the Committee on the Status of Endangered Wildlife in Canada (COSEWIC). Declines have been attributed to pesticide use, habitat loss, and pathogen spillover from managed bumble bee colonies. This species has been collected foraging on raspberries, blueberries, cranberries, fireweed, sheep laurel, and clover, as well as on many other plants.

- Size: workers 10-15 mm body length; queens 19-21 mm
- Habitat detail: nests underground in areas with dense vegetation, close to or within woodlands
- Distribution: northeastern North America, recorded in Newfoundland and Labrador

Yellow toadflax flower that has been robbed of its nectar (see holes).

 The yellow-banded bumble bee, a short-tongued bumble bee, is a frequent nectar robber of flowers that have long corollas. Nectar robbing is a foraging behaviour that involves biting a hole at the base of the flower and collecting the nectar, rather than entering the flower's natural opening. Nectar robbers do not come in contact with the reproductive parts of the flowers and therefore do not contribute to the reproductive success of the plants.

European Honey Bee
Apis mellifera
Western Honey Bee

Seven species of honey bees (*Apis*) are recognized in the world; all produce and store honey and construct perennial colonies from wax. The European honey bee is the primary species that has been domesticated and moved around the world with humans. It is not native to North America but was brought by European settlers in the early 1600s.

Today, this species is frequently seen in urban and agricultural areas and recognized by its slender, golden brown body covered with pale hairs. Honey bees often dangle their legs down when they fly. Individuals can be highly variable in coloration, even within the same colony, with degrees of dark bands on the abdomen. Honey bees also have dense hairs on their eyes, a distinguishing characteristic. Males (drones) are slightly bigger than the female worker bees and their eyes meet on the top of the head, giving them a flylike appearance. The female worker bees are seen more often than males, as they collect pollen and nectar from a wide range of flowers.

The economic importance of honey bees is immense. Much of our food production relies heavily on this one species of insect. The fact that extremely large colonies of honey bees are easily managed and transported makes them the most widely used pollinator worldwide.

- Size: worker 12–16 mm body length; queen and drones larger
- Habitat detail: domestic hives
- Distribution: no feral colonies in Newfoundland and Labrador and thus usually found within ~5 km of a managed hive

Honey bee worker.

Unfortunately, with this intense use of bees comes the development and spread of pests and diseases. In North America, European honey bees are susceptible to a range of bacterial, fungal, and viral infections as well as pests such as tracheal mites, wax moths, small hive beetles, and Varroa mites. The last two are introduced pests from Africa (small hive beetle) and Asia (Varroa mite). Debilitating mites found elsewhere in North America are absent in Newfoundland (as of 2019) and local hives are relatively disease-free.

Nomada cressoni.

Nomad Bees
***Nomada* spp.**

- Size: worker 6–17 mm body length
- Habitat detail: usually similar to their ground-nesting bee hosts
- Distribution: worldwide; species-dependent

Nomad bees are wasplike kleptoparasitic bees in the family Apidae. Most are red and black with yellow markings and lack pollen-carrying scopae—there is no need to collect pollen when the host bee does it for you. Female nomad bees enter their host's nest while the owner is away foraging and lay eggs in the cells built and provisioned by the host bee. Some male nomad bees can mimic the scent of their host *Andrena* and can transfer the scent to female nomads to make it easier for them to sneak into the nests of their hosts. Eight species of nomad bees have been recorded in Newfoundland.

Nomada cressoni.

Heart-shaped face of a cellophane bee.

CELLOPHANE BEES
MASKED BEES

Family Colletidae

Two genera of Colletidae are found in Newfoundland: the cellophane bees (*Colletes*) and the masked bees (*Hylaeus*).

Cellophane Bees
Colletes spp.

Cellophane bees line their nests with a waterproof material that resembles clear plastic when dry. They are superficially similar to bees in the genera *Andrena* and *Halictus*: small to moderate in size (6 to 20 millimetres in length), hairy, and known to carry pollen on the outside of their bodies on scopae. The eyes of cellophane bees are angled—rather than parallel—which gives the face a heart-shaped appearance and helps distinguish them. They nest in the ground and, instead of providing larvae with a

- Size: 6-20 mm body length
- Habitat detail: nest underground (*Colletes* spp.) or in hollow woody stems (*Hylaeus* spp.)
- Distribution: worldwide

Compact cellophane bee.

pollen ball to feed on, cellophane bees leave a soupy mass made of pollen mixed with nectar and water. Three species of cellophane bees have been recorded in Newfoundland.

The compact cellophane bee, *Colletes compactus*, is a late summer bee that feeds on late-blooming asters and goldenrods. A female compact cellophane bee will construct and provision a cell in her nest, and then attach an egg to the side of the cell at a 35 degree angle from the liquid mass of nectar and pollen. As the egg develops, it arches toward the liquid mass. Once it touches the liquid, hatching is triggered. The larva slips into the gooey mass to feed and develop.

Masked Bees
***Hylaeus* spp.**

Masked bees are small, wasplike, non-hairy bees. They are often matte black with yellow or white areas on the face, giving them their common name. Females have a yellow-white pattern beside the eyes; on males, the colour extends across much of the lower face. *Hylaeus* females carry pollen and nectar in a crop and most nest in the hollow woody stems of dead berry canes. Five species of *Hylaeus* are recorded from Newfoundland.

Female masked bee, *Hylacus* sp.

Face of a male modest masked bee.

Sweat bee, *Lasioglossum* sp.

SWEAT BEES
Family Halictidae

Sweat bees are a diverse family of shiny metallic and non-metallic bees. Female halictids carry pollen on the tibia and femur of their hind legs. Three diverse genera are recorded in Newfoundland and Labrador: *Halictus*, *Lasioglossum*, and the kleptoparasitic *Sphecodes*.

- Size: 3-11 mm body length
- Habitat detail: variable, from wilderness to urban backyards
- Distribution: worldwide

Lasioglossum spp.

Lasioglossum is the largest of all bee genera worldwide. Ranging from minute to 11 millimetres in length, these bees are matte black to shiny metallic black, commonly seen in backyards, and often attracted to sweat, giving them their common name. Extremely difficult to identify to species even under the microscope, these bees are sometimes distinguished by the relative density of small punctures on their surface. About 15 species of *Lasioglossum* have been recorded in Newfoundland and Labrador.

Halictus spp.

Halictus are brown-and-black bees that, in North America, nest in the ground. *Halictus* have bands of hair restricted to the apical portion of each abdominal segment; the area between bands is usually hairless. The orange-legged furrow bee, *Halictus rubicundus*, is the only species of this genus in the province. It is usually 10 to 11 millimetres in length and has been recorded collecting pollen and nectar from a wide range of flowers. It

Orange-legged furrow bee near her nest entrance.

is a well studied bee due to the variation in degree of sociality. In warmer, southern climates, the orange-legged furrow bee is eusocial; it lives a solitary life in cooler temperate climates. This variation presents the opportunity to study the evolution of social behaviour.

Female kleptoparasitic *Sphecodes* sp.

Dirt-covered *Sphecodes* sp., likely waiting to sneak into a host nest.

Sphecodes spp.

Sphecodes are wasplike in appearance in that they are slender and mostly hairless. They are often shiny black with a red abdomen that makes them easy to recognize. Females lack pollen-carrying structures, as they rely on the provisions of other bees to feed their young. They differ from other kleptoparasites: the female *Sphecodes* enters the host nest, eats the host egg, and lays an egg of her own in its place—as opposed to laying her egg and relying on the hatched larva to eat the host. Sometimes adult *Sphecodes* bees move into host nests and live there with them, presumably eating the hosts' eggs and laying their own eggs as the cells are provisioned.

Leafcutter bee, *Megachile* sp.; scopa on the abdomen underside is characteristic of bees in this family.

CARDER, LEAFCUTTER, AND MASON BEES
Family Megachilidae

This large and diverse family of bees is represented in the province by four genera: *Anthidium*, *Megachile*, *Osmia*, and *Coelioxys*. Many megachilids use plant material to line their nests and have large mandibles for cutting leaves, moving rocks, and chewing wood. The pollen-collecting hairs of megachilids are located on the underside of the abdomen (except in kleptoparasitic species) and are a defining characteristic of bees in this family. Most are solitary, but they may nest in groups, building nests in the ground, hollow stems, or dead wood. They may also use other available holes/spaces such as pine cones, snail shells, or steel pipes. This feature has led them to take up residence in commercially bought "bee houses" or "bee condos," as well as being used commercially for pollination services.

Male wool-carder bee gripping flower with his mandibles. He most likely spent the night sleeping here.

Wool-carder bee entering a foxglove flower.

European Wool-Carder Bees
Anthidium manicatum

The genus *Anthidium* is represented in Newfoundland by one species, the European wool-carder bee. This fast-flying bee is most often seen in urban gardens where lamb's ear is grown. This bee resembles a yellowjacket (page 72), but European wool-carder bees are hairy while yellow jackets are not. Females are about 11 to 13 millimetres in length; males, 14 to 17 millimetres.

Female European wool-carder bees scrape dense hairs off the leaves of lamb's ear, *Stachys byzantine*, and carry it back to their nest in a ball. They use this material to line nest cavities, earning them the name wool-carder bees. This European species was introduced into the United States in the early 1960s and was first recorded on the island of Newfoundland in 2011. The spread of this species

- Size: female 11-13 mm body length; male 14-17 mm
- Habitat detail: urban gardens where lamb's ear is grown
- Distribution: recent introduction in the province; confirmed in St. John's, Grand Falls-Windsor, and Corner Brook

is likely due to their nesting choice in pre-existing cavities in wood, which can be easily transported to new areas. Male wool-carder bees are very territorial. They have five spines on the apical tergum that can inflict serious damage to victims. They are aggressive toward conspecific males as well as other visitors to "their" flowers. They have been known to dive-bomb and kill other bees, competing for territory. It is not known whether the territorial nature of this species will diminish the utility of urban gardens as reservoirs of native pollinators in urban habitats.

Face of a female wool-carder bee.

Expect to see wool-carder bees early in the summer. They are a generalist forager and can be found foraging on sage, mint, catnip, lavender, Russian sage, and lamb's ear. The wool-carder bee is a solitary bee, with one generation a year. Females nest in pre-existing cavities such as beetle holes in dead wood and prefer to nest in aerial cavities.

LEAFCUTTER BEES
Megachile spp.

Leafcutter bees are uniquely shaped, making them relatively easy to identify. Their abdomens are slightly flattened and taper at the ends and the head is broad with large jaws; they tend to rest with their abdomens up when they are on a flower. Female bees in the genus *Megachile* have large mandibles for cutting leaves into pieces which are used to line the cells of their nest, gaining them their common name. The variations in structure and the number of teeth on these large mandibles are often used to distinguish between species. Many leafcutter bees use rose leaves as a favourite nesting material; plants with circles cut out of the edge of the leaves likely indicates the presence of these bees. Seven species of *Megachile* have been recorded from Newfoundland, with two to three of these in Labrador.

Perfect circles chewed out of rose leaves by a leafcutter bee.

Frigid leafcutter bee; its large mandibles are used for chewing leaves for nest lining.

Frigid Leafcutter Bees
Megachile frigida

Frigid leafcutter bees are robust and eye-catching. The females have bright orange scopal hairs and a mane of pale hairs on the sides of the thorax and on the fronts of their faces around the antennae. Males look quite different, with enlarged, pale front legs fringed with hairs and orange-and-black markings. It is thought that the males use these enlarged front legs during mating to subdue the female; as well, he uses odour glands to reassure her that he is the right bee for the job.

The frigid leafcutter bee has been recorded foraging on thistle, sedum, alfalfa, clover, vetch, and fireweed. They usually excavate nests in rotting logs (page 39).

- Size: female 12–25 mm body length; male 11–15 mm
- Habitat detail: nests in rotting logs
- Distribution: North America; widespread across Newfoundland and Labrador

Osmia bucephela female.

Osmia inermis nest under flowerpots placed in a blueberry field.

MASON BEES
Osmia spp.

Mason bees, *Osmia* spp., are a group of solitary bees that often use mud as a nesting material. Like others in the family Megachilidae, females carry pollen on the scopal hairs on their abdomens. Most mason bees have a metallic sheen to their stout bodies (8 to 16 millimetres) and are fast fliers. Many species are important crop pollinators. They often use pre-existing holes to nest in, and they readily use commercial bee condos, bundles of straws, or holes in a block of wood. Six species of mason bees have been recorded in Newfoundland—none to date from Labrador.

Coelioxys sp. female.

KLEPTOPARASITES

Coelioxys spp.

Coelioxys species are kleptoparasites primarily on bees in the genus *Megachile*. Of all the kleptoparasitic bees, this genus is the most diverse, with over 500 species worldwide. *Coelioxys* is Greek for "sharp belly" and all females have a characteristic sharp point to their abdomens. The tip of the male abdomen has spines. With large eyes, a broad black thorax, red or black legs, and a distinct abdomen, this genus is fairly easy to recognize. Two species have been recorded in Newfoundland: Porter's cuckoo leafcutter bee, *Coelioxys porterae* (9 to 12 millimetres body length) and *C. moesta* (7 to 12 millimetres). *Megachile relativa* has been recorded as a host for both and *M. frigida* as a host of *Coelioxys porterae*.

Bald-faced hornet.

WASPS
BALD-FACED HORNET
Dolichovespula maculata

- Size: 12–15 mm body length
- Habitat detail: build nests in trees and bushes
- Distribution: throughout North America (except very dry regions)

Although it has no yellow markings, the bald-faced hornet is actually a species of yellowjacket. True hornets are in the genus *Vespa*, of which only one species, *Vespa crabro*, is found in North America—it arrived from Europe in the 1800s and was first noticed in New York. *Vespa crabro* have not been recorded in Newfoundland and Labrador; they will be recognized if they do show up: individuals are up to 40 millimetres long and they live in colonies of hundreds.

The bald-faced hornet has a similar life history to that of the eastern yellowjacket (page 72) and also eats insects. One strong difference between the species is nest location. The eastern yellowjacket prefers cavities; the bald-faced hornet locates its paper-covered nests in bushes or among the lower branches of trees.

Fraser Piccott and his grandson, Liam, regularly walk around Bowring Park in St. John's, but it was not until autumn 2017, when the leaves had started to drop, that they noticed a large nest made by the bald-faced hornet. The nest they discovered was finished for the season, but over the summer it had attained the size of a soccer ball (at the higher end of the nest size range) and probably contained up to 400 individuals at its peak of activity.

 The common name "bald-faced" does not refer to its hairless face but is a shortening of "piebald," referring to this species' black-and-white markings on its face and body.

EASTERN YELLOWJACKET
Vespula maculifrons

The common name yellowjacket is used for a variety of species in the subfamily Vespinae, but none of these species should be confused with the more distantly related and easier-to-live-with honey bee (page 54). The eastern yellowjacket is about the size of a honey bee worker, but it has bright yellow markings and is shinier than the fuzzy, golden brown honey bee.

Eastern yellowjackets are social insects. The queen founds a colony in spring within a subterranean cavity such as an abandoned rodent nest. She makes a paperlike material out of wood fibre and saliva and uses it to create a comb surrounded by an envelope. She lays eggs in the comb cells, which are destined to be daughters (the queen chooses the sex, a common trait in Hymenoptera). She forages for insects to feed her developing brood until the workers emerge and take over the colony chores: nursing, nest building, and defending the colony, primarily from mammals. Colonies can be made up of hundreds to thousands of individuals.

Eastern yellowjackets can inflict multiple painful stings—imagine a sewing machine needle at work. They may also bite their prey, to get better purchase for stinging. Humans frequently and inadvertently build attractive cavities (in between storm windows or in the eave of a shed, for example) for yellowjacket nest building. In early summer, the workers show up at backyard picnics, primarily looking for protein sources to feed developing larvae, at times pulling charred meat from a cooled barbecue or dead insects from a car's grill.

Eastern yellowjacket.

- Size: 12–16 mm body length
- Habitat detail: urban and woodland
- Distribution: eastern North America

In late summer, colonies are at their maximum size, and queens and male offspring are produced. Congregations of hundreds of males looking for mates may be seen, for instance, flying around a prominent tree.

Most males die in the fall with the first sub-zero temperatures, but mated queens find a protected cavity and hibernate until spring. They do not re-use their old nest sites.

HORNTAILS
Family Siricidae
Timberflies

Horntails are large insects known in Newfoundland and Labrador as timberflies. Females have a long slender ovipositor (egg-laying structure) at the end of the abdomen. Both sexes have a spearlike plate, the cornus, or horn, at the tip of the abdomen, giving them their common name. A female uses the ovipositor to drill into the wood of weakened and dying trees, where she lays one or more eggs. It can take 10 to 15 minutes to penetrate the wood in order to lay eggs.

Eggs hatch into soft, whitish, wrinkly larvae which bore through the wood as they feed, making tunnels. The larvae do not actually feed on wood—rather, they live in a symbiotic relationship with fungi: adult females carry

Black horntail, female.

fungi and inoculate the tree host when they lay eggs. The fungus grows in the tree and the larvae feed on it.

Of the 21 species of horntails in Canada, seven occur in Newfoundland and Labrador. One of the most common species provincewide is *Sirex cyaneus*, the blue horntail. The black horntail, *Urocerus albicornis*, is probably the most commonly encountered and familiar horntail in forested areas on the island. *Urocerus albicornis* has not been recorded from Labrador but a related species, *Urocerus flavicornis*, the banded horntail, occurs in both Labrador and western Newfoundland. Larvae of all three species occur in fir, spruce, and pine.

The blue horntail is about 25 millimetres long and primarily attacks balsam fir. Females have metallic blue-black bodies and yellowish legs. Males are similar in appearance, except a large part of the abdomen is pale reddish brown and the hind legs are overall dark. The area behind the eyes of both sexes is black. Adults are present from late summer through the fall.

- Size: 12–40 mm body length
- Habitat detail: forested areas; areas with wounded, stressed, or dying trees, including near logging operations and burnt-over areas
- Distribution: worldwide

RHYSSA PERSUASORIA

Rhyssa persuasoria (family Ichneumonidae, see photo page 28) is a large parasitic wasp: males are 10 to 20 millimetres long; females are 40 to 80 millimetres long, including the ovipositor. These distinctive insects have a thin black body, several whitish spots on the head, thorax, and abdomen, and reddish legs. A female will use her antennae to detect horntail and other larvae inside trees; she uses her long ovipositor to drill into the wood and lay a single egg on the horntail larva. Upon hatching, *Rhyssa* larva feed on the horntail. *Rhyssa persuasoria* is most often found in clearings and pathways in forests, especially coniferous forests, where horntails are found. Humans are often alarmed when they encounter horntails and parasitic wasps like *Rhyssa*. The ovipositors are used only to lay eggs, however, and these insects are not aggressive.

Adult black horntails are about 25 millimetres long and present from mid-summer through fall. Females are mostly black, with white markings on their antennae and distinctive black-and-white bands on their legs. Both males and females have a white spot behind each eye. Males have a reddish abdomen and legs which are mostly black with white marks smaller than those on the female.

Blue horntail female.

Adult banded horntails range from 12 to 40 millimetres long and are present from mid-summer to fall. Males and females are black with prominent yellowish bands at the end of the abdomen. Both sexes have black heads with a white spot behind each eye. Females have light reddish brown legs and antennae; males have black antennae and legs mostly black with some paler bands. Male banded horntails sometimes aggregate at high ground, where they wait to intercept females. This behaviour is called "hilltopping."

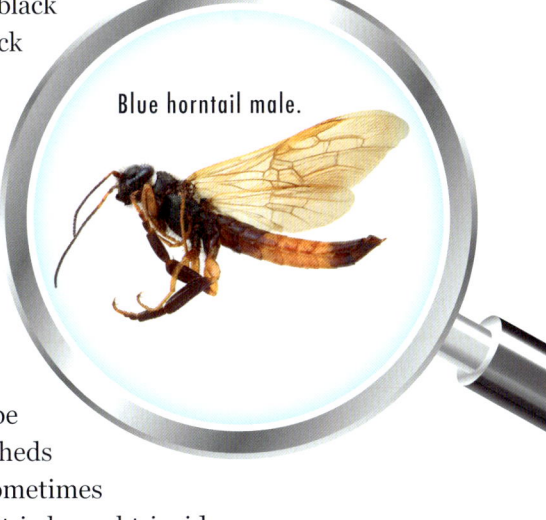

Blue horntail male.

Horntail larvae spend one to three years tunnelling inside wood before becoming adults. Adult horntails may be encountered in homes and sheds where firewood is stored: sometimes larvae are in the wood when it is brought inside, and after their development, adult horntails emerge. As horntail larvae occasionally are accidentally moved in lumber, adults can be found far outside their natural range.

DIPTERA: TRUE FLIES

Green bottle fly.

A mating pair of phantom crane flies.

Deer fly.

Hover fly, *Sphaerophoria* sp.

Hover fly, *Sericomyia militaris*.

DIPTERA
TRUE FLIES

If a house fly sitting on a kitchen table detects an approaching human hand, she jumps. The sudden contractions and stretchings of leg muscles trigger her flight muscles. She does not even have to think about starting to beat her wings. But there is a pause, a tiny fraction of a second, at the top of her jump before her wings are beating at full throttle (approximately 200 beats a second) when she can be caught. Sweep your hand quickly toward her from the front, she will jump slightly forward, and plan to close your hand about an inch above where she had been standing, and amaze friends and family (and maybe yourself).

The common house fly is just one of approximately 125,000 true fly (Diptera) species in the world that have been described by entomologists. Some estimate the total number of Diptera species to be over 1 million. Worldwide, the beetles (Coleoptera) are a more diverse order, but Newfoundland and Labrador hosts many more fly than beetle species. This book could easily be filled with fly species alone; what follows is a vastly shortened list that shows some of the range of fly diversity in the province.

Only species in the order Diptera are true flies. Common names that include *fly* as a separate word, such as *house fly* or *deer fly*, are named species of true flies. The names of non-true flies, such as *dragonflies* or *caddisflies*, are not separated with a space. This convention is used throughout this book.

Despite vast diversity in appearances, the Diptera are united by having one pair of flight-worthy wings (the forewings): *di* meaning two; *ptera*, wings. The hindwings have evolved into structures that detect the fly's body movements in flight. The hindwings, in the shape of small chicken drumsticks, are called halteres (our large crane fly is the easiest to observe halteres on). If you are wondering if the insect you caught, perhaps using the technique described above, is a true fly, count its wings.

CABBAGE MAGGOT

Delia radicum
Cabbage Root Maggot, Root Maggot

- Size: 10 mm body length
- Habitat detail: gardens, agricultural fields
- Distribution: Canada, Europe, other locations worldwide where its host plants grow

The cabbage maggot, accidentally introduced from Europe via ships' ballast, is a serious agricultural pest found throughout Newfoundland and in parts of Labrador. The maggots are whitish, legless larvae which live in soil and feed on the roots of their host plants, including broccoli, cabbage, cauliflower, Chinese cabbage, radish, rutabaga, turnip, and other members of the brassica family. As a result of this feeding, the maggots can kill young plants and severely stunt the growth or lower the quality of older plants. The cool, moist weather of Newfoundland and

Cabbage maggot fly on a leaf.

Cabbage maggot larvae in rutabaga.

Labrador promotes the survival of eggs and larvae, and plant damage can occur throughout the growing season from early summer through to fall harvest.

Adult cabbage maggots resemble house flies (page 84) in appearance but are lighter in colour. The flies spend the winter in the soil in the pupal stage and emerge in May and June to lay eggs on susceptible plants. A related species, *Delia floralis*, the turnip maggot, occurs in southern parts of Labrador. Its larvae feed on the same range of host plants as the cabbage maggot but it emerges from its overwintering areas in July. Gardeners and farmers in Labrador may have to deal with both species at the same time.

 A great deal of research has been conducted at the Agriculture and Agri-Food Canada Research and Development Centre in St. John's, with the goal of managing the cabbage maggot in farms and gardens. Entomologists Ray Morris and Peggy Dixon and Memorial University graduate students Juanita Cutler and Carolyn Parsons studied the biology, natural enemies (see page 147), and management of the cabbage maggot. Successful management techniques developed include intercropping/relay cropping and the use of insect netting.

Barges collecting ballast, to be transferred to larger transatlantic fishing vessels, at low tide in Northern Devon, UK, around 1900.

INSECT STOWAWAYS

That noe Ballast, Prest stoned nor anything else hurtful to the Harbours bee throwne out to the prejudice of said Harbours, but that it be carried ashore and layd where it may not doe annoyance.
—Lawes, Rules, & Ordinances Whereby the Affairs & Fishery of Newfoundland Are to Be Governed, 1653

In the 17th and 18th centuries, ships travelling from Europe to Newfoundland to pick up codfish used soil and rock from their home ports as ballast. Laws of the time prohibited dumping ship's ballast in the ocean—so it was transported to shore. Numerous plant seeds and soil insects made their way across the Atlantic in this way.

CARROT RUST FLY

Psila rosae

- Size: 5-7 mm body length
- Habitat detail: gardens, agricultural fields
- Distribution: Canada, Europe, New Zealand; introduced to Newfoundland

This small fly can be identified by its coloration: shiny green-black body, reddish head, and long yellowish legs. It is a major pest anywhere in Canada and Europe where carrots are grown. The carrot rust fly prefers carrots, but it will also attack parsnips, celery, and parsley. The carrot rust fly was accidentally introduced to Canada in 1885 but was not reported in Newfoundland until the 1930s. Since then, it has spread through most of the carrot-growing areas of the island. A trapping study in 1995 and 1996 did not find the insect in Labrador.

Carrot rust fly.

Carrot rust flies overwinter in soil as pupae. From late June through July they emerge and lay eggs on carrots and other host plants. The larvae (maggots) tunnel in the vegetable's roots as they feed, causing substantial crop damage. The creamy white, legless larvae can be found in the soil around the plant roots or in the carrot itself. Damage may occur in the summer and into the fall as the vegetables mature. In general, carrot rust fly is most serious in locations with shelter from weeds, shrubs, or hedges, where the adults can rest during the day. These delicate flies do not fly well in open, windy areas.

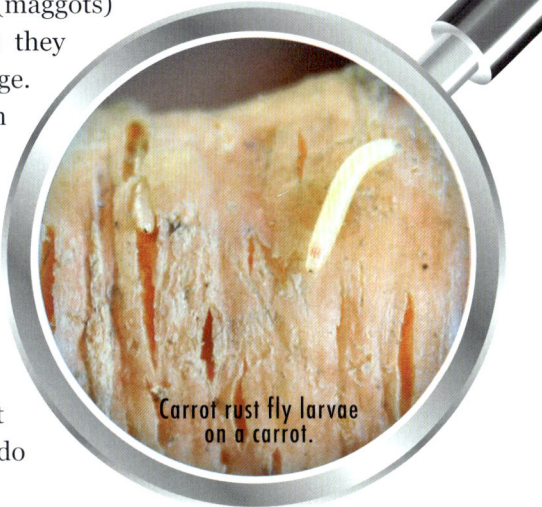

Carrot rust fly larvae on a carrot.

COMMON GREEN BOTTLE FLY

Lucilia sericata

Common green bottle flies are metallic green, sometimes copper green—beautiful, if one ignores the fact that this fly's larval stages were definitely spent crawling through some serious filth. Common green bottle flies are the first

Common green bottle fly.

- Size: 10–14 mm body length
- Habitat detail: breeds in carrion, feces, and garbage
- Distribution: primarily Holarctic, but now found in Australia and some South and Central American countries

insects to arrive at a corpse, their preferred place to lay eggs. Temperature, humidity, and nutrient quality impact the rate at which this insect passes through each life stage. Typically, their shiny white eggs hatch within a day. Transitioning from the first to the second larval stage can take another day, and the same to moult into the third and last larval stage.

During the third stage, larvae crawl away from the corpse to pupate in the soil. They remain there for more than a week before emerging as adult flies. Armed with this information, forensic investigators note the life stage of green bottle flies on a corpse and use this information to help determine when that person died.

Common green bottle flies can also prevent death. Maggot therapy involves the application of living green bottle fly larvae to a wound that has significant dead, or necrotic, tissue. Untreated, the wound might lead to the

Common green bottle fly.

loss of limb or life. The larvae feed on and remove the necrotic tissue from the wound, avoiding healthy tissue, while releasing antimicrobial enzymes that promote new tissue growth. This therapy is growing in importance in modern medicine, but it has been used traditionally in Newfoundland and Labrador for some generations.

Susan Felsberg, a nurse, historian, and long-time resident of Happy Valley-Goose Bay, Labrador, recounts a story she heard in the 1960s from Uncle John Broomfield, one of the original settlers of Happy Valley. According to Broomfield, the generation before his—circa late 1800s—gathered maggots from rotting fish or seal entrails and packed them into a person's wound if it wasn't healing. The maggots would be held in place with heavy wrappings. The species of fly is not certain, but it was likely the green bottle fly.

Common house fly.

COMMON HOUSE FLY
Musca domestica

Common house flies are difficult to identify and easily confused with many other flies. To be certain that a specimen is even in the same family (Muscidae) requires careful observation of wing venation patterns. But if a fly has red eyes, grey stripes on its back, and, more importantly, is in a kitchen, it is likely a common house fly. Male flies have a narrower gap between their compound eyes than females.

The flies seek out semi-liquid foods. They taste through their feet, and a yummy signal through the feet will trigger the proboscis to extend from the head. The proboscis is tipped with a spongelike structure that sops up runny food. Common house flies also make sopping up food easier by drooling and/or vomiting on it: the digestive enzymes from the previous meal begin digestion of the next one immediately. The flies also defecate frequently, and often while they are feeding, which means that they regularly defecate on their food.

- Size: 8–12 mm body length
- Habitat detail: human habitations and associated organic waste (feces, carrion, rotting vegetation)
- Distribution: worldwide, having perhaps originally evolved in the Middle East; likely dispersed via commensalism with humans

Common house flies lay their eggs on rotting organic material such as animal corpses and feces. Each female lays about 100 eggs at once, and she may live long enough—two or three weeks—to repeat this seven times. Consequently, a female fly landing on a plate of food is likely to have previously walked on garbage, feces, or carrion, or all three. Due to their feeding habits and hairy bodies, flies pick up disease-causing agents that may be transferred to food. The common house fly has been implicated in the transmission of dozens of human diseases, including cholera, leprosy, tuberculosis, and typhoid. However, indoor toilets, regular garbage removal, and backfilling landfill sites have greatly diminished the risk that flies pose to Newfoundlanders and Labradorians.

House flies in northern latitudes (e.g., Newfoundland and Labrador) have a Y sex chromosome that contains a single gene that alters development of the male sex; in southern latitudes, house flies have no Y sex chromosome, and the male-determining gene occurs on one of its other five chromosomes.

DEER FLY

***Chrysops* spp.**
Stout, Horse Fly, Three Corner Fly

Deer flies are among the smaller and more delicately built members of the horse fly family, Tabanidae. Deer flies have wide or stout bodies (inspiring one of their common names), short antennae, and bands or blotches of dark colour on their wings. Their striking eyes are streaked with bright colours and bands or blotches of darker areas. Male heads are almost completely covered by their colourful eyes, an ideal feature when searching for mates. People, however, usually only notice the female.

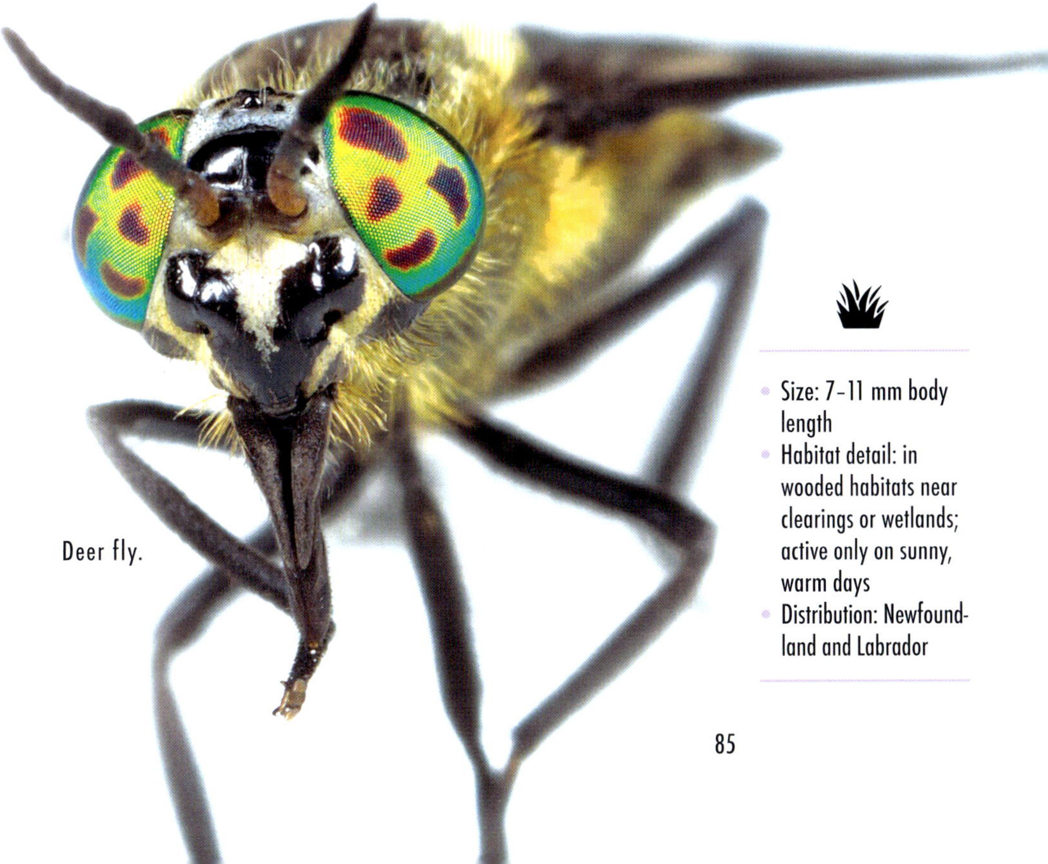

Deer fly.

- Size: 7–11 mm body length
- Habitat detail: in wooded habitats near clearings or wetlands; active only on sunny, warm days
- Distribution: Newfoundland and Labrador

This female deer fly has mouthparts for cutting through the skin of mammals and birds in order to sip blood. Male deer flies do not have mouthparts for cutting; they only sip nectar.

Like Newfoundland and Labrador's other biting flies (black flies, page 98; mosquitoes, page 99), the female deer fly can increase her egg production only after obtaining a blood meal. A deer fly bite hurts, and it usually leaves a welt—not surprising, given her tactics. The female deer fly lands hard on her victim. She grips the skin with her clawed feet and drives a robust proboscis into her victim's flesh. She moves the impaled proboscis around to further lacerate the skin, and wreaks even more damage with additional flesh-cutting mouthparts. All this activity induces blood flow, which she sops up with a spongy mouthpart, a modification at the base of the labium characteristic of most flies.

When her eggs are fully developed, the female will lay them on vegetation that overhangs larval habitat, typically wet earth or along the margins of ponds and streams.

At least four species of deer fly are encountered in Newfoundland and Labrador: *Chrysops excitans*, *Chrysops frigidus*, *Chrysops mitis*, and *Chrysops nigripes*.

The drain fly's feathery wings resemble those of a moth.

DRAIN FLIES

Family Psychodidae
Moth Flies

Drain flies are tiny and stout and have hairy wings, leading them to resemble a small moth more than a fly. Flies in this family are also commonly called moth flies and can be found in areas that have films of moist microorganism-rich sludge, like streamsides, sewage discharge pipes, and household sink drains. With over 2,600 species worldwide, only a few have moved into our homes and buildings, making use of drainpipes for their habitat. *Psychoda alternata* is the most common drain fly in North America. Their colour varies, from yellowish to grey to black, depending on the species.

Drain flies can be considered a nuisance but they are completely harmless. Adults are weak fliers and are usually seen crawling around sinks and bathtubs. Females lay eggs on the surface of the slimy film on the inside

- Size: adult 1.5-4 mm; larvae 3-10 mm
- Habitat detail: in the home around sink and tub drains, sewage discharge pipes, streamsides
- Distribution: cosmopolitan

surfaces of drains and sewage pipes. Larvae are eyeless and legless; the head is darker and narrower than the body. The larvae feed on the organic sludge that forms on inner surfaces of the drains and sewage pipes.

EUROPEAN CRANE FLY
Tipula paludosa
Daddy Longlegs, Leatherjacket (larval stage)

- Size: female 40–50 mm body length; males slightly smaller
- Habitat detail: lawns, agricultural fields, pastures, and other grassy areas
- Distribution: throughout much of Europe and the east and west coasts of North America

The European crane fly is a large insect with a slender slate grey body and narrow pale grey wings with dark front edges. Its long slender legs give it the common name daddy longlegs—confusing, because harvestmen (page 301) are also often called daddy long legs. Harvestmen, however, do not have wings; adult crane flies do. Crane flies are common, appearing from mid-July through the fall, depending on temperature. They often are most abundant, and therefore most noticeable, in August and September.

Soil-dwelling larvae are known as leatherjackets for their leathery outer layer. They are about 2.5 centimetres long when mature and dark grey, fleshy, and legless. Leatherjackets eat the roots and crowns of grasses and, when numerous, can cause serious damage to lawns, pastures, hayfields, and golf courses. There is some evidence that leatherjackets feed on and damage vegetable seedlings.

Leatherjackets in a lawn.

The family Tipulidae, which includes the European crane fly, is the largest known family of flies, with some 14,000 species worldwide. With long narrow wings and long legs, the phantom crane fly, *Bittacomorpha clavipes*, superficially resembles the crane fly but is actually in a related family, the Ptychopteridae (page 76). These look-alikes are black with distinctive white bands on their legs. The black-and-white part of each leg is enlarged toward the feet.

European crane fly.

Flesh fly.

FLESH FLIES
Sarcophaga spp.

Scarlet eyes and a red-tipped abdomen are clues that a fly might be a flesh fly in the genus *Sarcophaga*. These flies are most commonly associated with decaying flesh. They typically arrive at a corpse after the common green bottle fly (see page 81), but they make up for lost time by laying either larvae or eggs that hatch almost immediately. Some flesh flies are alternatively or additionally attracted to feces.

Flesh flies play a critical role in the decomposition of carrion and feces, but they also play an important, if less heralded role, in the dispersal of moss spores. Two species of mosses (in the family Splachnaceae) in Newfoundland and Labrador grow especially well on moose feces. When these mosses mature and produce spores, they exude a dung smell that attracts flies. While exploring the moss, the flies will inadvertently pick up moss spores that may get deposited again when the flies visit a real pile of fresh moose dung. Memorial University professor Paul Marino and his students have been studying the interactions between these mosses and flies for decades. By setting simple traps above fresh moose dung, they have captured thousands of specimens composed of many different fly families, including two species of flesh flies, *Sarcophaga sarraceniae* and *Sarcophaga nearctica*.

- Size: 10-14 mm
- Habitat detail: mainly associated with carrion
- Distribution: throughout US and southern Canada

FLOWER FLIES
Family Syrphidae
Hover Flies

Hover flies are among the most collected and photographed flies. Many are brightly coloured and their behaviour is easy to observe. Adult hover flies are often seen hovering and manoeuvring above flowers; they frequent flowers in search of pollen and are important pollinators. The approximately 6,000 described species of hover flies are separated into

Hover fly, *Eupeodes* sp.

Drone fly.

- Size: 10–20 mm
- Habitat detail: species-dependent
- Distribution: worldwide; 125 species in Newfoundland and Labrador

three subfamilies: Eristalinae, Syrphinae, and Microdontinae. The larval habits correspond to the subfamily divisions: Eristalinae larvae feed on decomposing organic matter; the majority of the Syrphinae are predaceous, feeding on aphids and other soft-bodied insects; and the rarer Microdontinae are known to live in ant nests.

One of the most widespread and familiar hover flies in the subfamily Eristalinae is *Eristalis tenax*, the drone fly (adult) and rat-tailed maggot (larva). This beelike fly is often mistaken for a honey bee as an adult. To distinguish it, look for two wings (bees have four wings) and a robust waist (bees have a thin waist). Females lay eggs in masses near the surface of wet decomposing organic material; this species is often associated with animal agriculture.

Hover fly, *Syrphus* sp.

Syrphid larva (bottom right), sucking juices from an aphid.

The maggot has a breathing tube that resembles a rat tail that it uses when feeding. The tube is retractable and allows the maggot to search for food at varying depths without having to return to the surface to breathe.

Syrphus ribesii, the common banded hover fly, is widespread and typical of the familiar black-and-yellow hoverflies seen in the garden. It is, however, difficult to identify to species from a photo. Belonging to the subfamily Syrphinae, its larvae are predaceous and an important natural enemy of aphids. Encourage hover flies to the garden by providing pollen for the adults and by leaving a few aphid colonies in which the females can lay their eggs.

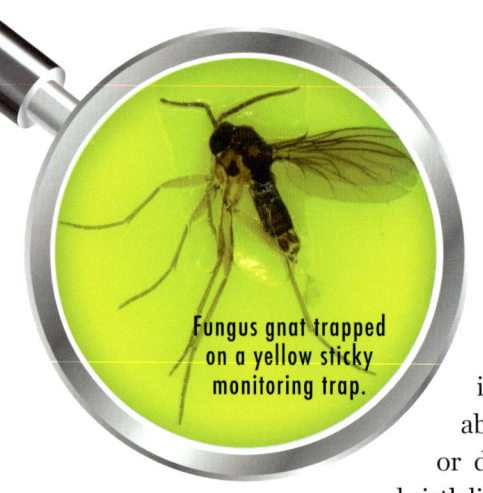

Fungus gnat trapped on a yellow sticky monitoring trap.

FUNGUS GNATS

Families Mycetophilidae, Sciaridae

Most of the commonly encountered fungus gnats belong in the family Mycetophilidae but the name is also used for the closely related Sciaridae (dark-winged fungus gnats). Fungus gnats are mosquito-like in appearance in that they have long legs and a slender abdomen and are often black, brown, or dull yellow. They have long legs with bristlelike hairs and spurs on the tibia. Upon close inspection, look for enlarged coxae, which can be a distinguishing feature of flies in this family.

Anyone with houseplants or a greenhouse will likely encounter these tiny flies at some point in time. They are most often seen hopping or slowly flying around the soil surface of potted plants, especially plants that have been overwatered. Adults live only about one week. Females can lay up to 200 eggs over the course of her short life and prefer to lay eggs on damp soil. The emerging legless larvae are white with black heads and feed on decaying organic matter in the soil. Larvae sometimes move onto water-logged damaged roots to feed.

The first step to control fungus gnats is to reduce the soil moisture in pots. Allow the soil surface to dry between watering. As fungus gnats are weak fliers, placing yellow sticky cards near the soil level of the pots often helps reduce their numbers.

- Size: 2–13 mm
- Habitat detail: moist wooded areas, moist potted houseplants, greenhouses
- Distribution: worldwide

LAKE MIDGE

Chironomus plumosus
Buzzer Midge

The lake midge is a member of the family Chironomidae. Species in this family have delicate bodies and are often mistaken for mosquitoes. Unlike mosquitoes, however, this midge family does not drink blood, as they lack a proboscis—the lake midge would be very large for a mosquito (it is also very large for a midge), so this is particularly good news. The midge wing lacks the scales that run along the wing veins of mosquitoes; like the proboscis, the presence of scales is difficult to ascertain without magnification. Males and females of the lake midge have brown bands that encircle and run the length of their abdomens.

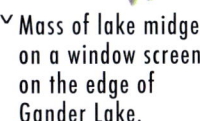

Lake midge antennae.

The lake midge lays eggs on the surface of a lake. The egg mass sinks to the bottom, where the larvae hatch. The larvae are called bloodworms, as they contain an analog to the oxygen-binding protein hemoglobin, which is rare in insects. Each larva constructs a bag out of silk, and from this protective structure it feeds on organic debris filtered from the water. In spring or early summer, the larvae pupate. When the pupae are ready to emerge as adults, they pop to the surface together before quickly wriggling out of their pupal cases to emerge as adults. The speed and coordination of this transformation is essential to limiting the chances of being eaten, particularly by trout. The pupal cases of the lake midge remain on the surface of the water and, through wind and wave, can noticeably accumulate on the shoreline.

Mass of lake midges on a window screen on the edge of Gander Lake.

The adults have atrophied mouthparts and cannot feed. Therefore, they quickly turn their attention to mating, and sections of the shoreline become mating zones. Adult males, who have larger and more feathery antennae than females, drift through the mating zones, gathering into large flying aggregations. At some point they agree—it is not known how—on a swarm marker that anchors the mating swarm to one location. The marker can be a stump or rock, but it can also be a person if that person is stationary or moving very slowly. Female lake midges are attracted to these swarms of thousands of males. Even within the din

- Size: adult 10-13 mm body length
- Habitat detail: associated with large lakes
- Distribution: throughout the northern hemisphere

of the swarm, males are able to hear (using their antennae) the specific sound of the beating wings of an approaching female of their species. The best-positioned male in the swarm likely becomes her mate.

LESSER HOUSE FLY
Fannia canicularis

- Size: 3.5-6 mm body length
- Habitat detail: homes, farms
- Distribution: Eurasia and North America

A fly circling erratically under a central interior light is likely a male lesser house fly. Females usually rest on kitchen walls—they do not go for endless circling, but they must find it an attractive attribute in males. Both sexes hold their wings in a narrow V when at rest and have yellow patches on their abdomens.

As their name suggests, lesser house fly bodies are smaller and narrower than the common house fly (page 84). Lesser house flies make up between 2 and 25 per cent of flies caught on the main floor of a home (Hewitt, 1912, summary of US and UK research), and 100 per cent in upper-storey rooms (Chilcott's 1960 Ottawa observation). It is on farms, however, where this insect is found in its greatest numbers.

Lesser house flies lay eggs on almost any rotting organic material, including decomposing vegetables or animal carcasses, but they prefer animal feces. One study suggested that the flies' favourite laying location is human feces, but in Newfoundland and Labrador mink feces and lesser house flies have made the news. Lesser house flies have been known to invade homes surrounding some mink farms, and this has caused concerns ahead of the expansion of the fur industry into other parts of the province. In 2014, a mink farm in Cavendish, Newfoundland and Labrador, installed automated mink feces removal and processing equipment, with the expectation of reducing the lesser house fly population. Starting in 2015, Memorial University student Srabani Saha assessed the project; her research demonstrated the lesser house fly numbers appear lower since the mechanization.

Lesser house fly, pinned specimen.

LOUSE FLY

Ornithomyia anchineura (possibly)

- Size: 4–12 mm
- Habitat detail: ectoparasite on birds
- Distribution: Nearctic

In May 2017, a merlin, *Falco columbarius*, a small highly migratory bird of prey, was blown offshore. At about 77 nautical miles east-northeast of Cape Freels, it came to rest on a research vessel. Unfortunately, the bird perished from this misadventure, but Department of Fisheries and Oceans biologist Megan Boucher secured the specimen and delivered it to Memorial University. Undergraduate biology student Christine Conlan, while preparing the specimen as a study skin, discovered among this merlin's feathers the strangely flattened fly pictured here.

The flattened appearance is natural. It is thought this shape more readily enables movement within a bird's plumage and enables the fly to gain purchase while it pierces the bird's skin and sups its blood. These flies are called pupa-bearers: eggs hatch (one at a time) within the female's modified reproductive tract, referred to as a uterus. The uterus is lined with modified accessory glands, sometimes called milk glands, that deliver nutrients to the larva. The uterus is laced with tracheal tubes that deliver oxygen to the larva. When born, the largely immobile larva quickly hardens into a roundish and dark-coloured pupa. These pupae are sometimes found in the nests of birds, but it is likely that female flies leave their host and deposit their offspring on soil. The pupae overwinter and complete their development to adulthood in the spring before seeking a host bird and a fly mate.

Ornithomyia anchineura has been collected from at least 68 genera of birds (22 families and seven orders).

The louse fly has a flattened profile to enable it to ride comfortably within the feathers of a bird.

MIXED-UP BLACK FLY
Prosimulium mixtum

- Size: 3–6 mm
- Habitat detail: wooded tracts; breeds, especially, in small shaded streams
- Distribution: eastern North America

Thirty-three species of black flies in North America, at least 12 of which occur in Newfoundland and Labrador, are known to cause significant human misery—they swarm, bite, and explore various orifices. All 33 species are small, usually dark in colour, and have a humped thorax. Their heads appear to be attached much lower than they are in other flies. Black flies use a feeding style called *telmophagy*, which means that they penetrate and lacerate skin using specialized mouthparts—the opposite of the delicate and precise syringe of the mosquito, a feeding style called *solenophagy*.

In early spring, the mixed-up black fly is one of the most vicious biters of people in Newfoundland and Labrador. Even so, and as violent as telmophagy sounds, the bite of the mixed-up black fly is usually painless. To keep the blood flowing, this fly spits an anticoagulant into the wound. Enough of these little painless bites close together might result in a drip of blood coming from the wounds. About 10 per cent of people have an allergic reaction to black fly bites, and many more experience itchiness that could lead to scratching and, perhaps, to a secondary infection.

Mixed-up black flies lay their eggs in streams. Upon hatching, the larvae attach themselves to rocks by making a silk pad into which they engage their hooks.

A handful of reports suggest that people have died from black fly bites. The Reverend Louis L. Noble tells a short story in *After Icebergs with a Painter: A Summer Voyage to Labrador and around Newfoundland* (1861) about a sailor's death by black fly bites. The sailor was likely running from St. John's toward Torbay:

Mixed-up black fly.

A few years ago, a sailor ran away from his vessel, at St. John's and took to these bushy wilds, in which, at length, he got lost, and finally perished from the bites of this pestilent fly [possibly *Prosimulium mixtum*, but maybe another vicious black fly in this area, *Simulium venustum*]. *He was found accidentally, and in a state of insensibility, being covered with them, and so devoured that he died within a few hours after his discovery.*

The first substantial study of black fly hosts (published in 1960) was conducted by Professor Gordon Fraser Bennett. Bennett taught at Memorial University from 1969 to 1995, where he established himself as a world authority, not on black flies but on avian haematozoa. A highly regarded gymnastics coach, Bennett was admitted to Newfoundland and Labrador's Sports Hall of Fame in 1988.

Memorial University professor (1975–2006) Murray Colbo made significant contributions to black fly biology (both in Australia and Newfoundland and Labrador). The Australian black fly, *Austrosimulium colboi*, is named in Colbo's honour.

MOSQUITOES
Family Culicidae
Nippers, Garnippers, Skitties, Skeeties

> ***Cold and mosquitoes***
> ***Those two pests***
> ***Come never together***
> —Ivaluardjuk, in Rasmussen (1929)
> *Intellectual Culture of the Hudson Bay Eskimos*

Sharks, spiders, and snakes occupy our nightmares more often than mosquitoes do. Perhaps this should not be the case: among animals (excluding humans), mosquitoes are the number one killers of humans and they do this by transmitting disease. The threat mosquitoes pose in Newfoundland and Labrador is currently very low but not zero.

Over 3,000 species of mosquitoes have been described worldwide, but only a small proportion pesters humans. Newfoundland and Labrador has at least 37 recorded species of mosquitoes (as of early 2019). The total is an estimate because the earliest mosquito provincial record keeping was done in the 1950s, and only a handful of studies have been conducted since. These studies are typically regionally narrow "snapshots"—a researcher or agency takes a one- or two-year interest in mosquito diversity, and decades follow before the interest is renewed.

A group of Memorial University biologists (Chapman and colleagues) have been trapping mosquitoes since 2010, concentrating on St. John's and its immediate surroundings, as well as in Salmonier Nature Park (approximately 80 kilometres southwest of St. John's). As a result, this group can say with some certainty that 25 species of mosquitoes are in the area (as of 2018). They are rarely encountered together, and only a few are a pest or a worry. Not all mosquitoes are interested in human blood; a few species prefer frog blood. Depending on location—the cabin or the backyard, for example—only one species would likely be a pest at a time.

Of the diversity of mosquitoes in this province, seven species are highlighted here. Four were chosen because of their potential as disease transmitters; the other three illustrate that not all mosquito species are life-threatening and can have interesting life histories to boot.

- Size: 5–12 mm
- Habitat detail: tundra and coastal grasslands
- Distribution: Arctic; *Aedes nigripes* has been collected in Labrador and on the Northern and Avalon Peninsulas; *Aedes impiger* has been seen in Labrador

Arctic Mosquitoes
Aedes nigripes and *Aedes impiger*

These two species of Arctic mosquitoes are known pests that can "form swarms thick enough to asphyxiate caribou," according to science journalist Janet Fang. They are not, however, disease vectors. Some researchers suggest that humans tend to exaggerate the size of mosquito swarms because they irritate us, but most also agree that these Arctic mosquitoes make up a greater proportion of the Arctic biomass than mosquitoes do in any other climatic zone.

Both species have scattered setae on the scutum; that is, they have hairy backs. Separating these two species comes down to a slight difference in the shape of their hind tarsal claw.

Would we not be just fine without mosquitoes? Maybe—everywhere other than the Arctic. The removal of these mosquitoes would profoundly alter biodiversity and abundances of some species. The impact mosquitoes have on caribou is extreme, but often indirect. Caribou will often move in response to mosquito swarms and, thus, some caribou will weaken from continued travel. This, as well as moving into areas caribou may otherwise avoid, can make some in the herd more vulnerable to wolf attacks. Good for the wolves, bad for the caribou. Removing mosquitoes would reduce predation by wolves, which would lead to increased grazing by caribou—in other words, removing mosquitoes would change everything.

Arctic mosquitoes emerge in huge numbers, and the females can vary greatly in their relative size.

Entomologist Tom Chapman spent a summer in Canada's high Arctic (Truelove Lowlands, Devon Island). While walking across the tundra, he saw swarms of mosquitoes (likely *Aedes nigripes*) rise into the air 5 metres ahead of him and then fly directly into his face. During the peak emergence, the field station's double-paned kitchen window accumulated a 10-centimetre-deep band of dead mosquitoes.

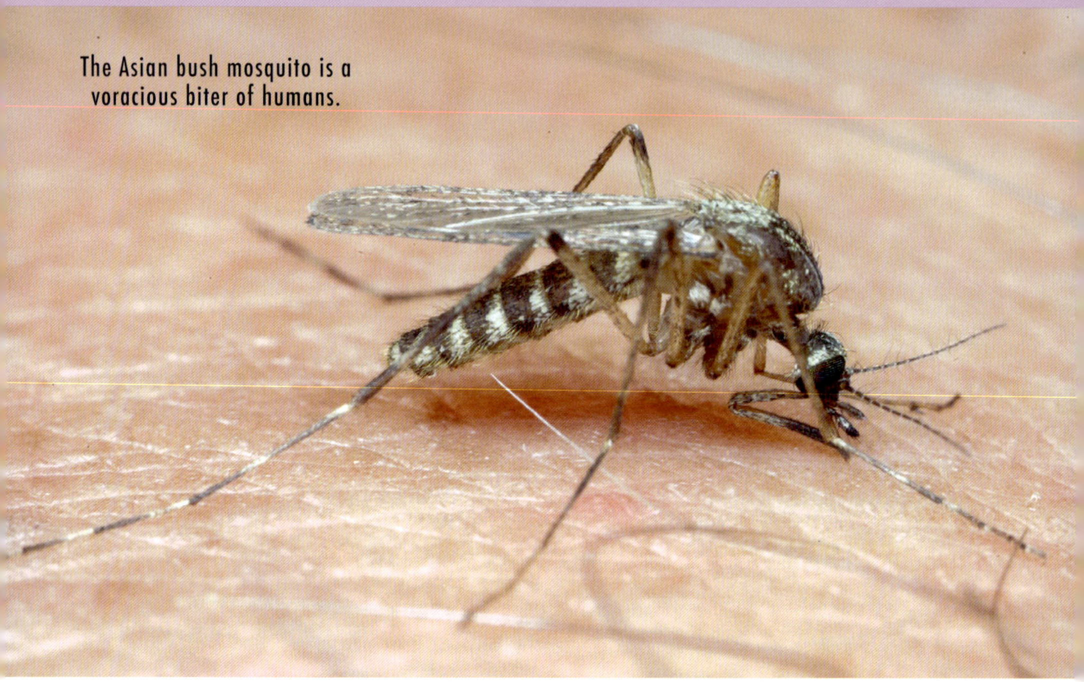

The Asian bush mosquito is a voracious biter of humans.

Asian Bush Mosquito
Aedes japonicus
Asian Rock Pool Mosquito

- Size: 5-9 mm (medium)
- Habitat detail: urban container-breeder (likes small fetid pools of water)
- Distribution: eastern Asia, arrived in North America in 1998

The Asian bush mosquito arrived in St. John's fast on the heels of the detection of *Culex pipiens*. Middle Cove resident Mardon Erbland first noticed this mosquito in 2013. He posted a photograph and an identification to NLNature.com, a citizen science site. Memorial University student Miles Fielden started to see this mosquito in his breeding traps, which he had set in St. John's east to attract egg-laying females of *Culex pipiens*, that same year.

Attracting a container-breeder like the Asian bush mosquito requires two things: a container (in this case, an empty ice cream bucket) and fetid water. Fielden ground up grass, mushrooms, and moose dung and added the mixture to tap water. Dung is not necessary, but it does make the water fetid fast. A bucket left outside on Memorial University's St. John's campus and containing rainwater, garbage, and cigarette butts was found to be harbouring hundreds of bush mosquito wrigglers.

In Europe, this mosquito's movements were linked to the transportation of used tires. While the exact vessel that transported Asian bush mosquitoes to Newfoundland is not known, it is certain that the movement of some sort of container brought this mosquito to our shores. Memorial graduate student Andrew Chaulk used a genetic dataset to determine that Newfoundland's population of this species is likely to have come from Quebec or Ontario. This suggests that trucking was the likely conduit for this mosquito's movements from the mainland.

The Asian bush mosquito is an aggressive people-biter. While it has been implicated in the transmission of a number of diseases, including dengue, chikungunya, and maybe West Nile elsewhere, as of 2018 no evidence of disease activity in Newfoundland and Labrador related to this mosquito has been recorded. Getting rid of standing water and cleaning out gutters regularly, however, helps reduce potential breeding grounds.

Golden Bog Mosquito
Aedes aurifer

With so many wetlands, you would think the golden bog mosquito would love Newfoundland and Labrador. But it was not collected in the province until 2010, when a specimen was identified on the Avalon Peninsula. Why so slow getting to the province? It is abnormal for females of this species to travel significant distances from their breeding site, the bog, so while they clearly can prosper in Newfoundland and Labrador, they just took their time to get here—a few thousand years perhaps.

Golden bog mosquito.

The common name for this mosquito comes from the gold-and-white scales on their thoraces and abdomens, which can be seen clearly on the otherwise dark-coloured

- Size: 5-9 mm
- Habitat detail: near bogs
- Distribution: mainly in the northeastern US, but range extends into southern Ontario and New Brunswick

mosquito. Golden bog mosquitoes bite mammals, including humans, but they are not well known as a transmitter of human disease. A 2008 study in Connecticut, however, suggests that the golden bog mosquito is a good vector of the Jamestown Canyon virus, a member of the California serogroup viruses (see *Aedes canadensis* for more detail).

 Knowing the habits of this insect is useful. It can be a real pest near bogs during peak abundances in spring but, if you have set up camp near a bog and are being bitten by mosquitoes, you only need to reset your tent another 50 to 100 metres from the bog and the golden bog mosquito will leave you alone.

Northern House Mosquito
Culex pipiens pipiens, Culex pipiens molestus

Culex pipiens is a species complex, which means its members are closely related and often hard to tell apart. The complex includes two forms of *pipiens* that are important in Newfoundland and Labrador: *Culex pipiens* form *pipiens* and *Culex pipiens* form *molestus*. Form *molestus* is restricted to human-built underground structures, and famously molested those seeking safety in London's underground railway system during the Blitz. Form *pipiens* differs in that it does not breed in confined spaces, and it would rather bite birds than people (*molestus* likes birds and people).

- Size: 5-9 mm
- Habitat detail: urban container-breeder
- Distribution: native to Africa, but now in temperate regions of the northern and southern hemispheres

Form *pipiens* is found in northeastern North America, but genetic studies have revealed that this population (along with other populations outside the United Kingdom) has some evidence of hybridization with *molestus*. The outcome is a "bridge vector": a mosquito that is more likely to carry viruses between host types. In this case, the avian virus, West Nile, has been transmitted to humans via form *pipiens*. Since 2002, thousands of Canadians have been infected with West Nile virus, resulting in a few dozen deaths. As of 2018, there has been no known instance of an infection (resulting in death or otherwise) occurring in Newfoundland and Labrador in humans or birds.

This northern house mosquito specimen does not look menacing (it is dried out and missing legs), but its sisters have the capacity to transmit disease to humans.

Form *pipiens* was first collected on Newfoundland's west coast in 2004 by Sarah Hustins, and it was first collected in St. John's (specifically the neighbourhood of Georgetown) by Kate Carson in 2012. A genetic study conducted by Andrew Chaulk (2016) found evidence of the bridge vector hybrid on the west, but not the east, coast of Newfoundland. All three were Memorial University graduate students at the time.

WEST NILE VIRUS PREVENTION
Two important actions will help fight West Nile virus:
- Report any significant bird deaths (crows and other corvids such as ravens, blue jays, and grey jays) to a local conservation officer or the Animal Health Division.
- Inspect your property and remove any standing water. Rain accumulating in a blocked rain gutter, for example, is all the water this mosquito needs to breed.

Pitcher plants (top) are home to the pitcher plant mosquito (adult, middle; larva, bottom).

Pitcher Plant Mosquito
Wyeomyia smithii

The larvae of this mosquito develop in the water held within the juglike leaves of the northern pitcher plant, the floral emblem of Newfoundland and Labrador. Yes—while this plant kills insects and spiders, it also hosts an entire ecosystem. It is not surprising that an ecosystem that can be contained in a teacup has been attractive to biologists for study, and within this one, *Wyeomyia smithii* is the best-known inhabitant. As interesting as it is, the pitcher plant mosquito is a weak flier and not likely to be a pest.

The larvae can be found within the pitcher plant leaves anytime. In fact, if you ventured out in February and removed the solid ice from within a plant you might find wrigglers (larvae) once the ice thawed, but that will damage the plant. However, during warmer periods, a turkey baster can be used to sample for larvae (do not eat turkey at a mosquito specialist's house), thus leaving the plant uninjured. Within days, the larvae will develop into pupae, which will, in turn, emerge as adults.

When the adult is at rest, this mosquito strikes a rather elegant pose, with hind legs raised and arched forward. It has grey scales on the top of its thorax. If we were ever to have an insect emblem for the province, at least one of the authors of this book would vote for the pitcher plant mosquito.

- Size: 2–4 mm (possibly the smallest mosquito in the world)
- Habitat detail: bogs
- Distribution: from Florida to Labrador (island of Newfoundland too), and as far west as Manitoba

The woodland pool mosquito is one the first species of mosquitoes to arise in spring and pester human.

Woodland Pool Mosquito
Aedes canadensis

Throughout its North American range, peak abundance for the woodland pool mosquito is usually early spring. A local study (Kate Carson 2011, St. John's) of the species, however, suggests that this pattern is not true in Newfoundland and Labrador. This mosquito was found to be active from mid-June to mid-September, with peak abundance in mid-August. As this study was narrow in place and time, it is not definitive.

In a mid-August sample taken near Middle Cove, snowshoe hare virus was detected within the bodies of these mosquitoes. This virus belongs to the California serogroup, a group of viruses that show genetic similarities.

The snowshoe hare virus was first detected on the island of Newfoundland in the 1980s along with another type of California serogroup virus. It is possible to contract this disease without knowing it—most people experience no symptoms, or symptoms akin to a mild flu, which are easily dismissed. Only rarely do these viruses infect the central nervous system and result in serious illness or death.

As of 2018 there is no evidence of a human death or serious illness in Newfoundland and Labrador due to snowshoe hare virus, although they have occurred in Canada. Any risks from mosquitoes are outweighed by the health benefits of being active outdoors. Wear brightly coloured clothing and mosquito repellent and go for a hike.

- Size: 5-9 mm (medium)
- Habitat detail: in wooded areas close to shallow pools of water (its breeding habitat)
- Distribution: throughout Canada and the eastern US (except southern Florida)

SIPHONAPTERA: FLEAS

Car flea, dog flea, human flea, and flea from a red squirrel.

Human flea.

Cat flea showing structures used in determining species.

SIPHONAPTERA
FLEAS

Fleas are blood-feeding insects that have been long known as an unwelcome companion of human civilization. Flea bites are annoying, can spread disease, and may generate an allergic reaction in their host. Over 2,500 species of flea have been identified worldwide. Individual flea species may feed off a single species or family of animals.

In contrast to the louse (page 260), which is flattened from back to front (dorsoventrally), the flea is flattened sideways (laterally). The flea is wingless but, with its large hind legs, is well known for its ability to jump long distances, up to 50 times its own length.

The human flea, *Pulex irritans*, the cat flea, *Ctenocephalides felis felis*, and the dog flea, *Ctenocephalides canis*, are of concern to the public, although almost all domestic or wild animals have one or more species that affects them (including squirrel, mink, ground nesting bird, and seabird fleas). Species identification is not as easy as host identification: red squirrels, for example, have been known to harbour at least 25 different flea species, and precise identification of a flea requires microscopic examination.

Eggs laid by the female hatch after a few days. The larvae transform into pupae and subsequently adults—at which point they need a blood meal to survive. The life cycle of a flea can be completed in less than two months in favourable environmental conditions.

In Newfoundland and Labrador, the human flea is no longer a common pest. The cat flea and the dog flea are both encountered regularly, with the cat flea being most prevalent. A tapeworm parasite, *Dipylidium caninum*, may be carried by these fleas and infect a dog or cat or, more rarely, a human. Cat scratch fever, caused by the bacterium *Bartonella henselae*, can be transmitted between cats by the cat flea.

Differentiating between the dog and cat flea requires a microscope and a good quality flea specimen. It primarily involves an examination of the head region: the cat flea's head is more elongate than the dog's, and the combs on the head are different.

Red squirrel fleas may also become a household pest if a red squirrel, *Tamiasciurus hudsonicus*, nest is near a home or cabin.

- Size: up to 3 mm long
- Habitat detail: on host animal and surrounding environment
- Distribution: worldwide

 The bubonic plague, or Black Death, killed thousands of Europeans, resulting in major social upheavals. This disease, caused by the bacterium *Yersinia pestis*, was carried by rats and transmitted by the Oriental rat flea, which could also bite humans.

 Traditional Newfoundland prevention for fleas: Place mint or tansy between the bottom sheet and the mattress of the bed (*Home Medicine: The Newfoundland Experience*, John K. Crellin).

COLEOPTERA: BEETLES

European ground beetle.

Seven-spotted lady beetle.

Long-horned flower beetle, *Evodinus monticola*.

Viburnum leaf beetle, *Pyrrhalta viburni*.

Red-shouldered pine borer, *Stictoleptura canadensis*.

COLEOPTERA
BEETLES

Beetles represent one-quarter of all species on the planet. It is estimated that there are more than 387,000 species of beetles in the world, of which 8,300 occur in Canada. At least 1,100 species are found on the island of Newfoundland, and more than 500 have been recorded from Labrador.

Thickened outer wings (elytra) protect the beetle's soft abdomen and the membranous inner wings. These delicate inner wings are folded underneath the elytra when not used for flight. The elytra meet in a line down the middle of the beetle's back. Many aquatic beetles are streamlined and compressed top to bottom, with legs adapted for swimming. Rove beetles have shortened elytra which expose their abdomens. The heads of weevils are modified with a long snout.

BURYING BEETLES
Family Silphidae
Carrion Beetles

Burying or carrion beetles are members of the family Silphidae, of which there are at least six species in Newfoundland and Labrador. Silphids are most active at night, typically associated with dead vertebrates, and not encountered often by the general public. The two examples of burying beetles described below were highlighted in a Memorial University study published in *Northeastern Naturalist* in 2001. The authors were Sabina Wilhelm and professors David Larson and Anne Storey. Their investigation was motivated by an anecdote from 1999: a bucket of dead puffins was left outside in a rainstorm and attracted and drowned 179 specimens of the burying beetle *Nicrophorus investigator*, presumably attracted to the decomposing puffins. This event suggested that burying beetles might be an important ecological component of a seabird colony. Focusing on Great Island (off the southeastern shore of the island of Newfoundland), the researchers found two burying beetle species, *Nicrophorus investigator* and *Nicrophorus defodiens*, in large numbers. As it turned out, these species were found more often in the burrows of Leach's storm-petrels than in the burrows of puffins. The authors speculated that the smaller size of the petrels was more attractive to the beetles, which attempt to bury, at least partially, carrion that they lay their eggs on; as well, petrel burrows are often found in wooded areas with moist soil, which may facilitate burying carrion.

Silphidae are relatively flat bodied compared to other beetles. All have clubbed antennae. Most are black, but some additionally have vivid splashes of yellow or orange.

Burying beetle.

Banded sexton beetle.

Banded Sexton Beetle
Nicrophorus investigator

With orange- to red-tipped antennae and orange to reddish bands on its elytra, this is an eye-catching beetle. Banded sexton beetles, 15 to 25 millimetres long, are thought to fly many kilometres to rotting carrion (bird, mammal, or sometimes a beached fish). If the dead animal is a vole or a songbird or something else small enough to bury, and it has also attracted a crowd of banded sexton beetles, these beetles will battle. Males fight males and females fight females. The result will be a strong and scrappy lone banded sexton beetle couple. They will struggle together to hide their carrion by excavating beneath it until the carrion sinks out of sight—this can take a full work day— and is then covered over. The cavity the beetles create for the carrion is called a crypt.

In a crypt, the beetles form the carrion into a ball. They also remove the feathers or hair from the animal and use this material to line and reinforce the crypt walls.

- Size: 12-25 mm
- Habitat detail: found on carrion, most often associated with boreal forest in Newfoundland and Labrador
- Distribution: Holarctic

The beetles cover the now-bald carrion with their own excretions that contain antifungal and antibacterial agents. These excretions slow the decay of the carrion and reduce the smell. The beetles themselves do not mind the smell—they just do not want to attract flies and more beetles that they have to drive away from their carrion ball. More importantly, though, they are preserving the carrion as a food source for their offspring.

The number of eggs the female lays is related to the size of the carrion ball. When the eggs hatch, the beetle pair will chew and partially digest carrion pieces that they then regurgitate for their begging offspring to eat. Offspring beg by touching their parents with their legs. It sounds like a warm family scene ... but if the mother beetle has produced too many offspring for the carrion ball to sustain, she will cull her family by eating a few, thereby spoiling her chances of receiving the insect mother-of-the-year award.

Burying Beetle
Nicrophorus defodiens

- Size: 13-20 mm
- Habitat detail: found on carrion, most often associated with boreal forest in Newfoundland and Labrador
- Distribution: Holarctic

The burying beetle (see photo, page 112) is similar in shape to the banded sexton beetle, and it also has similar flashy orange or reddish markings on its elytra, but it is smaller and lacks a reddish tip on its antennae. The life history of this species is similar to that of the banded sexton beetle but, perhaps due to its smaller size, the breeding pair excavates at most a shallow bowl under the carrion. The pair will then cover the carrion with leaf litter, which leaves them vulnerable to having their carrion ball stolen by members of larger species of burying beetles.

This vulnerability likely at least partially explains why this species is associated with carrion found in trees. Many birds and a few mammals in Newfoundland and Labrador are cavity-nesters. The death of chicks or pups will attract many species of burying beetles, but *Nicrophorus defodiens* is one of two species (the other, *Nicrophorus tomentosus*) that is known to breed on carrion in trees.

CONFUSED FLOUR BEETLES
Tribolium confusum

The confused flour beetle, *Tribolium confusum*, was given its name because it was confused with a similar species, *Tribolium castaneum* (red flour beetle), for many years. The two can only be distinguished as adults with the aid of magnification of the antennae. The antennal segments on the confused flour beetle increase in size gradually from base to tip; the segments on the tip of the antennae of the red flour beetle are abruptly much larger than the preceding ones. The adults are small (3 to 4 millimetres long), shiny, reddish brown elongated beetles.

Adults of these species were found in jars containing grain in the tombs of pharaohs around 2500 BC and can still be found infesting grain today. Adults live up to three years; both adults and larvae feed on flours and broken kernels of grain. In addition to directly damaging the flour by leaving behind dead bodies, fecal pellets, and liquids, these beetles exude pungent odours that reduce the quality of the grains they infest.

Female beetles can lay 300 to 400 eggs over a period of five to eight months. Thus, the introduction of a few beetles can create quite an infestation in a short period of time. Careful sanitation, regularly cleaning cupboards, and storing flours and other cereals, bran, dried fruits, seeds and beans in containers, can prevent a major infestation.

Red flour beetle; note the abrupt enlargement of the last three antennal segments.

- Size: Adults 3–4 mm; larvae 4–5 mm
- Habitat detail: food cupboards, granaries
- Distribution: worldwide; more common in cooler, northern regions

< Confused flower beetle; its antennal segments gradually become larger.

Red flour beetle feeding on grain.

DERMESTID BEETLES
Family Dermestidae
Skin Beetles

Carpet Beetles
Anthrenus verbasci and *Attagenus unicolor*

- Size: black carpet beetle 2.8–5 mm body length; varied carpet beetle 1.7–3.5 mm body length
- Habitat detail: primarily household pests, larvae hide in dark undisturbed areas
- Distribution: cosmopolitan

The common name "carpet beetle" can refer to a number of different species with the most common being *Anthrenus verbasci*, the varied carpet beetle, and *Attagenus unicolor*, the black carpet beetle. These species are found in most parts of the world. Homeowners most often notice the larvae, exuvia, and/or feeding damage of the carpet beetle, rather than the adults. The larvae range in size from 4 to 8 millimetres, depending on species. All have bristles.

Black carpet beetle larvae are the largest of these two species and are light brown to black. They have a carrotlike shape, with a tapered rear end and long tufts of bristles (almost as long as the body) at the rear end. In contrast, the larvae of the museum beetle, *Anthrenus museorum*, and varied carpet beetles are smaller, less tapered, and stouter; they are light brown, with bristles organized in strips of light and dark, giving a striped appearance. Larvae are scavengers and feed on a range of protein-rich plant and animal products such as natural fibre fabrics (silk, wool, and linen), animal carcasses and hides, feathers, dried meats, dog food, and grains in kitchen cupboards.

Varied carpet beetle adult.

Black carpet beetle larva, pupal case, and adult.

Adults prefer to live outside and feed on pollen and nectar. They gain access to the house via flowers or other plant material being brought inside; females may lay eggs on lint or dead insects around window ledges. The larvae can also be introduced into the home on old carpets and draperies. Carpet beetles become a nuisance if the population is large enough and left unchecked.

The adult black carpet beetle is 2.8 to 5 millimetres long and ranges from black to reddish brown. The head is concealed from above and it has clubbed antennae. The varied carpet beetle is 1.7 to 3.5 millimetres with an overall round shape with white and yellowish brown scales on its body. Its name comes from the great variation in the colour pattern on the dorsal surface.

MUSEUM PESTS
In addition to being house pests often found in cupboards and drawers, larvae of beetles in the family Dermestidae are notorious museum pests and can cause considerable damage to fabrics, papers, stuffed animals, hides, skins, and insect collections. (Above: dermestid larva and feeding damage to moth specimens.)

Larder beetle.

Larder beetle larva.

Larder Beetle
Dermestes lardarius
Bacon Beetle

This beetle's common name came from its being found near and on cured meats, especially bacon, traditionally stored in larders. The use of refrigeration has decreased the economic importance of this insect but it can still be found regularly in homes, museums, and anywhere that contains a suitable food source. Known to feed on dried dog food, furs, hides, feathers, and dead insects, the larvae of this beetle have the characteristic long rear-end bristles of dermestid beetle larvae. Larvae are dark brown and covered in brown bristles, with two spines at the end of the abdomen that curve backwards.

Adults are small, oval, dark brown to black beetles with a distinct pale yellow transverse band and six to eight small black spots on the elytra. Antennae are relatively short and clubbed.

- Size: 7-9 mm body length
- Habitat detail: primarily a household pest
- Distribution: cosmopolitan

After overwintering outdoors or in wall spaces, in the spring adults seek cracks in buildings and homes in search of suitable food sources. When they do, the females lay eggs. Larvae hatch and feed, moulting up to five or six times before seeking a solid place to bore into and pupate. The last moulted skin is used to plug the entrance to the hole in which they pupate. Under ideal conditions, the life cycle can take 40 to 50 days.

DOR BEETLE

Geotrupes stercorarius
Dung Beetle, Lousy Watchman

Flip over a dry cow patty and in the soil beneath you might observe chambers and tunnels that lead to more chambers. These excavations are the work of the dung-loving dor beetle. Adult dor beetles line the subterranean chambers with dung that nourishes their larvae.

Dor beetle nests can also be found in woodland settings where, instead of dung, brood chambers are lined with

- Size: 25 mm body length
- Habitat detail: grazing pastures, forests, near livestock barns
- Distribution: Europe, Asia, and eastern Canada

Dor beetle.

decaying fungus and rotting vegetation. Whether they are dung or vegetable matter collectors, these beetles play an important role in soil conditioning and are essential to ecosystem health. In recent decades, reductions in dor beetle numbers have been noticed in the United Kingdom. It is thought that residue from ivermectin-based wormers (anti-worm treatment used in the intensive rearing of cattle) in cattle dung may be killing dor beetle larvae. This is of concern, because dung beetles can actually help reduce greenhouse gas emissions. By dispersing dung, beetles reduce methane (a greenhouse gas) production. The impact is more significant in agricultural areas where manure is left on the fields.

Dor beetles can be distinguished from Newfoundland and Labrador's other large beetles by their shiny bluish bodies, oval shape, and lamellate-clubbed antennae (the antennae end with a series of lobes that can be closed). They may be called lousy watchmen because they can be found covered in copper-coloured mites.

GROUND BEETLES
Family Carabidae

Ground beetles make up one of the largest families of beetles, encompassing an estimated 40,000 species around the world, with 983 in Canada, 178 on the island of Newfoundland, and 96 in Labrador. The majority of ground beetles live on or in soil, especially under rocks and sand near the edges of ponds and rivers. Most do not have common names. Ground beetles are usually predators or opportunistic scavengers—but some feed on seeds and pollen. Because the majority of ground beetle adults and larvae are predators of other invertebrates, including many insect pests, they are considered a beneficial insect group. They are important biological control agents in many ecological systems, and their conservation is important.

Ground beetle larva.

The majority of ground beetles hibernate over the winter as adults. They are therefore most numerous early in the spring and late in the fall—other species overwinter as larvae and need time in the spring to complete their development, with numbers peaking in mid-summer. Ground beetles are abundant and generally found on the ground underneath rocks, logs, and leaf litter. Most, but not all, are nocturnal. Many species have individuals with long hindwings as well as individuals with short hindwings. To the observer, short- and long-winged individuals may be difficult to distinguish, as the hindwings are folded and hidden under the hardened front wings, the elytra. Several representative ground beetles are described here.

Amara fulva

Amara fulva is a brownish red ground beetle of 8 to 10 millimetres in length. Adults are nocturnal and fly readily. Introduced from Europe, the first record of *Amara fulva* in North America is from 1905 at Codroy in western Newfoundland. It is found in open country, especially on dry, sandy, or gravelly areas near sand dunes and near the seashore, at the top of riverbanks, and in vacant lots. Unlike most ground beetles, adult *Amara* feed on seeds and other plant material. *Amara fulva* occurs province-wide.

- Size: 8–10 mm body length
- Habitat detail: dry areas, near the sea
- Distribution: Europe and eastern Canada; found in Newfoundland and Labrador

Amara fulva.

Bembidion carinula.

Bembidion transversale.

Bembidion scopulinum.

Bembidion spp.

- Size: 3–7.4 mm body length
- Habitat detail: species-dependent
- Distribution: worldwide; *Bembidion lampros* in Newfoundland only

With almost 200 species in Canada, it is no surprise that *Bembidion* occupy many different habitats. Some of these small ground beetles are common on farmland or in gardens and parks. Others live only on sphagnum bogs, and many on gravelly river and stream banks and lakeshores. Several species are found on dry, open, sandy soil; others live in marshes close to the ocean. Native species include *Bembidion grapii* and *Bembidion scopulinum*, both of which occur in both Newfoundland and Labrador. *B. grapii* can be found on dry gravel but *B. scopulinum* is a shore-living beetle on all kinds of soil close to water.

Bembidion lampros is a European introduction widespread on the island of Newfoundland but has not been documented in Labrador. It has a metallic, brassy appearance and like many *Bembidion* prefers dry, open soils. Many species of *Bembidion* are active during the day and are readily observed running around on the soil surface in gardens and agricultural fields.

Carabus meander.

Carabus meander

Species in the genus *Carabus* are some of the largest ground beetles. They are slender with long legs and undeveloped hindwings and are unable to fly. *Carabus meander* is a native ground beetle most commonly seen in spring and early summer. The adult colour varies from a bright copper to greenish to matte black. The elytra have noticeable pits and furrows. Adults are 19 to 23 millimetres long. *Carabus meander* prefers open ground that is moist, with moderately high vegetation, on meadow slopes or mainly in sedge bogs or close to the borders of fresh water.

- Size: 19-23 mm body length
- Habitat detail: meadows, bogs, or near fresh water
- Distribution: worldwide; found in both Newfoundland and Labrador

European ground beetle.

- Size: 21-26 mm body length
- Habitat detail: varied human-disturbed habitats
- Distribution: Europe and North America; not recorded from Labrador

European Ground Beetle
Carabus nemoralis

The European ground beetle, *Carabus nemoralis*, was accidentally introduced from Europe and is one of the largest species of ground beetle in Newfoundland, with an adult body length of 21 to 26 millimetres. Adults are bronze to greenish bronze with violet edges. Mostly nocturnal, this ground beetle is often present in areas disturbed by human activity—lawns, gardens, agricultural fields, and gravel pits, parks, and forests. It has not been reported from Labrador. In the spring, European ground beetle adults are often seen on driveways and sidewalks.

Elaphrus clairvillei.

Elaphrus clairvillei

Elaphrus clairvillei are medium-sized ground beetles that are overall bronze with green-and-violet hues. They are easily recognized due to the distinctive, elaborate punctuation on the elytra and their enormous protruding eyes. Like all species of *Elaphrus*, *E. clairvillei* occurs in very damp places—in bogs and near water, and may be seen on muddy shorelines. Adults fly readily. This beetle is found in both Labrador and Newfoundland. Species in the genus *Elaphrus*, including *E. clairville*i, are called marsh ground beetles.

- Size: 8–10 mm body length
- Habitat detail: in bogs, near fresh water
- Distribution: North America; including Newfoundland and Labrador

Pterostichus adstrictus.

Pterostichus adstrictus and *Pterostichus melanarius*

- Size: 10-19 mm body length
- Habitat detail: variable, including vacant lots, farmland, grassland
- Distribution: worldwide

Pterostichus melanarius (12 to 19 millimetres long) and *Pterostichus adstrictus* (10 to 13 millimetres long) are large nocturnal ground beetles. Both species are black and non-metallic and frequent open country, including gardens and agricultural areas. *P. adstrictus* is a native species found in both Newfoundland and Labrador. It is widespread in open areas, including cultivated ground and grassland, and one of the most common ground beetles in the province. *P. melanarius* is introduced and so far has only been reported from the island. Some *P. melanarius* individuals have long wings and can fly; others have short wings and are incapable of flight. They are found in open but not dry areas, common in gardens and on farmland, vacant lots, gravel pits, and other human-disturbed places, as well as grassland and forests. The larvae of both species are soil-dwellers and may be encountered while digging in the soil in gardens and similar habitats.

Pterostichus melanarius.

Strawberry seed beetle.

Strawberry Seed Beetle
Harpalus rufipes

Like *Amara*, the genus *Harpalus* contains a large number of species which prefer open country and feed on seeds and other plant material. One common species, the strawberry seed beetle, *Harpalus rufipes*, was accidentally introduced from Europe and sometimes feeds on fruit such as strawberries. It has a black body of 10 to 17 millimetres in length and distinctive reddish brown legs. It is common and widely distributed in open, dry habitats, often on disturbed sites like cultivated fields, pastures, gravel pits, and dumps—but also undisturbed habitats like forests throughout Newfoundland. *H. rufipes* has not been found in Labrador but a total of nine species of *Harpalus* occur in the province, including seven from Labrador.

- Size: 10-17 mm body length
- Habitat detail: variable, including forests and open areas
- Distribution: Europe and North America; found in Newfoundland, not recorded from Labrador

Close-up of tiger beetle head.

Tiger Beetles
Subfamily Cicindelinae

Tiger beetles, a subfamily of the family Carabidae, are active predators with long legs and huge eyes which help them hunt. They run quickly and fly readily, making them a challenge to observe or collect. In relation to body length, they are among the fastest land animals on earth. Unlike most ground beetles, tiger beetles are active during the day and are most likely to be seen in bare, open areas such as sandy beaches, paths, and dirt roadways, especially when the sun is shining. Their powerful mandibles help them catch and subdue ants, caterpillars, flies, and other insects. The young live in vertical tunnels in the ground; they wait at the top of the tunnel to grab insects passing by. The majority of the tiger beetle species in North America are in the genus *Cicindela*, including the twelve-spotted tiger beetle and the long-lipped tiger beetle.

Twelve-spotted tiger beetle.

Twelve-Spotted Tiger Beetle
Cicindela duodecimguttata

The twelve-spotted tiger beetle is native and common in both Newfoundland and Labrador. Its colour is variable, but specimens with a greenish lustre are common. The number of spots is also variable, despite the common name. Some individual beetles have 12 spots but others have fewer than 12. They are good fliers, and adults are between 12 and 15 millimetres in length. They are not aquatic but they live close to the edges of ponds and streams and are often abundant on riverbanks and lakeshores on open, sun-exposed gravel and sand.

- Size: 12–15 mm body length
- Habitat detail: near ponds and streams
- Distribution: North America, including Newfoundland and Labrador

Long-lipped tiger beetle.

Long-Lipped Tiger Beetle
Cicindela longilabris

- Size: 13-15 mm body length
- Habitat detail: open, sunny areas
- Distribution: North America, including Newfoundland and Labrador

The long-lipped tiger beetle is native to Newfoundland and Labrador and is often observed sitting or running on roadways and gravel or forest paths. Look for them in sunny spots in areas with sparse vegetation, sometimes on peaty ground. Long-lipped tiger beetles are good fliers and are usually between 13 and 15 millimetres in length.

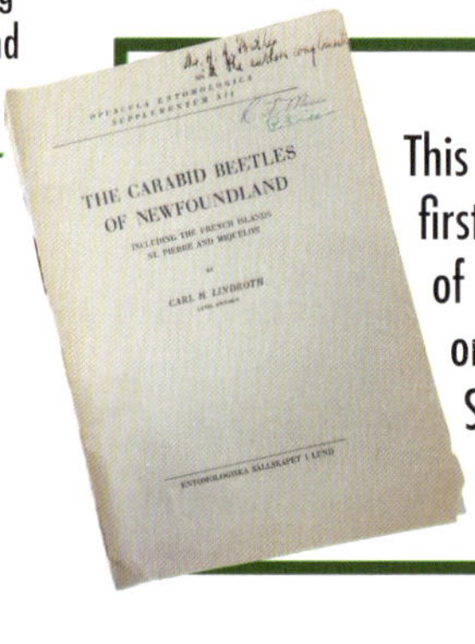

> This book, by Carl Lindroth, was one of the first comprehensive summaries of any group of insects in North America. It was based on collections of ground beetles made by Scandinavian biologists in Newfoundland in 1949 and 1951.

Seven-spotted lady beetle.

LADY BEETLES
Family Coccinellidae
God's Cow, Lady-Bird Beetle, Ladybug

Most lady beetles are easily recognizable as round or oval red or orange beetles, often with distinct spots and/or bars. Some people call them ladybugs, which is perfectly acceptable—however, entomologically speaking, true bugs are insects in the order Hemiptera, and lady beetles are members of the order Coleoptera, the beetles.

Some species are elongate rather than oval, and some have no spots at all. Of the 5,000 to 6,000 species of lady beetles in the world, about 500 species are found in North America and 160 in Canada. As of 2019, records show 24 species in Newfoundland and Labrador, 13 of which occur in Labrador and 22 on the island of Newfoundland.

The head of an adult lady beetle is partly covered by the pronotum, the plate directly behind the head. Legs and antennae are relatively short, and the antennae have clubs at their tips. Lady beetles fly readily and are usually active during the day. A number of other insects can be confused with lady beetles—generally because they are red or orange with black markings—including beetles in the family Chrysomelidae and some of the true bugs (page 241). Precise identification requires looking at tiny features using a microscope, but in general, these other candidates have longer antennae.

Lady beetle larvae look so different from the adults that most people would never guess they are related. The soft-bodied, caterpillar-shaped larvae are black or dark grey with spots, covered in spines, and elongate with a tapered body. They have six legs and no wings, are very active, and run about after their prey. Lady beetle larvae may look alarming to some, but they are harmless—unless you are an aphid. Most lady beetles, both adults and larvae, are carnivores and eat aphids (page 242) and other soft-bodied insects. Lady beetles are often easiest to find where aphids are plentiful. A single lady beetle can eat hundreds or even thousands of aphids in its lifetime.

Lady beetle larvae on a carrot.

Females lay groups of bright yellow eggs on the undersides of leaves and other locations near their prey. Young larvae will often eat their own eggshells, aphids, and even each other when there is insufficient prey. When the larva has eaten enough, it attaches itself to a leaf or other object and becomes a pupa. The adult beetle develops inside the pupa and eventually emerges and continues the cycle.

Lady beetle pupa.

Counting the spots on a lady beetle might be fun and a good way to help identify species, but it has nothing to do with a lady beetle's age. Most individuals live less than a year. A lady beetle's bright colours are a signal to predators to stay away. Anyone who has picked up a lady beetle might notice orange-brown fluid on their hands—this fluid is released from joints in their legs and serves to deter predators because of its foul taste.

Lady beetle adults seek shelter in the fall, sometimes in large congregations. Overwintering sites include protected locations like leaf litter and, for some species, inside homes and other buildings, and under verandahs and decks.

Eye-spotted lady beetles.

- Size: 7-8 mm body length
- Habitat detail: forest
- Distribution: North America; not recorded from Labrador

Eye-Spotted Lady Beetle
Anatis mali

The eye-spotted lady beetle, *Anatis mali*, at 7 to 8 millimetres in length, is one of the province's largest lady beetles and is usually found in the forest, on coniferous trees and other vegetation where prey is found. Its pattern and coloration are distinctive: on a background colour of brownish red are eight black spots on each elytron and each spot is surrounded by a yellowish ring, creating the namesake eye-spots. These lady beetles darken as they get older and the yellow rings may be less obvious in older beetles. They occur outside from May to September and spend the winter hibernating in sheltered locations like under leaf litter. Like other lady beetles, both adults and larvae feed on soft-bodied insects, including aphids.

Marsh lady beetle.

Marsh Lady Beetle
Anisosticta bitriangularis

The marsh lady beetle, *Anisosticta bitriangularis*, is small—just 3 to 4 millimetres in length—and distinct due to its pale yellow-and-black colouring. The marsh lady beetle is elongate rather than oval and generally found in bogs and fens, near bodies of water, and on sedges and grasses in wet areas. Adults and larvae eat soft-bodied insects.

- Size: 3–4 mm body length
- Habitat detail: bogs and other wet areas
- Distribution: North America, including Newfoundland and Labrador

Multicoloured Asian Lady Beetle
Harmonia axyridis

Halloween Lady Beetle, Harlequin Lady Beetle, Asian Lady Beetle

The multicoloured Asian lady beetle, *Harmonia axyridis*, is what people often imagine as a typical lady beetle—round and convex—but it occurs in a wide variety of

Multicoloured Asian lady beetle.

- Size: 6–8 mm body length
- Habitat detail: urban parks, meadows, and marshes
- Distribution: Europe, Asia, North America

colour forms and can be tricky to identify. The most common form has multiple irregular black spots on a reddish orange background and a white, M-shaped mark behind its head. It is native to Asia but was deliberately introduced to several parts of North America and Europe to control aphids on crops. The multicoloured Asian lady beetle is probably established on the island of Newfoundland although, so far, there have been few reports and, of those, all are from the Avalon Peninsula. Adults are 6 to 8 millimetres long and usually found in forests, marshes, and meadows, although they are most commonly observed in urban gardens and parks and on crops in agricultural areas.

Although an impressive predator of aphids and other small insects, in many areas the multicoloured Asian lady beetle is considered a nuisance. It invades homes, buildings, and even beehives in large numbers looking for sheltered places to hibernate, and it has a reputation for nipping humans when handled. These lady beetles sometimes feed on small fruit like grapes; wine made from grapes affected by multicoloured Asian lady beetles often has an unpleasant, bitter taste called "ladybug taint."

Three-Banded Lady Beetle
Coccinella trifasciata

The three-banded lady beetle, *Coccinella trifasciata*, has orange-red wing covers with black markings often outlined with yellow. The markings consist of a black band across the shoulders and two broken bands farther back on the elytra. A hint to the pattern of black markings is given in both its common name, three-banded, and its scientific name; *trifasciata* means three bands. Adults are 4 to 5 millimetres long and most often seen in backyard gardens, agricultural fields, parklands, and boreal forest.

Like other lady beetles, adults and larvae of this species eat aphids and other small insects.

Three-banded lady beetle.

- Size: 4-5 mm body length
- Habitat detail: gardens and boreal forest
- Distribution: North America

Transverse Lady Beetle
Coccinella transversoguttata

Transverse lady beetles have orange to red wing covers with a single black more-or-less continuous band just behind the head, and four irregular spots. This lady beetle inhabits agricultural areas, suburban gardens, parks, coniferous and deciduous forests, grasslands, meadows, and other natural areas. This broad habitat range reflects this species' ability to exploit seasonal changes in prey availability across different vegetation types. In some parts of Canada, steep declines in abundance of this species have been observed, potentially due to land-use changes and the arrival of other lady beetle species.

Transverse lady beetle.

- Size: 6-7 mm
- Habitat detail: farm, forest
- Distribution: Europe and North America

Two-spotted lady beetle.

Two-Spotted Lady Beetle
Adalia bipunctata

The two-spotted lady beetle, *Adalia bipunctata*, is likely the most commonly observed lady beetle in the province. This small (3.5- to 5-millimetre-long) beetle has an orange-red background with one prominent black spot on each wing cover. Its scientific species name, *bipunctata*, means two-spotted.

Although the majority of the two-spotted lady beetles in the province are in fact orange red with two black spots, this species is highly variable with many colour forms. Some have two black bands or four black spots; others, no spots at all. Like other lady beetles, adults and larvae of the two-spotted lady beetle eat aphids and other small soft-bodied insects and live almost anywhere their prey is found, although they prefer trees and shrubs. They have been collected outside from mid-May to late September in Newfoundland and Labrador.

- Size: 3.5–5 mm body length
- Habitat detail: damp places, including in leaf litter and under logs
- Distribution: Holarctic; found in Newfoundland and Labrador

Seven-spotted lady beetles.

This species overwinters as adults, hibernating in sheltered areas under leaf litter, under logs, on trees, and sometimes in buildings. Two-spotted lady beetles are often encountered in homes during the winter and spring when warm inside temperatures bring them out of hibernation. Although there is little evidence that their numbers are in decline in the province, there is concern for this lady beetle in other areas.

Seven-Spotted Lady Beetle
Coccinella septempunctata

The seven-spotted lady beetle, *Coccinella septempunctata*, is oval and red orange with seven black spots: three on each elytron and one in the middle where the elytra meet. It is one of the most common lady beetles on the island of Newfoundland. Adults and larvae primarily feed on aphids but eat other small insects like thrips. Adults are 6 to 8 millimetres long and found on low shrubs

- Size: 6–8 mm body length
- Habitat detail: on low shrubs, plants, and roadsides
- Distribution: worldwide; no records from Labrador

and plants, grassland, agricultural fields, gardens and parks, and roadsides.

The seven-spotted lady beetle is native to Europe, North Africa, and Asia but, due to its voracious appetite for aphids, it was deliberately released in many areas of North America for aphid control, including in western Newfoundland and on the Avalon Peninsula in 1983 and 1984. This species can occur in huge numbers and adversely affect populations of native species, presumably through competition. Adult seven-spotted lady beetles hibernate in groups in leaf litter in parks and gardens, in protected sites near the fields where they feed, and near the foundations of buildings.

- Size: 4-6 mm body length
- Habitat detail: gardens, lawns, and near fresh water
- Distribution: North America, including Newfoundland and Labrador

Thirteen-Spotted Lady Beetle
Hippodamia tredecimpunctata tibialis

Thirteen-spotted lady beetle, *Hippodamia tredecimpunctata tibialis*, is a native lady beetle with an elongate rather than oval shape, and the adults are 4 to 6 millimetres in length. It is orange with 13 black spots: six on each elytron and one in the middle where the elytra meet. The thirteen-spotted lady beetle's legs are distinctive; each femur (the visible part closest to the

Thirteen-spotted lady beetle.

body) is black, and the other two parts (tibia and tarsi) are orange. This species is common in man-made areas like gardens and lawns, and in agricultural crops; its natural habitat is marshy meadows and reed beds and near water. As with other lady beetles, adults and larvae feed on aphids and other small, soft-bodied organisms.

Fourteen-Spotted Lady Beetle
Calvia quatuordecimguttata

The fourteen-spotted lady beetle, *Calvia quatuor-decimguttata*, also known as the polkadot lady beetle, occurs in a number of different colour forms, especially in North America. The most common form in Newfoundland and Labrador appears to be orange yellow with 14 black spots, although the reddish pink form with pale-coloured spots might be seen. These lady beetles are usually 4 to 6 millimetres long and live high in trees—particularly deciduous and mixed forests—but also in parks, gardens, and meadows and on agricultural crops where prey is found. As with other lady beetles, fourteen-spotted adults and larvae eat aphids and other insects. Adults overwinter in leaf litter and similar protected situations.

- Size: 4-6 mm body length
- Habitat detail: often in deciduous trees and gardens
- Distribution: North America, northern Europe, and Asia

Fourteen-spotted lady beetle.

Twenty-Spotted Lady Beetle
Psyllobora vigintimaculata

The twenty-spotted lady beetle, *Psyllobora vigintimaculata*, is also known as "wee-tiny lady bug" due to its size—adults are just 2 to 3 millimetres in length. Individuals are tan with black markings. It occurs across North America, including on the island of Newfoundland, but to date has not been recorded from Labrador.

Twenty-spotted lady beetle.

- Size: 2-3 mm body length
- Habitat detail: on trees and shrubs
- Distribution: North America; not recorded from Labrador

Unlike most lady beetles, which are carnivores, adults and larvae of the twenty-spotted lady beetle feed on mildew growing on leaves of roses, willows, birches, maples, and other woody plants and that growing on aphid honeydew. The twenty-spotted lady beetle has been tested for its ability to eat and control powdery mildew, a serious plant pathogen.

LONG-HORNED BEETLES
Family Cerambycidae

Long-horned beetles gain their common name from their extremely long antennae, which can often be as long as or longer than the length of the beetle's body. Over 25,000 species are recorded worldwide; two species common in Newfoundland trees and woody plants are described here.

Elderberry Borer
Desmocerus palliatus

The elderberry borer is one of Newfoundland's most recognizable long-horned beetles. The elderberry borer has characteristic long antennae and is a metallic dark blue black with a gold to yellowish orange band on the upper part of the elytra. The adults are most often seen eating the pollen of elderberry flowers or resting on elderberry leaves in late June to July.

Elderberry borer.

Feeding damage at the base of an elderberry shrub.

Females lay eggs on the stems of elderberry and the emerging larvae bore into the stem and feed inside stems and roots until they mature and move into the roots to pupate. Feeding damage can be observed as coarse fibrous frass that collects at the base of the stems. Exit holes are usually seen 15 to 20 centimetres above the soil line. Not much is known about the elderberry borer's life history in Newfoundland, but it is thought to have a two-year life cycle.

This beetle was first recorded in Newfoundland in St. John's on 30 July 1962. Local records indicate it is present in St. John's and surrounding area but its distribution on the island is not well known. It is locally called the St. Bon's beetle as its colours are those of St. Bonaventure's College in St. John's.

- Size: 18-27 mm
- Habitat detail: gardens with elderberry
- Distribution: northeast North America, eastern Newfoundland, not known from Labrador

White-spotted sawyer.

White-Spotted Sawyer
Monochamus scutellatus

- Size: 20–25 mm body length
- Habitat detail: coniferous forests
- Distribution: Canada and US

Large conspicuous long-horned beetles, white-spotted sawyer adults usually emerge from July to August. The adults are a dull dark reddish brown to black with a white scutellum and very long antennae that extend well beyond the elytra in both males and females. The antennae on the males can be up to twice the body length and, if intact, can be used to sex these beetles. The body can appear mottled, especially in the females, as the elytra often have dense patches of white hairs.

After emerging, adult beetles feed for a few weeks on coniferous needles and bark before laying eggs on damaged, dying, or recently burned or felled pine, larch, and spruce. The larvae hatch and tunnel into the tree or log and bore tunnels through the sap and heartwood, often taking up to two years to complete its life cycle.

The white-spotted sawyer is sometimes confused with the Asian longhorn beetle, *Anoplophora glabripennis*, which is not present in the province and considered an invasive insect pest. The Asian longhorn beetle has a shiny black body with bright white spots, black-and-white long banded antennae, and a black scutellum.

PREDACEOUS DIVING BEETLES
Family Dytiscidae

Predaceous diving beetles are a large diverse group, with almost 300 species in Canada, 81 in Labrador, and 79 on the island of Newfoundland. These elongate-oval, dark brown to black beetles are abundant in ponds, streams, bog pools, and lakes. They are well adapted to swimming due to their streamlined bodies and flattened hind legs, which are fringed with bristles. The beetles use these specialized hind legs as paddles.

- Size: 2-40 mm body length
- Habitat detail: most freshwater habitats
- Distribution: worldwide

Adult predaceous diving beetles are also strong fliers and can move to new areas if conditions become unfavourable. They are often attracted to lights.

Like many aquatic insects, predaceous diving beetle adults and larvae breathe air and can often be observed coming to the surface of the water to replenish their air supply. Beetles store a supply of air under their wings for breathing while underwater, and larvae store air inside their bodies.

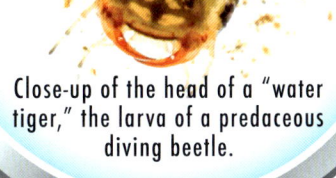

Close-up of the head of a "water tiger," the larva of a predaceous diving beetle.

Dytiscus dauricus, male (left) and female (right).

True to their names, adults and larvae are voracious predators, eating other insects, small fish, and crustaceans. Larvae, called water tigers, have large mandibles for catching prey (see photo page 145). These mandibles have channels for sucking prey contents; water tigers do not bite or chew their prey.

Depending on the species, adult predaceous diving beetles in Newfoundland and Labrador vary greatly in length. *Liodessus affinis*, just 2 millimetres in length, is abundant in many shallow water habitats, but because of its size it is often overlooked. At the other extreme are some species in the genus *Dytiscus*; *Dytiscus dauricus*, at 30 to 40 millimetres long, is one of the province's largest aquatic insects.

ROVE BEETLES
Family Staphylinidae

At first glance a rove beetle does not look like a beetle at all. Most have elongate, slender bodies with elytra so short that much of their abdomen is exposed—unlike most beetles, where the abdomen is completely covered by the elytra. The rove beetle's delicate hindwings are used for flight and are intricately folded under the elytra when not in use. Many rove beetles will flex their abdomen upwards if they are disturbed, and most species are good fliers.

Rove beetles usually live in the top few centimetres of soil, in leaf litter and other decomposing organic matter. Their habits are diverse: they may also be found in nests and on moss, fungi, and vegetation. They play an important role in many terrestrial ecosystems. Most rove beetles are beneficial, as both the larvae and adults are active predators of a wide range of insects and other arthropods. Rove beetles are very common: a study in Newfoundland balsam fir forests found that almost 80 per cent of the beetles present were rove beetles. No doubt many species are still unknown and, in fact, two new species were recently described from this province.

Over 56,000 species of rove beetles are recorded worldwide, with 1,774 from Canada, including 317 from Newfoundland and 149 from Labrador.

Aleochara bilineata.

Parasitic Aleochara bilineata larva inside a cabbage maggot pupa.

Aleochara bilineata

Aleochara bilineata, a glossy black rove beetle, is an enemy of several species of pests, including the cabbage maggot, the seedcorn maggot, and the onion maggot, and is important in their natural control. *A. bilineata* has several host flies, including the cabbage maggot, and was likely introduced from Europe along with these hosts. Female members of

- Size: 2-6 mm body length
- Habitat detail: gardens and fields where its host flies are found
- Distribution: worldwide; not recorded from Labrador

- Size: 13-21 mm body length
- Habitat detail: in or near dung, carrion, or compost
- Distribution: eastern North America

this species lay eggs near the pupae of their host fly in the soil. When the eggs hatch, the young beetle larvae chew holes in, and enter, the fly pupae. The beetle larva spends the winter protected inside and, in the spring, it kills and eats the fly. As a result of this insect warfare, an *A. bilineata* beetle emerges from the pupa instead of a fly.

Adult *A. bilineata* rove beetles also eat the eggs and larvae of their fly hosts and are thus most often found in gardens and agricultural fields where its host is found. Adults are strong, active fliers.

Gold-and-Brown Rove Beetle
Ontholestes cingulatus

The gold-and-brown rove beetle, *Ontholestes cingulatus*, is a large (13 to 21 millimetres in length) native species which is widespread and common in eastern and northwestern North America, including Newfoundland. It has not been recorded in Labrador. Its body colour is overall brown, but clumps of dark hair form spots. This species can be identified by the tip of its abdomen, which is covered with distinctive golden yellow hairs. Like many species of rove beetle, adult gold-and-brown rove beetles tend to curl the tip of the abdomen upwards when they walk. Adults and larvae are predators of maggots (fly larvae) associated with dung and carrion, but they also are attracted to compost piles and other decaying organic matter such as fungi. They are generally found in woodlands and fields where their food (carrion, dung, decaying organic material) is found.

Gold-and-brown rove beetle.

Hairy Rove Beetle
Creophilus maxillosus

Hairy rove beetle.

The hairy rove beetle, *Creophilus maxillosus*, is one of the largest and most distinctive species of rove beetle in North America. It is shiny black with greyish yellow patches and bands on the elytra and abdomen. Hairy rove beetles live in various habitats, including open fields, forests, and coastal areas. They are avid predators of fly larvae, or maggots, and generally are found anywhere there is a supply of maggots, including on dung and carcasses.

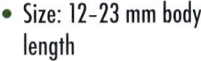

- Size: 12-23 mm body length
- Habitat detail: usually in gardens or along the seashore
- Distribution: Holarctic, South America, Hawaii

Tachinus rufipes

Tachinus rufipes is a 4.5- to 5.5-millimetre-long, shiny, black rove beetle introduced from Europe. It prefers shaded and damp, but not wet, habitats: forests, near streams, and in decaying logs, matted vegetation, compost, and even dung. A related species, *Tachinus luridus*, occurs in Labrador. *Tachinus luridus* has pale reddish brown elytra rather than black like *Tachinus rufipes*. These rove beetles are predators of aphids and other small insects.

- Size: 4.5-5.5 mm body length
- Habitat detail: in decaying material
- Distribution: Europe, Canada, not recorded in Labrador

Tachinus rufipes.

Atheta pseudovestita.

Silusa prettyae.

> Rove beetle species are still being discovered and recorded for the first time in Newfoundland, including these two:

Atheta pseudovestita, a 3.5- to 3.9-millimetre-long, shiny, dark rove beetle, is widespread across Newfoundland but is known from nowhere else in the world. The first specimens were found in 2011 under debris such as seaweed along seashores and sandy beaches, and in vegetation and gravel on riverbanks.

Silusa prettyae, another tiny (2.7- to 3.0-millimetre-long) rove beetle, is yellowish brown to brown. It is known only from Butterpot Provincial Park in eastern Newfoundland, where it was first collected in 2012 in coniferous forest.

WEEVILS
Family Curculionidae
Snout Beetles

Weevils come in many shapes, sizes, and colours and are one of the most specious families of insects on the planet. According to the last checklist published, there are about 825 species of weevils in Canada, with 95 recorded from Newfoundland and 15 from Labrador.

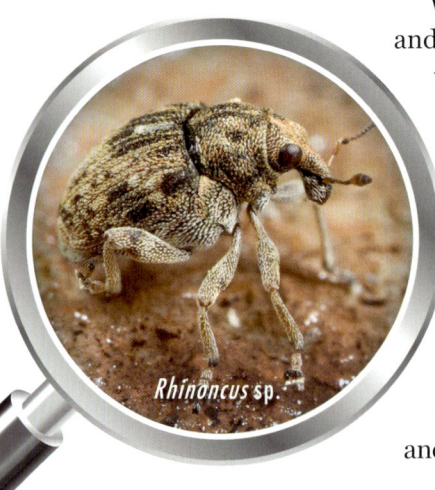

Rhinoncus sp.

Weevils have hard sculptured elytra and a long snout, called a rostrum, from which elbowed antennae arise. Found in almost every habitat, most weevils are herbivorous and some are considered pests that can cause extensive damage to important crops. The black vine weevil, *Otiorhynchus sulcatus*, for example, extensively damages a range of economically important plants, including yews, rhododendrons, raspberry, strawberry, and cyclamen. The slate grey to black adults

Black vine weevil on a strawberry leaf.

are 9 to 13 millimetres long, with small patches of short golden hairs on the elytra. They are most active at night, when they feed on the leaves of their host plants. Females lay hundreds of eggs in the soil near the base of the host plant. The emerging C-shaped larvae burrow below ground to feed on root hairs, progressing to larger roots as they grow, eventually leaving the plant with no means to uptake water and nutrients, resulting in plant death.

Green immigrant leaf weevil.

A recent introduction to Newfoundland within the past 15 years is the green immigrant leaf weevil, *Polydrusus formosus*. This species, most likely encountered on the west coast of Newfoundland, is a bright metallic green due to the green scales covering its body. Its legs are brown yellow and the elytra appear to have dark black grooves running down its length. The green immigrant weevil has root-feeding larvae, but not much is known about its life history in the province. It is reported as a day feeder on a number of different plant species, including rose, birch, apple, and blueberry.

WHIRLIGIG BEETLES
Family Gyrinidae

Whirligig beetles have divided eyes so they can see both above and below the water.

Small, shiny, dark, oval whirligig beetles can often be seen in large numbers on the surface of still and slow-moving waters in ponds and streams. Their front legs are long, but the middle and hind legs are short and flat and used like paddles for swimming. Their common name comes from their habit of swimming in circles on the water surface with fast, zig-zagging motions.

Gyrinus is a common and widespread genus. *Gyrinus sayi* (right) is the most frequently collected species on the island of Newfoundland.

- Size: 2–18 mm body length
- Habitat detail: on the surface of freshwater ponds, lakes, quiet streams, marshy areas, and bog pools, often in large groups
- Distribution: worldwide

Whirligig beetle eyes are divided into lower and upper parts, allowing them to watch for predators and prey both above and below the water surface. Adults and larvae are predators, eating other insects such as mosquito larvae. Elongate larvae have several pairs of feathery gills and live on the bottom of ponds and slow streams. Although they usually occur on the water surface, adults carry a bubble of air underneath their elytra, which allows them to breathe underwater.

Thirty-four species of whirligig beetles are known in Canada, with 11 in Labrador and 13 on the island of Newfoundland.

NEUROPTERA: LACEWINGS

Brown lacewing.

Green lacewing on a cabbage leaf.

Lacewing larva, also called an aphidlion.

NEUROPTERA
GREEN LACEWINGS, BROWN LACEWINGS, APHIDLIONS

About 20 species of lacewing are recorded in Newfoundland and Labrador from two different families: the green lacewings, family Chrysopidae; and the brown lacewings, family Hemerobiidae.

Green lacewings are the largest and most familiar family of the two. The adults generally have long slender green bodies, large golden or copper-coloured eyes, long delicate antennae, and the namesake lacy wings. Despite their delicate appearance, the adults are predators of aphids, thrips, and other soft-bodied insects. The adults also feed on nectar and pollen.

To prevent predation by other insects, females lay eggs on long stalks that they construct and attach to leaves. The eggs hatch into larvae that are often called aphidlions, as they are voracious predators, especially of aphids. Larvae are highly mobile and have long mandibles for capturing and sucking the fluids of their prey. Some species, as larvae, make "trash packets" on their backs. These trash packets can be small pieces of leaves or the body remains of their prey, which are attached to their backs as a means of camouflage. Commonly found in gardens and agricultural areas, green lacewings are natural enemies of some important insect pests and a welcome addition to the garden.

Brown lacewings are not as frequently encountered as their green counterparts but have the same general appearance, except they are usually smaller and overall yellow to dark brown. Brown lacewings do not put eggs on stalks; instead they attach eggs directly to leaves, and the larvae do not make trash packets on their backs.

- Size: adult 15-20 mm body length (green lacewings); 6-15 mm (brown lacewings)
- Habitat detail: variable; brown lacewings often associated with wooded areas, hedgerows
- Distribution: worldwide

Green lacewing.

Green lacewing eggs on a cabbage leaf.

Green lacewing pupa on a blueberry.

TRICHOPTERA: CADDISFLIES

Caddisfly larva (top) and case (bottom).

The central part of this necklace was constructed by a caddisfly larva.

Caddisfly.

Caddisfly.

TRICHOPTERA
CADDISFLIES

Adult caddisflies are long and slender and have long, slender antennae. Their wings are covered in hairs, and in fact Trichoptera means hairy wings (*trichos*, hairy; *ptera*, wings). Coloration varies with species, but generally, caddisflies are beige, brown, or black, often with irregular dark wing markings. The wings are held tentlike over the body when the adult caddisfly is at rest. Adult caddisflies are active at night and can often be seen flying near ponds, lakes, and streams, or resting on vegetation or buildings near bodies of water. They can occur in large numbers near lights.

Most adults are short-lived and do not feed, a trait shared with mayflies. At certain times of the year large mating swarms occur.

The aquatic, caterpillar-shaped larvae have three pairs of walking legs. Most have gills on the outside of the body. Larvae of several caddisfly species are amazing architects: they construct cases of silk strengthened with small stones, sand grains, twigs, shells, plant material, or combinations of these. The cases are a protected place to live. If the insects live in running water, the stone cases help to prevent them from being swept away by the current. Other, free-living, caddisfly larvae construct silken nets across the current to trap food particles. Caddisflies are useful as bioindicators, as they are sensitive to polluted water.

Picking stones out of all types of rivers and streams in Newfoundland and Labrador will often reveal species in the caddisfly family Hydropsychidae. These are widespread and their larvae live inside cases attached to rocks; each case has a woven net at the opening which the insect uses to catch plankton.

There are 635 species of caddisflies recorded from Canada. Of a total of 141 species in the province, 133 are from Newfoundland and 32 from Labrador.

- Size: 3-15 mm body length
- Habitat detail: larvae, in a wide variety of freshwater aquatic habitats: lakes, ponds, fast-flowing rivers and streams, and bog pools; adults, near the water bodies where they lived as larvae
- Distribution: worldwide

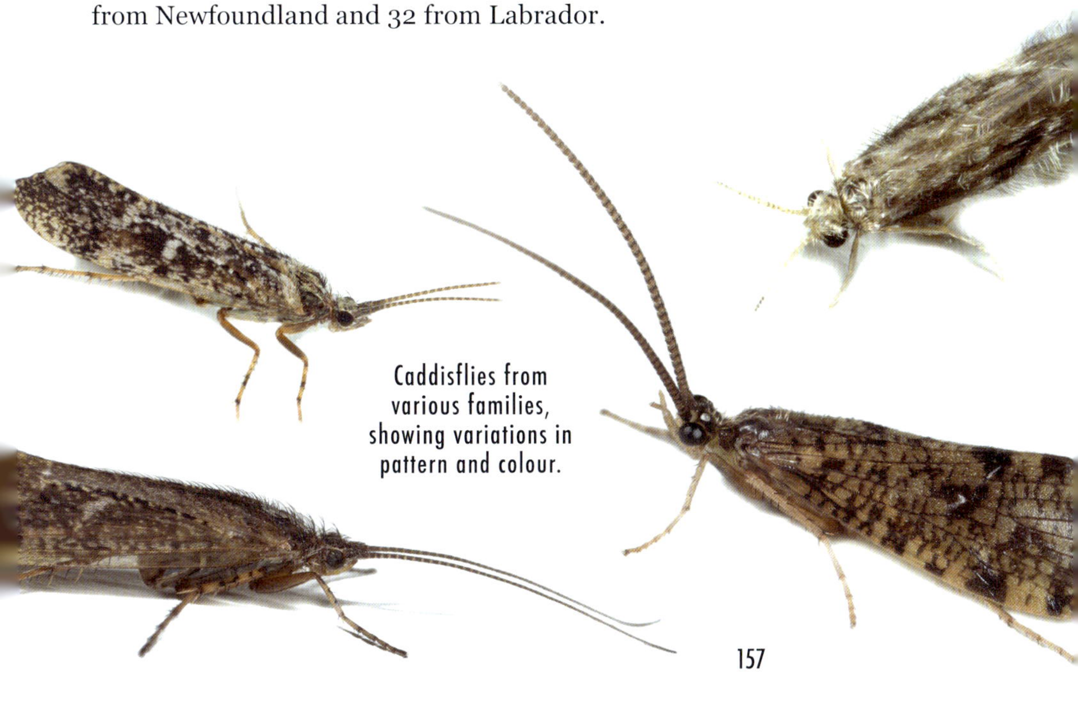

Caddisflies from various families, showing variations in pattern and colour.

LEPIDOPTERA: BUTTERFLIES·MOTHS

Elm spanworm moth laying eggs on a maple tree.

Moth expanding its wings after emerging from its cocoon.

Characteristic scales on a moth's wing.

Wing of an armyworm moth, *Mythimna unipuncta*.

LEPIDOPTERA
MOTHS AND BUTTERFLIES

Members of the order Lepidoptera, which include butterflies and moths, have four scale-covered wings. The presence of these wing scales—often but not always brightly coloured—is unique to this order.

The colours of the scales on the fore- and hindwings (both upper- and undersides) are used to identify many species of butterflies and moths; the presence of spots or continuous bands of colour and the general size and shape of the wings are also used in identification. In cases where species look very similar, identification requires an expert eye and, often, dissection to use genitalia characteristics to distinguish between species.

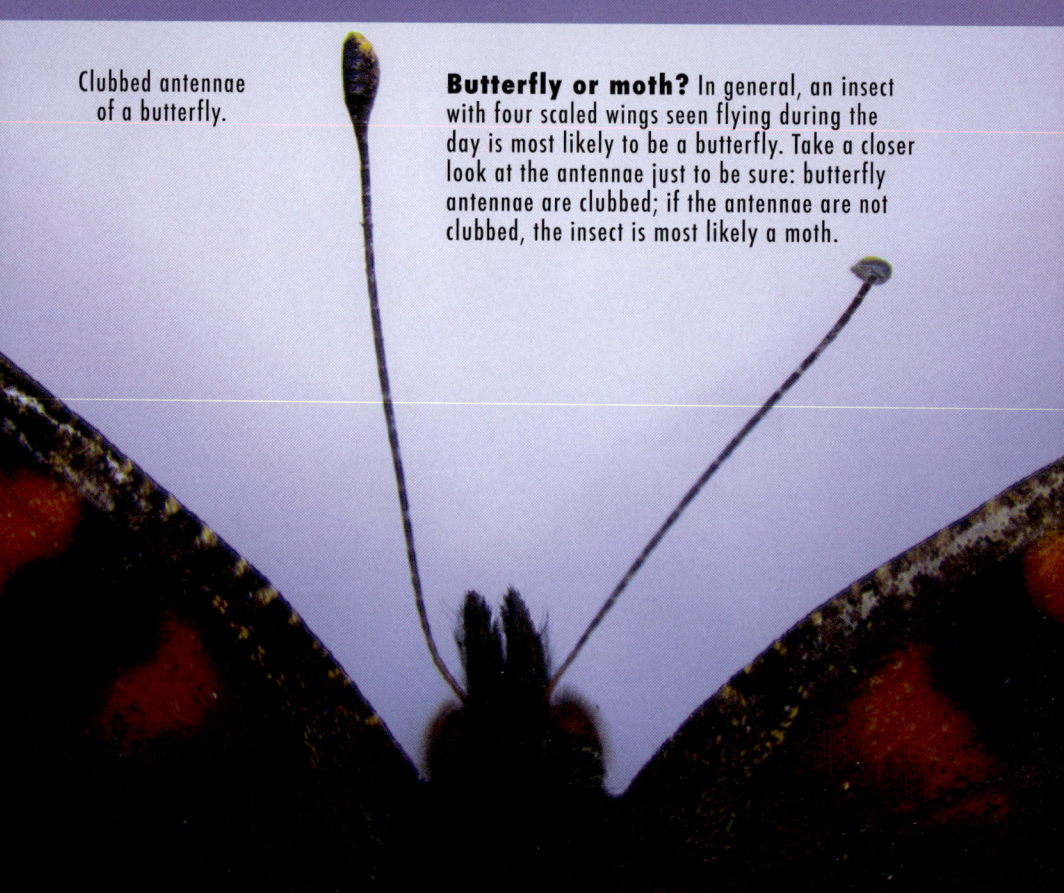

Clubbed antennae of a butterfly.

Butterfly or moth? In general, an insect with four scaled wings seen flying during the day is most likely to be a butterfly. Take a closer look at the antennae just to be sure: butterfly antennae are clubbed; if the antennae are not clubbed, the insect is most likely a moth.

The majority of species in this order are herbivores. Females lay their eggs on a host plant, on which the emerging larvae—caterpillars—feed. Caterpillars go through growth stages, known as instars, and shed their exoskeleton at the end of each. The number of instars a caterpillar goes through depends on its species. After the caterpillar has reached its last instar and is fully grown, it begins to pupate, often forming a cocoon. Some caterpillars pupate on the plant on which they were feeding, others drop into the soil, and some travel away from the host plant.

The metamorphosis from caterpillar to adult butterfly/moth is complete: wingless larvae transform into winged adults. This is in contrast to incomplete metamorphosis in which the life cycle consists of egg, nymph, and adult, and the immature nymphs look similar to the adult.

Feathery antennae of a moth; not all moth antennae are feathery.

As with other insect groups, it is impossible to describe all species of Lepidoptera found in Newfoundland and Labrador. In many cases, where the number of species recorded within a family is small, a brief description of each is included. In other cases, the variety is too great—for example, over 270 species of noctuid moths have been recorded on the island alone. Not all families of moths are discussed; we have selected a handful of the most conspicuous or interesting of the 44 families present in the province.

Species accounts have been verified in the annotated checklist of *Lepidoptera in Canada and Alaska*, the most up-to-date and comprehensive list of species for the country compiled by some of the country's top taxonomists. New records are constantly being found and these lists are always changing.

ARE MILLERS MOTHS?

Moths appear under three names in the *Dictionary of Newfoundland English*:
- lamp-lighter: a variety of large moth with dusty wings; miller
- Johnny Miller: a small moth; young miller; a small, light-coloured moth
- dows'y poll: a moth, miller; large moths attracted to lamp

Using "miller" to refer to moths is not unique to Newfoundland. In the midwestern United States the often-abundant armyworm moth, *Euxoa auxiliaris*, is referred to as a miller. According to the United States Department of Agriculture, "miller moth" is the term given to any type of moth particularly abundant in and around homes. The word is thought to come from the fact that millers—people who mill grain into flour—would be covered in flour/dust which is similar to the scales that come off moths when they knock their wings.

MOTHS

Includes Families Erebidae, Geometridae, Noctuidae, Plutellidae, Sphingidae, Tortricidae

EREBID MOTHS

Family Erebidae

Virginian tiger moth caterpillar.

The family Erebidae contains the largest number of described moth species worldwide; this is in part due to the recent combining of previously recognized families and subfamilies based on a unifying wing venation character. Although variable, moths in this family tend to be medium to large with stout, thicker bodies. This family includes the tiger moths, tussock moths, and underwings, as well as other subfamilies.

TIGER MOTHS
Subfamily Arctiinae
Woolly Bear

Moths in this subfamily, often called tiger moths, are some of the most colourful moths found in the province. The adults generally have stout bodies of between 1.5 and 3.5 centimetres in length and closely resemble moths in the family Noctuidae. Most produce distasteful chemicals as a means to avoid predation. The larvae are known as woolly bears and have colourful long hairs that are often incorporated into their cocoons when they pupate. Some larvae are also called tussock moths, a name also used for the larvae in the subfamily Lymantriinae (page 166). Most species overwinter as young larvae.

Opulent Moth
Arctia opulenta

The opulent moth occurs in Labrador (not Newfoundland) and is a day-flying moth on the alpine and Arctic tundra. It is a large moth—the body can be 3.5 centimetres or longer—with white and dark brown-grey markings on the forewing and bright red hindwings with black spots. The head and thorax match the dark brown grey on the forewings, and the abdomen tends to be a darker red than the hindwings, also with black spots. Females lay eggs on willow and birch. The antennae are white on the back sides.

- Size: 45–55 mm wingspan
- Habitat detail: alpine and Arctic tundra
- Distribution: north-western North America; present in Labrador, not Newfoundland

Opulent moth laying eggs on a dwarf birch in Labrador.

- Size: 35–45 mm wingspan
- Habitat detail: boreal deciduous forest
- Distribution: Canada and US, present in Newfoundland and Labrador

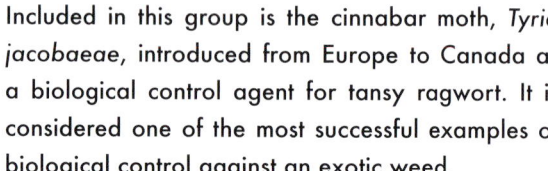

Included in this group is the cinnabar moth, *Tyria jacobaeae*, introduced from Europe to Canada as a biological control agent for tansy ragwort. It is considered one of the most successful examples of biological control against an exotic weed.

Spotted Tussock Moth
Lophocampa maculata
Yellow Woolly Bear

Spotted tussock moth.

Usually seen in the fall crawling around looking for a place to pupate, the yellow woolly bear is a fuzzy caterpillar that has a distinct black-yellow-black banded pattern. Often, black spots are present along the caterpillar's back on the yellow band, and white tufts come from the black bands. The larvae feed on a variety of trees, including alder, poplar, maple, and willow. This insect overwinters as a pupa. Adults emerge in the spring, normally flying in July on the island and mid-August in Labrador. The adults have a wingspan of 35 to 45 millimetres and are an example of a drab tiger moth, with pale yellow forewings which have light brown bands.

Yellow woolly bear caterpillar, which will turn into the spotted tussock moth above.

Virginia Ctenucha
Ctenucha virginica

This distinctive day-flying moth has brown-black forewings, black hindwings, a metallic blue thorax and abdomen, and an orange head. It has a wingspan of 40 to 50 millimetres and the wing tips sometimes have white fringes.

Virginia ctenucha caterpillars feed on grasses, and outbreaks of this species in Newfoundland have damaged hay and pasture fields. The caterpillars are often found in fall or early spring in grassy fields and can be recognized by a row of black tufts among cream-coloured hairs down the back, and white or cream-coloured subdorsal and subspiracular stripes. These moths overwinter as larvae and are usually seen flying in June and July.

- Size: 40–50 mm wingspan
- Habitat detail: open grassy areas in boreal regions
- Distribution: Canada and eastern US; present in Newfoundland and Labrador

Virginia ctenucha moth sipping nectar.

Virginia ctenucha moth.

Caterpillar of the Virginia ctenucha moth gripping a blade of grass with its red feet.

Mating pair of rusty tussock moths; the female (right) is wingless.

Rusty tussock moth caterpillar.

Tussock Moth
Subfamily Lymantriinae

This subfamily was, until 2010, its own family, the Lymantriidae. Six species have been recorded in Newfoundland and four in Labrador. Commonly known as tussock moths, all lymantriids have larvae with distinct bristles on their bodies. Similar to the woolly bears of the tiger moths, the hairs are also often incorporated into their cocoon when they pupate. Many adults rest in a characteristic triangular fashion with their hairy front legs held out in front of the body.

Rusty Tussock Moth
Orgyia antiqua

The rusty tussock moth caterpillar has an impressive arrangement of hairs. The caterpillars themselves are black with a black dorsal stripe of hairs, four cream-coloured tufts of hair, and bright red spots along the sides. They also have long black lateral tufts of hair and long black lashes on each end of their bodies. The caterpillars feed on a wide range of woody plants, including alder, apple, cherry, fir, larch, and blueberry.

- Size: 30 mm wingspan (male)
- Habitat detail: variable
- Distribution: throughout North America; native to Europe

Adults are sexually dimorphic: males have a wingspan of approximately 25 to 30 millimetres with red-brown forewings with a large white spot on the inner margin and red-orange hindwings; females are wingless. Females mate shortly after emerging from the cocoon and lay eggs directly on the cocoon.

This species overwinters in the egg stage. Early in the spring the young caterpillars emerge and often disperse by ballooning on threads of silk to find suitable host plants.

 Ballooning, a mode of dispersal used by spiders (Araneae), spider mites (Acari), and the larvae of some moths (present in nine families of moths), involves the production of silken threads by the organism, which are used to catch the wind, and disperse. In moths, ballooning is often used by larvae of species with flightless or weak flying females.

Satin Moth
Leucoma salicis

This snow-white, stout moth has black stripes on its legs. It was accidentally introduced to North America from Europe around 1920 and is currently found in eastern North America from Newfoundland and Labrador to Ontario and into the eastern United States. It is also present from Alberta west to Vancouver Island and down into California.

- Size: 24–47 mm wingspan
- Habitat detail: larvae feed on poplar and willow
- Distribution: Holarctic

Adults are usually in flight from early July to late August. Females lay eggs on the branches and trunks of

Satin moth.

Satin moth caterpillar.

poplar and willow trees. This species overwinters as young caterpillars. In some years, when populations are high, they have caused extensive defoliation. The caterpillars have cream-coloured spots along the middle of the back and tufts of red-brown hair on the back and sides.

Underwings
Catocala spp.

Using common names can lead to confusion in identifying insects, and the term "underwings" for moths with brightly coloured hindwings is a prime example. The presence of bright colours on the hindwing of a moth does not necessarily mean it is a true underwing. This common name generally refers to moths in the genus *Catocala*; many other moths, however, from other families, have brightly coloured hindwings, for example, the yellow underwing, *Noctua pronuba* (family Noctuidae), and the infant moth, *Archiearis infans* (family Geometridae).

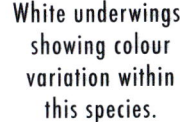

White underwings, showing colour variation within this species.

Adult true underwings usually have cryptically coloured forewings used to camouflage while resting on trees or rocks, and a brightly coloured banded hindwing that is normally hidden but used as a scare mechanism against predators. Four species of *Catocala* are recorded on the island of Newfoundland and none in Labrador.

The relict or white underwing, *Catocala relicta*, is a fairly common species found in woodland habitats. This moth has a wingspan of 65 to 75 millimetres and is readily attracted to lights. The forewings are variable but often white with grey to black markings. The thorax is dark and the hindwings are distinctively black with a white stripe. In flight from

Briseis underwing pinned specimen.

- Size: 50–65 mm wingspan
- Habitat detail: most abundant in deciduous forests
- Distribution: Holarctic

June to early October, this species overwinters as an egg and has one generation per year. Host plants include poplar, cottonwoods, and aspen.

Another species that uses poplar and willow as a host plant is the briseis underwing, *Catocala briseis*. This species has the familiar black-banded orange-red underwing colouring that many of the underwings have. The forewings are black, grey, and white and slightly scalloped on the edges. The briseis underwing is smaller than the relict and flies from early August to early September.

Other underwings recorded in the province include *C. blandula* and *C. unijuga*.

GEOMETER MOTHS

Family Geometridae
Loopers, Inchworms, Spanworms

Over 150 described species of geometer moths are recorded from the province. The geometers are often associated with forests and wooded areas, as many feed on woody plants, but they can be found in most habitats.

Geometrid moth.

Adults usually have a slender body and many hold their broad, delicate wings horizontally when at rest. The caterpillars are unique in that they have two pairs of well-developed prolegs at the hind end (most lepidopteran caterpillars have five pairs) that create the looping or inchwormlike movement typical of caterpillars in this family. When startled, many larvae adopt a stiff twiglike pose and attach themselves to the substrate by these prolegs.

About 23,000 named species of Geometer moths are found worldwide; 538 are reported from northern North America (Canada and Alaska); 167 in Newfoundland and 121 in Labrador.

Elm spanworm moth being attacked by a centipede.

Elm spanworm caterpillar striking a stick pose after being threatened.

Elm Spanworm
Ennomos subsignaria

Prior to 2000 most people in St. John's would not have heard of the elm spanworm, and the insect was considered rare in Newfoundland and Labrador. But thanks to an elm spanworm population outbreak in the centre of the city in 2004 to 2006, this insect is now infamous. The outbreak affected nearly every sycamore maple in the area and residents moved homes, cut down trees, slipped on caterpillar frass, and even wrote songs about the event.

- Size: 28-90 mm wingspan
- Habitat detail: woody plants
- Distribution: eastern North America

Despite the horrendous mess that the masses of hungry caterpillars created, the adult elm spanworm is a delicate snow-white moth that is a little less slender than a typical geometrid. Usually active in August, the females lay masses of eggs on the underside of branches and main trunk of the host tree (see page 158), where the

Elm spanworm larvae and frass covering a car during the 2005 outbreak.

eggs overwinter. Upon emerging in the spring, caterpillars feed on leaves of elm, maple, birch, apple, and oak. The caterpillars vary in colour from green to mottled brown; they usually have a dark body with a golden head and are typical of this family in that they move inchwormlike.

Hemlock Looper
Lambdina fiscellaria

- Size: 32–35 mm wingspan
- Habitat detail: forest
- Distribution: native to North America; found in all Canadian provinces (not in territories)

Adult hemlock loopers have a single flight in the fall, often in late August to October. Coloration of the adults is variable, from beige to brownish grey, with a connecting dark purplish line across its fore- and hindwings and a second line on its forewing. The degree of shading between the two lines is variable, from none at all to being noticeably darker than the rest of the wings. Females lay eggs on the bark of host trees or on lichen growing on the tree where the eggs overwinter. Larvae feed on the needles of its host—primarily balsam fir in Newfoundland—eventually pupating in bark crevices on the tree. When populations reach large numbers, larvae have been known to feed on black spruce, white birch, and white pine.

Hemlock looper.

Records of hemlock looper outbreaks in Newfoundland date to the early 1900s, with infestations lasting on average three to six years and causing losses of over 10 million cubic metres of balsam fir forest. Natural factors such as pathogens and parasitoids play an important role in regulating these large outbreaks.

Spear-Marked Black Moth
Rheumaptera hastata

This day-flying conspicuous geometrid is usually seen flying from mid-June to July. The adults are black with varying degrees of white markings that create spear marks on each wing.

- Size: 26–30 mm wingspan
- Habitat detail: boreal forest
- Distribution: Holarctic, all Canadian provinces

The caterpillars feed on birch and alder and can skeletonize the leaves by feeding just on the upper side of the leaf. The larvae feed as a group, often within a shelter made between two leaves, and can cause extensive damage if numbers are high enough. Once mature, larvae drop to the ground on silken threads and pupate in the leaf litter. They overwinter in this stage.

Spear-marked black moth.

Antler moth nectaring.

OWLET MOTHS
Family Noctuidae
Cutworm Moth, Armyworm Moths

Noctuidae are recognized by their heavy bodies, which vary from about 1.5 to 3.5 centimetres in length. Forewing patterns of noctuids tend to be drab shades of brown and grey, with pale or solid-coloured hindwings. They are generally strong fliers. At rest, they fold their wings over their bodies and often also tuck their antennae back over their bodies.

Most noctuid moths are night-fliers, as their name suggests. Many feed on sap, nectar, and fermenting fruit and can be lured into the garden for observation by painting trees with a sugary fermenting solution. Noctuid identification relies heavily on colour and the location of specific spots and lines on the forewing. This can be tricky, especially in older individuals with wing scales rubbed off.

Larvae are usually smooth or have few hairs and feed on a wide range of plant species and plant parts, including roots, stems, and leaves. Many noctuid larvae are called cutworms which rest during the day in the soil but come up at night to feed on the stems of their host plants.

As of 2018, 272 named species of noctuids are recorded in Newfoundland and 163 in Labrador.

Antler moth.

Antler Moth
Cerapteryx graminis

The antler moth is a northern European species that was first detected on the island of Newfoundland in Mount Pearl in 1966. It is now known province-wide, including in Labrador (as of 2014), but is found in no other place in North America.

The adult has a 34- to 36-millimetre wingspan with reddish brown forewings and a distinct pattern of cream branching streaks that resemble the antlers of a stag. Its hindwings are dark grey with a pale central area and pale fringes.

- Size: 34-36 mm wingspan
- Habitat detail: grassy fields, meadows
- Distribution: Europe, Newfoundland and Labrador

- Size: 40-55 mm wingspan
- Habitat detail: agricultural
- Distribution: worldwide; migrant into Canada

Adults are active from mid-July to mid-August and can be seen around fields and lawns. Larvae feed on grasses and have been known to reach high numbers in some years, causing damage to lawns, pastures, and hayfields.

Black Cutworm
Agrotis ipsilon
Ipsilon Dart Moth, Dark Sword-Grass Moth

The black cutworm is a common cutworm that arrives in Newfoundland and Labrador as a migrant from the United States almost every year. One of the most widespread moths in the world, it is a serious agricultural pest when populations reach high numbers. Caterpillars have been known to feed on corn, beets, carrots, leafy greens, peas, snap beans, and squash.

Black cutworm moth.

Adults have brown-grey forewings with a wingspan of 40 to 55 millimetres, with a black dagger-shaped mark toward the outer edge of the forewing. Adults are active from early June to late September.

Eight-Spotted Forester
Alypia octomaculata

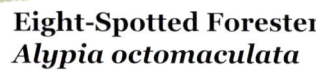

- Size: 30-37 mm wingspan
- Habitat detail: woodland edges where host and nectaring plants are found
- Distribution: eastern North America

Not all noctuids are drab—or night-fliers. This brightly coloured day-flying black moth has two cream-white spots on each of its four wings, giving it its common name. Its legs have distinct tufts of orange hairlike scales that make it look like it is wearing orange leg warmers.

The eight-spotted forester is found in Canada from Saskatchewan east to Newfoundland, but absent from Prince Edward Island and Labrador. Larvae have been recorded feeding on grape, Virginia creeper, and peppervine. This moth is most likely to be encountered in central and western Newfoundland in July.

Eight-spotted forester.

- Size: 45-55 mm wingspan
- Habitat detail: gardens
- Distribution: Palearctic; across Canada

Large Yellow Underwing
Noctua pronuba

These noctuid moths fly about lawns in mid-summer, showing a flash of yellow-orange hindwing as they make short flights and land again. An introduced species from Europe, the large yellow underwing is most easily identified by its hindwings, which are bright yellow orange with a black band border. The forewings are variable but are generally light to dark brown.

The caterpillars of this species feed on a wide range of plants, from grasses to brassicas, and can cause economic damage when populations are high enough. Overwintering as a large late instar larva, the caterpillars are also called winter cutworms, as they can be active in cool temperatures. The caterpillars have distinct broken dashes of black and cream on either side, which helps with identification.

Large yellow underwing moth.

The large yellow underwing resembles underwings of the genus *Catocala* (family Erebidae) but does not have a second black band through the brightly coloured hindwing, characteristic of the true underwings.

DIAMONDBACK MOTH

Family Plutellidae
Plutella xylostella

- Size: 12-15 mm wingspan
- Habitat detail: anywhere a host plant exists
- Distribution: cosmopolitan agricultural pest

The adult diamondback moth is greyish brown and about 6 millimetres long when it is at rest with the wings folded over its body. The wings have a light brown or cream band that comes together in a few places to form diamond shapes. When viewed from the side, the moth's wings appear to turn up at the tips. Females lay large numbers of eggs (150 or more) over their two- to three-week lifespan, usually on the undersides of leaves.

The larvae of the diamondback moth feed on plants in the family Brassicaceae, including cabbage, broccoli,

Diamondback moth adult.

and rutabaga. The first instar larvae are leaf miners—they eat the plant material between the upper and lower tissue layers of leaves. Second (3.5 millimetres long) to fourth instar (12 millimetres long) larvae are yellowish green to green and wider in the middle, tapering at both ends. Larvae have two prolegs on the last segment of the body which form a V shape that distinguishes them from other brassica-feeding caterpillar species. The larvae leave distinctive windowpane-like damage on the leaves they feed on. Mature larvae spin gauzy cocoons with the pupae visible inside. Multiple generations are produced each year.

Diamondback moth larvae.

The diamondback moth is one of the most challenging agricultural pests worldwide. The ability of this tiny moth to migrate long distances on high-altitude wind currents, coupled with its high reproductive capacity and fast developmental rate, means it can become a serious problem for growers in a short period of time. This moth does not overwinter in Newfoundland, but passively migrates every year on the wind from the southern US, landing in remote places in search of a host plant.

Susan Squires, working with Luise Hermanutz (Memorial University), has studied the impact of the diamondback moth on the rare native brassicaceous plants *Braya longii* and *B. fernaldii*, found only on the limestone barrens of the Northern Peninsula.

HAWK MOTHS

Family Sphingidae
Sphinx Moths, Horntails (larvae)

Sphinx moths are medium to large moths with elongated, narrow wings and a tapered body which gives them a distinctive fighter-jetlike appearance when at rest. Some species live for over a month as adults—this is considered long-lived for a moth—and are active feeders of nectar, which makes them important pollinators of flowering plants. Most have large eyes that help with locating flowers.

Sphinx moths are often various shades and patterns of browns, tans, and beige on the forewings, making it easy for them to blend in to tree trunks and leaf litter when resting.

A Canadian sphinx, *Sphinx canadensis*, resting like a fighter jet.

Apple sphinx moth caterpillar, *Sphinx gordius*; its horntail can be used for identification.

Pinned specimen of a clear wing moth.

Caterpillar of the laurel sphinx, *Sphinx kalmia*.

Many also have brightly coloured spots on the hindwings that are only seen occasionally, when the moths are startled. The larvae are also distinct: young caterpillars have a prominent horn on their rear end; some retain this horn as older larvae, in others it is reduced to a small knob or button.

As of 2018, 14 named species of Sphingidae are found in Newfoundland, and seven in Labrador.

Clear Wing Moth
Hemaris thysbe
Hummingbird Moth

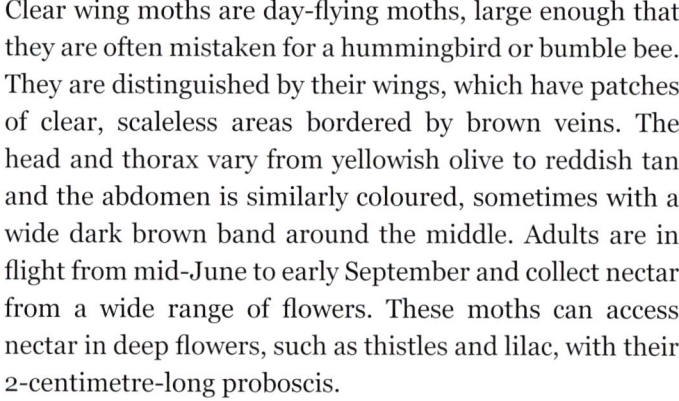

Clear wing moths are day-flying moths, large enough that they are often mistaken for a hummingbird or bumble bee. They are distinguished by their wings, which have patches of clear, scaleless areas bordered by brown veins. The head and thorax vary from yellowish olive to reddish tan and the abdomen is similarly coloured, sometimes with a wide dark brown band around the middle. Adults are in flight from mid-June to early September and collect nectar from a wide range of flowers. These moths can access nectar in deep flowers, such as thistles and lilac, with their 2-centimetre-long proboscis.

Caterpillars are bright green with yellow stripes on the sides that extend onto a slender tail horn. The horn is often bluish and curved; the larvae's head and body are peppered with small white bumps and the spiracles are orange red with white spots. The larvae have been recorded feeding on viburnum, hawthorn, honeysuckle, and snowberry.

In Newfoundland, this species produces one generation per year. Individuals spend the winter as pupae on the ground under leaves. One other species of *Hemaris* has been recorded from the island, *H. gracilis*, which is less common, similar in appearance to *H. thysbe* but slightly smaller, with a clear forewing cell that is not divided by a row of scales.

- Size: 20–24 mm wingspan
- Habitat detail: meadows, open forest, urban gardens
- Distribution: eastern North America; not recorded in Labrador

Clearwing moth nectaring on Rhodora.

One-eyed sphinx moth wing; note
the single undivided eye-spot.

One-Eyed Sphinx
Smerinthus cerisyi

- Size: 62-90 mm wingspan
- Habitat detail: deciduous forests where host tree present
- Distribution: most of North America and Canada; Newfoundland and Labrador

The one-eyed sphinx moth has scalloped forewing edges and pink hindwings with a blue-and-black eye-spot. The forewing colouration and degree of scalloping is variable, but generally the forewings are narrow at the base (closest to the body) in varying shades of grey and grey brown. The adults are normally in flight from early June to mid-July.

The larvae vary in appearance but tend to have subdorsal stripes that run down most of the body, as well as a wide head stripe. The tail horn can be yellow, pink,

Twin-spotted sphinx moth; note the half-moon shape on the forewing tip and the divided eye-spot on the hindwing.

or blue. One generation is produced per year; individuals overwinter as pupae. The one-eyed sphinx moth belongs to a genus of sphinx moths that do not feed as adults—they live only long enough to reproduce. Larvae feed on willow and poplar trees.

The one-eyed sphinx moth is similar in appearance to the twin-spotted sphinx moth, *Smerinthus jamaicensis*. These two species are distinguished from one another by the division of the eye-spot on the hindwing. In the twin-spotted sphinx moth, the eye-spot is bisected into two patches. It also has a dark brown half moon-shaped spot banded by white on the tip of the forewing.

TORTRICID MOTHS
Family Tortricidae
Leafroller Moths

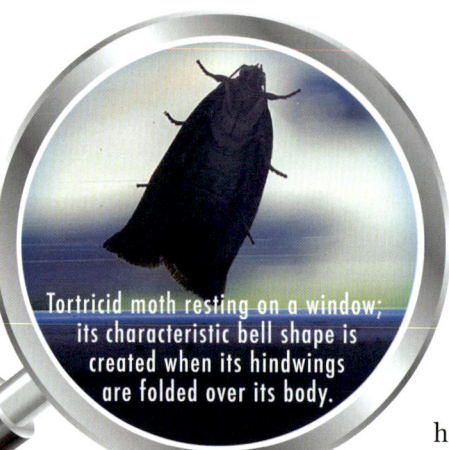

Tortricid moth resting on a window; its characteristic bell shape is created when its hindwings are folded over its body.

The Tortricidae is a huge family of primarily small moths. Many are brown, green, or greyish and often resemble bark, leaves, or bird droppings. Some, however, are brightly coloured, shiny, and metallic. Many have forewings that are square ended and, when resting, hold their wings rooflike over their bodies, giving them a characteristic bell shape. As larvae, many species have a habit of rolling and tying leaves together with silk.

Many tortricid moths are of great economic importance. In Newfoundland and Labrador, the blueberry leaftier, *Acleris curvalana*, lingonberry fruitworm, *Grapholita libertina*, and spruce budworm, *Choristoneura fumiferana*, are three notable tortricid moths.

Blueberry Leaftier Moth
Acleris curvalana

- Size: 14 mm wingspan
- Habitat detail: blueberry-growing areas
- Distribution: all provinces except PEI

The blueberry leaftier, as its name suggests, ties up the leaves of blueberry plants—but not before feeding on newly developing leaf and flower buds as a tiny larva. This insect has the potential to cause extensive damage to blueberry fields.

Blueberry leaftier eggs overwinter in leaf litter. The larvae hatch early in the spring, when blueberry plants are just forming tiny leaf and flower buds. The youngest larvae eat their way into the buds, where they feed; later instars roll and tie up the leaves to use as shelter. They leave their leaf shelters only to feed. Pupation usually occurs at about the end of June, and adults are active in July and August. Adult colours range from a pale yellow

Blueberry leaftier moth.

background with rust to chocolate brown markings and a yellow spot on each of the forewings to extremely pale with hardly any dark markings and no spot.

Lingonberry Fruitworm
Grapholita libertina

The lingonberry fruitworm is a tiny tortricid moth that is most likely encountered as a caterpillar because it infests lingonberry fruit (lingonberries are called partridgeberries on the island of Newfoundland; redberries in Labrador). In Canada this insect has been recorded in Newfoundland, Nova Scotia, and in British Columbia, although it is suspected to be in other areas as well, including Labrador.

Adults usually emerge in June and July and females lay eggs on the developing fruit. The larvae move between berries and consume the inside flesh. After the larva reaches maturity, it will exit the berry and overwinter in a prepupal stage in a hibernaculum constructed in debris on the ground. The Newfoundland and Labrador provincial government used to release updates on when partridgeberries would be "worm free"—after the larvae would have left the inside of the berry—and safe to harvest.

- Size: 11–14 mm wingspan
- Habitat detail: associated with lingonberry, barrens, heaths
- Distribution: British Columbia, island of Newfoundland, and Nova Scotia

Lingonberries (partridgeberries).

Lingonberry fruitworm on a partridgeberry.

In the late 1990s, Kirk Hillier (at Acadia University as of 2019), investigated the use of synthetic pheromones as a means to attract lingonberry fruitworms and to predict damage they would wreak in Newfoundland. The pheromone traps he used attracted male moths, allowing the estimation of population levels and timing of egg laying in the berries. This research involved the collection of mass numbers of berries with larvae and the discovery of a new species of parasitic wasp in the family Braconidae. This parasitic wasp, which lays its eggs inside the larva of the lingonberry fruitworm, has since been described as a new species, *Phanerotoma libertinecida*. Adults are tiny, just 3.3 to 4.4 millimetres long.

Phanerotoma libertinecida.

Pinned specimen of a spruce budworm moth.

Underside of a spruce budworm moth.

Spruce Budworm
Choristoneura fumiferana

The spruce budworm may be the most destructive foliage-feeding insect of the coniferous forests in North America. It is a small brownish moth with variable amounts of mottling on its forewings. Adults are active in July and August. After mating, females lay their eggs on the needles of balsam fir and white spruce. The larvae move to the crown of the tree and build an overwintering structure from silk, called a hibernaculum. Early in the spring the larvae become active and begin looking for new needles to feed on, continuing to eat until late June, when they pupate. This insect has caused extensive economic losses to the timber industry in many parts of Canada, including Newfoundland and Labrador.

- Size: 21–30 mm wingspan
- Habitat detail: spruce and fir forests
- Distribution: Canada and US

Upperside of an Arctic skipper.

BUTTERFLIES
SKIPPERS

Family Hesperiidae

Skippers, the common name of butterflies in the family Hesperiidae, have broad heads and wings that are usually brown, grey, and/or orange. They gain their common name from their fast, darting flight patterns. Over 4,100 named species of skippers are found worldwide; 74 reported from northern North America (Canada and Alaska); five in Newfoundland and Labrador.

Many skippers are difficult to identify to the species level, even for experts, and require genitalia dissection for proper identification. In Newfoundland and Labrador, however, given the lack of diversity of this family, all species should be able to be identified in the field.

Light red-orange underside of an Arctic skipper.

Arctic Skipper
Carterocephalus palaemon

The Arctic skipper, despite its name, is not a truly Arctic species. It can be found in boreal and mixed deciduous forests and flies from late May to mid-July. The adults are chocolate brown on the upperside with squarish orange spots on both wings. The undersides are light red orange with dark-rimmed cream-coloured spots. This butterfly is most often seen resting with its wings closed; it does open its wings to bask in the sun when it needs to warm up.

Females lay eggs on brome grasses and the larvae feed on and live in silk-tied leaf nests that they construct. The Arctic skipper overwinters as a mature larva and pupates in the spring, completing one generation per year.

- Size: 19–32 mm wingspan
- Habitat detail: open grassy areas; forest trails, clearings, edges
- Distribution: Canada, except the high Arctic; into northern US and along the mountains to California; Eurasia

European skipper, with narrow black wing margins and black outlined veins.

Common Branded Skipper
Hesperia comma borealis
Labrador Skipper

The common branded skipper (along with the European skipper and Peck's skipper) is one of three grass skippers encountered in Newfoundland and Labrador. The grass skippers, as their name suggests, have larvae that feed on grasses as their host plants. They are also known as the folded-wing skippers, as they have a characteristic posture when they land; the forewings are held at 45 degrees to the rest of the body, while the hindwings are held open and flat, giving them a fighter-jetlike appearance.

The common branded skipper can be differentiated from the other folded wing skippers by the presence of white spots on the undersides of the hindwings that sometimes form a continuous band of white. The uppersides of the wings are generally orange brown blending to a darker brown on the edges. Often flying in July, this species has been collected in northern Newfoundland and Labrador. This species' range extends well northward into the subarctic, where it is expected to have a biennial lifecycle.

- Size: 22-30 mm wingspan
- Habitat detail: grassy roadsides and forest clearings
- Distribution: boreal and subalpine regions of North America, Eurasia, and northwestern Africa

European Skipper
Thymelicus lineola

The European skipper is usually the most abundant skipper seen in Newfoundland and Labrador during the summer months. Of Eurasian origin, this species quickly spread throughout North America after its accidental introduction on imported timothy seed in London, Ontario, around 1910. This butterfly is bright shiny orange on its upperside, with narrow black borders on both wings;

European skipper.

European skipper, with its held-up wings showing the pale orange underside of its forewing and its extended proboscis (tongue).

- Size: 25-29 mm wingspan
- Habitat detail: open grassy fields, meadows, pastures, hayfields, and roadsides
- Distribution: Eurasian origin; North America

the wing veins are outlined in black as well. The undersides of the hindwings are greyish brown; those of the forewings, pale orange.

European skippers are most often found in open weedy habitats as well as near pastures, roadsides, woodland paths, and bog edges where host plants are present. Timothy grass is the preferred host plant, but individuals also feed on other grasses such as orchard grass and quackgrass. Females lay eggs in the leaf sheath or seed head.

The larvae are green with a dark dorsal stripe and a whitish green head with three distinctive reddish brown vertical bars. This species overwinters as eggs, with one generation per year.

Grizzled skipper resting with open wings, displaying black-and-white fringes on both hind- and forewings and squarish white checks.

Underside view of a grizzled skipper.

Grizzled Skipper
Pyrgus centaureae

The grizzled skipper is a small brownish black skipper with squarish white checks on the upperside of the wings and checkered black-and-white fringes on both wing margins. The underside is grey brown to black also with checkered spots and white veins. Subspecies *freiji* was first described from specimens collected in Labrador and is the most common subspecies found in Canada.

This butterfly has been seen nectaring on low-growing blueberry, wild strawberry, and Canadian cinquefoil from mid-June to early August, and often rests with its wings spread. Larvae feed on bakeapple. This species has one generation a year and, in some subarctic areas, it may even take two years to complete its life cycle.

- Size: 22–28 mm wingspan
- Habitat detail: depends on location; tundra, bogs, meadows, forest clearings
- Distribution: circumpolar, including Labrador and Northern Peninsula, Newfoundland

Brown upperside of a Peck's skipper.

- Size: 19-27 mm wingspan
- Habitat detail: wet marshes, roadsides, and gardens
- Distribution: all Canadian provinces, northern and central US

Underside of a Peck's skipper.

Peck's Skipper
Polites peckius

The Peck's skipper is the darkest, in terms of wing colouring, of the grass skippers found in Newfoundland and Labrador. The uppersides of the wings are brown with reddish orange patches; the underside of the hindwing has a characteristic large pale patch surrounded by a darker brown. This species regularly visits summer flowers for nectar and can be seen flying from mid-June to late July. Collection records indicate it may be more prevalent on the west coast of the island and the Northern Peninsula and Labrador.

Peck's skipper overwinters as a late instar larva or pupa and most likely has one generation per year.

GOSSAMER-WINGED BUTTERFLIES

Family Lycaenidae
Blues, Coppers, and Hairstreaks

The Lycaenidae are a family of butterflies that contain the blues (subfamily Polyommatinae), coppers (subfamily Lycaeninae), and hairstreaks (subfamily Theclinae). Generally, they are fast-flying, relatively small (bodies of 1.5 centimetres or less) butterflies, often seen resting with their wings folded back. Males are brightly coloured with iridescent blue, copper, or purplish scales; females, less bright.

The caterpillars are oval, flattened, and grublike. Many species secrete a sweet solution of sugars and amino acids which is attractive to ants. The ants protect the larvae from predators in exchange for the sugary drink.

Underside of an Arctic blue, with white-ringed black spots and a faint orange spot on its hindwing.

Seven species of this family have been recorded on the island of Newfoundland and eight in Labrador. Most are found in the wilderness.

Arctic Blue
Agriades glandon

The Arctic blue has a fast, erratic flight. It usually flies low to the ground and can be mistaken for a moth when in motion. The upperside of male wings are grey blue compared to the orange-brown wings of females. Both males and females have a dark cell spot on both wings that is sometimes ringed with lighter scales and a row of ringed dark spots on the hindwing margin. The underside of the wings is grey and has white-ringed black spots, and the hindwing may have an orange spot.

This butterfly usually flies in open dry areas in early to late July in Newfoundland and July to mid-August in Labrador. Host plants include pincushion plant, crowberry, and possibly others in the families Primulaceae, Fabaceae, and Saxifragaceae. This species has one generation per year and most likely overwinters as pupae. Its life history details in Newfoundland are not well known.

- Size: 17-23 mm wingspan
- Habitat detail: alpine and subalpine forests and meadows, bogs, and tundra
- Distribution: western and northern Canada and Newfoundland and Labrador, absent from the Maritimes and most of Quebec and Ontario

Arctic blue resting with open wings.

Greenish Blue
Icaricia saepiolus

- Size: 21–28 mm wingspan
- Habitat detail: open areas, roadsides, edges of bogs, and moist meadows
- Distribution: all provinces, except Prince Edward Island, island of Newfoundland, and southern Ontario

Present in Labrador but not Newfoundland, the greenish blue can be found in moist meadows, streamsides, and pastures. This butterfly is metallic blue with narrow dark brown to black borders on all wings and a row of dark spots near the hindwing margin. The female is dark brown with a blue sheen and has a row of faint orange-capped black spots on the hindwing margin. Both sexes have a small black dash at the end of the forewing cell. The underside of male wings is silvery grey; female, dark grey to pale tan. Each has two rows of small dark spots on both wings and a partial third row of spots on the hindwing.

The caterpillars vary in colour from green to greenish white or reddish brown and feed on many clovers, including white and alsike clover, but not red clover. This species overwinters as a second or third instar larva. Larvae are attended by ants.

Greenish blue resting on a blade of grass.

Northern Blue
Plebejus idas

Previously known as *Lycaeides idas*, this species, as its name implies, is a northerly species of blue and present in Newfoundland and Labrador—as well as in all other Canadian provinces, in northern Europe, and across Asia. Males are bright purplish blue on the upper wing surface, with very narrow black margins, rarely with black marginal spots on the hindwing. At least half of the outer edge of the upper side of the female's forewings is a dark brownish grey with a blueish sheen and often with a trace of orange marginal spots. Both male and female wing undersides are pale grey, with black spots in the central area, and a row of marginal black spots on both wings with metallic blue centres capped with orange.

Expect to find northern blues flying in late July to mid-August. They are often abundant on coastal headlands where black crowberry is present. Other larval hosts include Labrador tea and sheep laurel. This species overwinters as eggs.

- Size: 17-28 mm wingspan
- Habitat detail: open forest clearings, coastal headlands
- Distribution: all provinces, northern Europe and Asia

Underside of a northern blue.

Upperside of a northern blue.

Pinned specimen of a northern spring azure.

Northern Spring Azure
Celastrina lucia
Spring Azure

The spring azure is common and widespread and one of the first butterflies to fly in the spring. These blue butterflies are in flight from mid-May to mid-August. The male is predominantly blue on the upper surface with thin black lines on the outer margins of the forewing. The females also have a black marginal line on the upper forewing but to a much greater degree than the males—it can cover up to one-third of the upper forewing. The undersides of the wings are pale brownish grey with a zigzagged dark-grey-spotted submarginal line on the hindwing. There are three underside forms of this butterfly which vary in the degree of shading of the marginal and the central spots.

Host plants for this species include dogwood, sumac, blueberry, and other woody shrubs. The larvae

- Size: 19-22 mm wingspan
- Habitat detail: forest edges, open clearings, old fields
- Distribution: all provinces

Underside of a northern spring azure form *lucia*, with dark grey shaded margin and the central spots merged into one large central spot.

Underside of a northern spring azure form *marginata*, with no grey shading of marginal spots.

are variable in colour, in part depending on which host plant they are feeding. The sluglike caterpillars vary from pale, pastel green with little patterning to dark green with more pattern. A single generation is produced each year; individuals overwinter as pupae.

Some uncertainty surrounding the taxonomy of the genus *Celastrina* in Canada still exists and many field guides and websites list this species as *Celastrina ladon*.

Silvery blue nectaring from red clover; its underside has a single row of white-rimmed round black spots on both wings.

Silvery Blue
Glaucopsyche lygdamus

- Size: 18-28 mm wingspan
- Habitat detail: open edges of boreal forest, roadsides, and bogs
- Distribution: most of North America, all provinces

As its name suggests, the upper surface of this butterfly's wings is shiny, silvery light blue, with a dark grey to black border around both wings. Females often have a darker border. The underside of the hindwing is grey with one row of white rimmed, round black spots on both wings.

Host plants include vetch, lupines, and other legumes. Larvae are pale green, sometimes pinkish, with a pink or dark green dorsal line. They often feed on the flowers and fruit of their host plant as well as on newer leaves. Ants readily tend the caterpillars. If you see adults flying around (mid-June to mid-July), search for ants—chances are the butterfly larvae are close by. This species overwinters as pupae and has one generation per year.

This bog copper has fewer prominent orange markings on its hindwing than many, but they are still visible on the inner margin.

Bog Copper
Lycaena epixanthe phaedra

This butterfly's range is a band that includes the island of Newfoundland, the Maritimes, northeastern United States, and areas surrounding the Great Lakes. The subspecies *phaedra* is found in Newfoundland and Nova Scotia. Bog coppers can be found flying low and slowly over boggy habitats where cranberries grow. Adults drink nectar and caterpillars feed almost exclusively on cranberry.

Males have a faint purplish sheen on the upperside of the grey-brown wings and a prominent black spot in the middle of each wing. Inconspicuous smaller black dots may be found on the males but these are more prominent in the females. Both sexes may have orange markings on the outer margin of the upper hindwing. The underside is chalky white with small black dots and a thin submarginal

- Size: 18-28 mm wingspan
- Habitat detail: bogs with cranberries
- Distribution: band through eastern North America

Brown elfin sipping nectar.

Bog copper, showing its underside, resting on a leaf.

band of zigzagging orange. This species overwinters as an egg, which can withstand flooding.

The bog copper is similar to the Dorcas copper, *L. dorcas*, which is present in Newfoundland and also in Labrador. The Dorcas copper is slightly larger and has an orange-brown underside (unlike the chalky white of the bog copper) and more black spots on the uppersides of the wings.

Brown Elfin
Callophrys augustinus

This butterfly can be found in much of North America, including Labrador (subspecies *augustinus*) and the island of Newfoundland (subspecies *helenae*). Brown elfin are found early in the spring near bogs, barrens, and conifer woods where their host plants—blueberry, laurel, and Labrador tea—grow. Male brown elfins are grey brown on the uppersides and females appear a little more reddish. The undersides have a distinct division of pale brown on the outer half divided by an irregular line in the middle with dark brown on the basal part of the wings. A rich reddish brown is sometimes present along the hindwing margin.

Adults fly from mid-May to early June and like to sip moisture from the wet ground after it rains. The larvae are olive green to yellow green and have yellow-green markings. This species overwinters as pupae in the leaf litter at the base of its host plant.

- Size: 19–26 mm wingspan
- Habitat detail: any place larval food plants occur: bogs, barrens, and coniferous forests
- Distribution: much of North America, all provinces

BRUSH-FOOTED BUTTERFLIES

Family Nymphalidae
Brush-Footed Butterflies

The brush-footed butterflies are by far the most represented butterfly family in the province (26 species in Newfoundland and 29 in Labrador) and is so diverse that it was once divided into separate families. They all have reduced front legs that are covered with long hairs, giving them a brushlike appearance. This characteristic is hard to see in the field, but it does often give these butterflies the appearance of being four-legged. In Newfoundland the brush-footed butterflies are represented by the commas, fritillaries, monarch, ladies, admirals, and satyrs. Included here are the most conspicuous of the Nymphalidae as well as some of the more commonly seen.

Commas
Polygonia spp.
Anglewings

These distinctively shaped butterflies have a conspicuous white mark on the underside of each wing that resembles a comma, giving them one of their common names. Also known as anglewings, these butterflies have angular wing shapes and are known to nectar on flowers and feed on tree sap, rotting fruit, dung, and carrion.

Six species belonging to this genus are recorded in Newfoundland and Labrador. One, the question mark, *Polygonia interrogationis*, is a migrant and has not been observed reproducing in the province. The hoary comma, *P. gracilis*, only occurs in Labrador and the eastern comma (*P. comma*), satyr comma (*P. styrus*), and grey comma (*P. progne*) occur on the island only. The green comma, *P. faunus*, is the only species found in both Newfoundland and Labrador.

Green comma with closed wings resting.

Newly emerged green comma resting on a log; the adult will overwinter and look a little more worn and tattered in the spring.

The green comma overwinters as an adult in the province and has the most irregular looking wing edges of all of the anglewings. Individuals encountered in the spring are faded and battered looking and best recognized by the row of small green spots on the underside of the hindwing, near the outer margin. Using birch, willow, alder, and blueberry as larval host plants, green commas are most often seen in woodland habitats early in the spring and again in late summer/early fall.

- Size: 34-47 mm wingspan
- Habitat detail: boreal forest, roadsides
- Distribution: Canada, present in Newfoundland and Labrador

- Size: 28–64 mm wingspan
- Habitat detail: open meadows, tundra, bogs
- Distribution: most are Holarctic

Fritillaries
Speyeria atlantis and *Boloria* spp.

The fritillaries are a large group of butterflies in the subfamily Heliconiinae, most often recognized for their orange-and-black checkerboard wing pattern. These butterflies are widespread and usually seen on flowers in open meadows, bogs, or tundra. Some of the most useful defining characteristics of these species are on the underside of the wings but, unfortunately, these butterflies tend to rest with wings spread apart, making it difficult to distinguish them in the field.

This group is often separated into greater and lesser fritillaries based on size. One species of greater fritillary, *Speyeria atlantis*, as well as seven lesser fritillaries, *Boloria* spp., have been confirmed in both Newfoundland and Labrador: bog fritillary, *B. eunomia*; silver-bordered fritillary, *B. selene*; freija fritillary, *B. freija*; and Arctic fritillary, *B. chariclea*. Additional species have been recorded in Labrador: meadow fritillary, *B. bellona*; frigga fritillary, *B. frigga*; and polaris fritillary, *B. polaris*.

Underside of an Atlantis fritillary.

Atlantis fritillary, the only species of greater fritillary in Newfoundland and Labrador.

Milbert's Tortoiseshell
Aglais milberti
Fire-Rim Tortoiseshell

Another common name for this butterfly is the fire-rim tortoiseshell, which might help with identification in the field. Close to the body, wing uppersides have a large area of black rimmed with yellow, orange, and red. This rim of fire is surrounded by a black margin that often contains blue spots. Wing undersides are dark brown at the base but fade to a lighter brown toward the margins and look convincingly like tree bark or dead leaves. The forewings have a distinct squarish tip.

These butterflies are fast, erratic fliers and nectar on thistles, lilacs, and goldenrods from mid-May to early October. The adults also feed on rotting fruit, sap, and

- Size: 34–63 mm wingspan
- Habitat detail: moist pastures, woodland trails, and roads
- Distribution: all provinces, parts of US

Milbert's tortoiseshell resting on an aster.

Monarch butterfly, an occasional vagrant in the province.

dung. Females lay their eggs on nettles and the larvae are black with branched spines and flecks of white. Thought to overwinter as adults or pupae, this butterfly has multiple overlapping generations a year.

The only other tortoiseshell in Newfoundland and Labrador is the Compton tortoiseshell, *Nymphalis l-album*, which averages a little larger in size than the Milbert's tortoiseshell. The Compton tortoiseshell is a lighter rust brown with large black spots on the upperside of the wings; the wing shape is overall more angular, similar to that of the anglewings (page 212).

Monarch
Danaus plexippus

- Size: 93-105 mm wingspan
- Habitat detail: variable
- Distribution: migrant to Canada, only occasionally seen in Newfoundland

The monarch is one of the most recognized and well-known butterflies in North America due to its large size and fascinating life history. The uppersides of its wings are bright orange with black veins, and the edges of the wings have a black border with two rows of small white spots. Wing undersides have a similar pattern except in a lighter orange.

This species is migratory and usually arrives in Newfoundland in early August to November. It cannot reproduce in the province due to the absence of milkweed, the larval host plant. It is unlikely that the monarch's larvae—with its white, yellow, and black bands and pair of black filaments on its head—will be seen in the province.

The individuals that arrive in Newfoundland every year are part of the eastern population of monarchs that overwinter in Mexico. The overwintered butterflies leave Mexico in March or early April and make their way to coastal states on the Gulf of Mexico, where they produce their first generation. This generation continues the northward migration, stopping and producing subsequent generations along the way before reaching their northernmost sites. Varying numbers of monarchs arrive each year in the province; in some years and at some locations, mass numbers are reported.

Spiky caterpillar of the mourning cloak butterfly, with characteristic spines, small white dots, and red dorsal spots.

Mourning Cloak
Nymphalis antiopa

The mourning cloaks that are seen early in the spring often look like they have seen better days—because by then they have spent many cold days hibernating in a sheltered woodpile between logs. This species is one of the few butterflies that overwinters as an adult in the province. Once temperatures warm up in spring, these butterflies emerge in search of a mate and a place to lay eggs. They feed mainly on tree sap with a few visiting flowers for nectar.

- Size: 45–79 mm wingspan
- Habitat detail: parks, gardens, open woodlands, and near ponds, streams, forest borders
- Distribution: North America and Europe, widely distributed in Newfoundland and Labrador

Mourning cloak butterfly.

Underside of a mourning cloak butterfly.

Adults have dark brown-maroon wings with irregular edges. The wing tips are beige with blue spots on the inner edge of the beige border. Wing undersides are coloured to camouflage with its surroundings, overall dark brown with lighter brown edges. Host plants for the mourning cloak include a wide variety of deciduous trees, including willow (which seems to be a favourite), elm, poplar, and birch. The caterpillars, sometimes referred to as spiny elm caterpillars, are black with red-and-white spots and long spines. They are often found feeding together in large numbers; they will also often leave together in search of a safe place to pupate. Adults are seen in early spring and again in late summer and early fall.

Painted lady butterfly with spread wings resting.

American lady's two large eye-spots on the hindwing underside.

American lady butterfly nectaring on sedum.

Painted Lady
Vanessa cardui

- Size: 42–66 mm wingspan
- Habitat detail: open habitats, gardens, fields, farmlands, roadsides
- Distribution: all continents except Antarctica and South America

The painted lady is the most widely distributed butterfly in the world and often used as a demonstration of metamorphosis in classrooms, as they are relatively easy to rear on artificial diets. The adults have pointed wings which are overall orange pink in colour. Wing uppersides have intricate dark markings, and the forewings have black tips with a series of white spots. The hindwing marginal spots are black, rarely having blue centres. The underwing pattern is complex, with the hindwing having a row of five eye-spots on the outer margin.

Painted ladies are swift fliers and do not generally overwinter in Canada, although it is thought they may be able to overwinter in southern Ontario. They are a migratory species and their abundance is often dictated by the numbers that arrive in the spring. Unlike the monarch, another migrant, this species is capable of reproducing in

Painted lady butterfly nectaring on knapweed, showing underside row of five spots on hindwing.

Newfoundland and Labrador, as the larvae use thistles, hollyhock, burdock, and mallow as host plants.

American lady, *Vanessa virginiensis*, can be distinguished from the painted lady by the presence of two large eye-spots on each hindwing; the painted lady has five smaller spots. According to Morris (1980), the American lady is less common in Newfoundland. Larvae develop on various members of the sunflower family.

Red Admiral
Vanessa atalanta

The red admiral is common in Newfoundland and Labrador, often seen nectaring at a variety of wild and garden flowers. Wing uppersides are black brown with a distinct red-orange band on the middle of the forewing and a number of white spots on the tips. The underside of the forewing also has a red-orange stripe in the middle of the wing. The hindwing has a red-orange marginal band on its

- Size: 45-57 mm wingspan
- Habitat detail: variable; gardens, parks, open clearings in the woods
- Distribution: Holarctic; occurs as a migrant in all of Canada

Red admiral butterfly.

White admiral butterfly resting on a fir tree.

upperside and its underside is a mottled brown green.

In most of its range in Canada, including Newfoundland and Labrador, this species is a migrant and arrives each spring in search of suitable habitat and food plants. Adults have been seen in Newfoundland from May to mid-October. Known to be territorial, males will often claim a space and defend it, spending time perching and patrolling the space and driving away intruders.

Common food plants include stinging nettles and false nettle. The larvae are highly variable in colour, from white or yellow green to greenish black, usually with a speckling of white flecks and stiff hairs and spines. The young larvae build nests by tying up the leaves. This species produces a single generation in a season.

White Admiral
Limenitis arthemis
Red-Spotted Purple

- Size: 47–78 mm wingspan
- Habitat detail: clearings in wooded areas, roadsides
- Distribution: North America; present in Newfoundland and Labrador

The white admiral is a black-purple butterfly with broad white bands spanning both wings. Subspecies *Limenitis arthemis arthemis* is present in Newfoundland and Labrador; adults often have a row of blue spots (sometimes having a small amount of red) directly below the white band on the hindwing and rows of blue spots on the hindwing margins. The undersides of the wings are a paler reddish brown and have the same white bands with bright red spots along the outer margins and near the wing bases. This species has another form that was once thought to be its own species, the red-spotted purple. In areas where the two forms overlap, hybrids with many colour patterns are seen.

The white admiral is most often encountered on sunny paths and roads from mid-July to late July, flying with distinct quick wing beats followed by a glide. The females lay eggs on willow, poplar, and birch, and the larvae can easily be mistaken for bird droppings. This species overwinters as partially grown larvae and there is one generation per year.

Common ringlet butterfly resting on a leaf.

Common Ringlet
Coenonympha tullia

The common ringlet is a fairly common butterfly in Newfoundland and Labrador, taking flight from late May to late July. This species can be quite variable in coloration over its range and has eight recognized subspecies in Canada. When the butterfly is resting with its wings closed, the forewing is a light buff to orange brown with light grey on the outer margins. The underside of the hindwing is darker grey basally fading to a lighter grey at the margins. The upperside of the wings rarely have markings and are a light buff to orange brown.

- Size: 27–39 mm wingspan
- Habitat detail: grassy habitats, tundra, bogs, open meadows, roadsides
- Distribution: North America; present in Newfoundland and Labrador

Jutta Arctic resting on the tip of a spruce branch.

ARCTICS

Oeneis spp.

- Size: 33–50 mm wingspan
- Habitat detail: tundra, bogs, alpine
- Distribution: species dependent

The Arctics are medium-sized butterflies with pointed forewings and rounded hindwings. Many are brown or grey with very stunning hindwings marked to match the rocks, ground, trees, and other places they rest with their wings closed. They have hairy bodies and short antennae. There are four species of Arctics recorded in Newfoundland and Labrador. The white-veined Arctic, *Oeneis bore,* and Melissa Arctic, *O. melissa*, are both recorded from Labrador only and the jutta Arctic, *O. jutta,* and polixenes Arctic, *O. polixenes*, are recorded on the island as well as in Labrador. Most feed on grasses as larvae and commonly take two years to complete their life cycle.

A resting Canadian tiger swallowtail butterfly.

SWALLOWTAIL BUTTERFLIES
Family Papilionidae

The Papilionidae are commonly known as swallowtail butterflies. They are large colourful butterflies that often have a forked appearance to their hindwings, giving them their common name. They contain the fewest number of species of all the butterfly families; only two are found in Newfoundland and Labrador. The caterpillars are usually spineless and have an osmeterium, a foul-smelling forked organ that is used in deterring predators.

Canadian Tiger Swallowtail
Papilio canadensis

The Entomology Laboratory at Agriculture and Agri-Food Canada receives regular inquiries about the identity of the

Caterpillar of a Canadian tiger swallowtail butterfly turning brown before pupating.

- Size: 53-90 mm wingspan
- Habitat detail: a woodland species, but regularly found in fields, along roadsides, and in urban settings if host plants present
- Distribution: eastern US, all provinces

strange-looking caterpillar of the Canadian tiger swallowtail. This caterpillar is 55 millimetres long when mature and smooth green with a thickened thorax and tapered abdomen. It has a pair of distinct black, blue, and yellow eye-spots and a yellow-and-black stripe behind the eye-spots. When close to pupation, the caterpillar may turn a light brown. Typical of all swallowtails, this caterpillar has an eversible osmeterium (see page 234) on the prothorax, which looks like a snake tongue and is often foul-smelling and used as a defence mechanism. The larvae feed on a wide variety of trees, including willow, cherry, poplar, and ash. Canadian tiger swallowtails produce one generation per year and overwinter as pupae.

The Canadian tiger swallowtail is native to North America and common in forests and along rivers and streams as well as in urban and suburban habitats. Due to its large size, distinct yellow-and-black coloration, and long "tails" on its hindwings, it is one of the province's best-known butterflies. This butterfly flies high and fast from mid-June to late July and can often be found mud-puddling on moist sand/dirt.

> Mud-puddling is a behaviour most common in butterflies but also observed in other insects. A butterfly, for example, will seek out moist areas of sand, dirt, or even rotting plant/animal material to rest on and sip the fluids often rich in salts and amino acids.

Group of mud-puddling Canadian tiger swallowtail butterflies on the banks of the Terra Nova river.

Short-tailed swallowtail butterfly nectaring.

Short-Tailed Swallowtail
Papilio brevicauda

This species has three recognized subspecies, one of which, *Papilio brevicauda brevicauda*, only occurs in Newfoundland and Labrador and on Anticosti Island. Subspecies *bretonensis* occurs on Cape Breton Island and the north shore of New Brunswick, and subspecies *gaspeensis* is found in Quebec. These subspecies vary in the amount of orange present in the yellow spots on the upperside spot bands; with *brevicauda* having the most orange, *gaspeensis* the least.

Most papilionid butterflies have long tails on the hind wings (see Canadian tiger swallowtail) but, as its name suggests, this species lacks the long tail and may be easily separated from the Canadian tiger swallowtail by its predominantly black wings and short tails.

Adults usually fly from mid-June to late July, and larval host plants include cow parsnip (inland), Scotch lovage (along the coast), and other plants in the carrot family (gardens). Adults are frequently seen at Cape Spear,

- Size: 57–73 mm wingspan
- Habitat detail: gardens where host plants grow, clifftops and rocky beaches, inland meadows close to the treeline
- Distribution: Newfoundland and southern Labrador; Maritime provinces; Gaspé Peninsula, Quebec

Caterpillar of the short-tailed swallowtail, with osmeterium extended.

Newfoundland. Young caterpillars are brownish black with a white saddle and look like bird droppings; when they mature, they are green with a black band containing small yellow spots on each segment.

WHITES AND SULPHURS
Family Pieridae

The whites and sulphurs in Newfoundland and Labrador are medium-sized butterflies with bodies ranging from about 1.5 to 3.5 centimetres in length. They are predominantly yellow, orange, or white. The larvae of the whites tend to feed on plants in the family Brassicaceae; those of the sulphurs feed predominantly on plants in the family Fabaceae (legumes). The pupae of both groups are often attached to leaves or other surfaces by a silken girdle.

Six species of Pieridae have been recorded in Newfoundland and eight in Labrador.

Cabbage white butterfly resting on a leaf.

Cabbage White
Pieris rapae
Imported Cabbage Worm

The cabbage white is one of the most common butterflies found in urban habitats and agricultural areas; it is less often found in wilderness habitats. This species was introduced from Europe in the 19th century and has since spread across most of North America. As its common name implies, the cabbage white is a white butterfly and its larvae feed on cabbage and other plants in the family Brassicaceae. The upperside of the forewings is white with a black tip; males have one black spot, females have two.

Females lay eggs singly on the leaves of the host plant. Larvae are velvety green with a faint yellow stripe down the back and a row of yellow spots along the side of the body. Larvae feed until they reach maturity—this may take two to three weeks, depending on temperatures—and reach

- Size: 32-47 mm wingspan
- Habitat detail: urban gardens, weedy roadsides, agricultural
- Distribution: worldwide; present in Newfoundland and Labrador

Cabbage white butterflies.

approximately 30 millimetres in length before pupating into a distinct chrysalis secured onto the leaf by a silken girdle. Adults emerge and nectar from a wide variety of plants, including mustards, dandelion, red clover, asters, and mints before mating and starting a new generation. This species has multiple generations in a season. Most overwinter as pupae.

Many plants in the family Brassicaceae are vegetables commonly grown in Newfoundland (including cabbage, broccoli, cauliflower, and Brussels sprouts). Cabbage white larvae can be a major pest to gardeners and farmers and even has its own common name, the imported cabbage worm. The caterpillars can cause extensive damage by eating plant leaves and the copious amounts of frass discolour the heads of cauliflower and broccoli.

Mustard White
Pieris oleracea

- Size: 32–50 mm wingspan
- Habitat detail: woodland or open area near the woods
- Distribution: all provinces

Mustard white adults are seen flying from mid-June to August. The species often has two overlapping generations in Newfoundland and Labrador, and two forms can be seen, depending on the time of year. Both are white on the uppersides of the wings. The spring mustard whites have dark veins on wing undersides, however, and often a yellowish tinge to the hindwings and forewing tip. The summer form is solid white on the uppersides and undersides of both wings.

Similar to the cabbage white, mustard white larvae feed on plants in the Brassicaceae family. The mustard white, however, tends to feed on native brassicas as opposed to the cultivated varieties. Adults nectar on these same native brassicas as well as a wide variety of flowers. This species overwinters as pupae.

Mustard white butterfly.

Clouded sulphur nectaring on thistle.

Clouded Sulphur
Colias philodice

- Size: 32-54 mm wingspan
- Habitat detail: urban gardens, meadows, forage fields, and roadsides
- Distribution: all provinces and most of North America

Often found in agricultural areas, this species uses white clover, alfalfa, and other legumes as host plants and individuals are often seen flying and mud-puddling together in large numbers. Clouded sulphur are usually lemon yellow, although their colour can be variable and often a light yellow white, with the upperside of its wings margined with a dark brown-black border. Females have spots within this dark border. Both sexes have a black spot near the middle of the forewing. The undersides are usually lighter yellow, lack the dark margins, and are often rimmed with pink. The hindwing has distinct, often double, silver cell spots ringed with pink.

The orange sulphur, *Colias eurytheme*, is more orange than the clouded sulphur and the females tend to have a thicker dark border and an orange spot on the upperside of the hindwing.

Pink-edged sulphur nectaring on vetch.

Pink-Edged Sulphur
Colias interior

The pink-edged sulphur can be seen wherever blueberry, its host plant, is found—woodland clearings, woods roads, cut and burned areas, and forest edges are all good locations for finding this butterfly. Wing uppersides are yellow with black marginal bands that are thicker on the forewing than the hindwing; some females have no black margin on the hindwing at all.

The forewings can have a faint black spot or no spot at all and the uppersides of the hindwings have a faint orange spot. The underside of the wings is yellowish with a single pink-rimmed silver spot and a distinct pink fringe on the wing edge.

This species overwinters as a young larva and adults are active from mid-July to mid-August. Adults nectar from a wide variety of flowers, including clovers, hawkweed, goldenrods, and asters.

- Size: 35-47 mm wingspan
- Habitat detail: open woodlands, clearings where blueberry grows
- Distribution: all provinces

HEMIPTERA: TRUE BUGS

Aphids feeding on a young blueberry shoot.

Spittle bug nymph in protective foam.

Leafhopper.

Spiked shield bug, *Picromerus bidens*.

Water strider.

HEMIPTERA
TRUE BUGS

Hemiptera is a diverse order of more than 100,000 described species and 145 families, taking its name from the fact that the front wings (forewings) of most hemipterans have a thicker base than tip; in many cases, the forewings are hardened, giving the appearance of a half wing (*hemi*, half; *ptera*, wings).

Most hemipterans also share similar piercing mouthparts, a stylet designed to suck liquids from plants (most often) and animals, their main source of nutrients. Hemipterans undergo incomplete metamorphosis, meaning the young generally resemble adults. This order exhibits great variety in size, shape, colour, and habitat.

Although the word "bug" is often used for any creepy-crawly (ladybugs, for example, which are actually beetles), only insects of the order Hemiptera are true bugs.

Close-up of an aphid colony.

- Size: 1-5 mm body size
- Habitat detail: on plants
- Distribution: worldwide

APHIDS

Family Aphidae

Aphids are among the most abundant and destructive pests in agriculture. They are soft-bodied insects with piercing sucking mouthparts and are most often green—but some are pink, black, or brown. Aphids can be winged or wingless. The aphids commonly seen on garden and house plants often do not have wings. During summer, when populations increase, many aphids start producing winged forms. When present, the clear wings of aphids are held awkwardly back over their bodies. Most aphids are pear-shaped and have a short pointed process or tail at the rear end called a cauda and two tubes called cornicles or siphunculi.

The aphids use their sucking mouthparts to ingest juices from the sugary phloem in the plant. In many cases the sugar content is more than the aphid can use, and the excess is eliminated through the anus as honeydew. Some

Winged aphid.

Aphid live birth.

species of ants (page 33) feed on honeydew and, in return, protect the aphids against predators.

Depending on the species, aphids can be extremely host specific or feed on a wide array of plants from different families. They are important agriculturally, as aphids can reduce the health of the plant simply by sucking the plant juices. As well, some aphid species are vectors for serious plant diseases, and the sugary honeydew can create a medium for fungal growth, often called sooty mould.

The life cycles of aphids can be quite complex. Many reproduce parthenogenetically: they reproduce asexually, without males, and most give birth to live nymphs at some point in their life cycle.

Backswimmer.

BACKSWIMMERS
Family Notonectidae

These true bugs are wedge shaped and swim upside down, giving them their common name. Backswimmers propel themselves through water using their hind legs like oars. These long hind legs are fringed with hair. The antennae are short and barely visible. Backswimmers rest with their heads hanging down and their abdomens at the water surface. They live in ponds and slow, shallow streams and hold air trapped in pockets on their abdomens so that they can breathe underwater.

In general, the upper surface of the body is pale with a few dark markings, and the underside is black or dark brown. Backswimmers resemble water boatmen (family Corixidae), but backswimmers do not have the dark crosslines which are obvious on the uppersides of water boatmen. The easiest way to distinguish the two groups, at least when they are swimming, is that backswimmers swim upside down and water boatmen swim right side up.

Backswimmers are underwater predators, feeding on whatever they can catch, including other aquatic insects, tadpoles, and small fish. They use their short front and middle pairs of legs to grasp prey. Nymphs resemble small adults with undeveloped wings and are not sexually mature.

Backswimmers are strong swimmers—but the adults also have wings and can fly, allowing them to move to a more favourable area if conditions in their habitat deteriorate.

There are 12 species of backswimmers in Canada, with three occurring on the island of Newfoundland. Species in the genus *Notonecta* are common in the northern hemisphere.

- Size: 5-16 mm body length
- Habitat detail: calm freshwater bodies like ponds, lakes, and slow-moving streams
- Distribution: worldwide

Backswimmer.

BED BUGS
Cimex spp.
Bed Fly

Bed bug.

These reddish brown parasitic insects are wingless with a flat oval-shaped body. Bed bugs must feed on blood to survive in nymph and adult life stages. The adult female bed bug lays her eggs in sheltered areas behind baseboards and in the seams and crevices of a bed, leading to infestations that usually require professional extermination.

At least two related *Cimex* species are found in Newfoundland and Labrador: the bed bug *(Cimex lectularius)* and the eastern bat bug *(Cimex adjunctus)*. Species other than *Cimex adjunctus* exist on bats outside the province and may also live in the province, although, as of 2019, they have yet to be identified. The bed bug and the bat bug may have come from a common ancestor when humans shared dwellings, such as caves, with bats.

Although they may differ slightly in colour, the bed bug and the bat bug are differentiated by their pronotum. The bed bug's pronotum has a more deeply concave front end; the hairs on the pronotum are longer than the width of the eye in the bat bug and shorter than the width of the eye in the bed bug.

The bite of a bed bug causes no immediate discomfort, as the bug injects a local anesthetic into the skin. For a day or more afterward, however, the site of the bite may be swollen, red, and itchy. Unlike other biting insects, such as mosquitoes, lice, and fleas, bed bugs are not known to transmit disease.

Bat bug.

- Adult size: 5 mm body length
- Habitat detail: home and cabin
- Shape: flattened back to front, oval
- Distribution: worldwide

Brown-and-white leafhopper.

Yellow-and-black hopper.

BROWN-AND-WHITE LEAF HOPPER

Anoscopus serratulae

- Size: 3-5 mm body length
- Habitat detail: meadows, woodland edges, and roadsides
- Distribution: Europe, adventitious in North America

This species of leafhopper, found on grasses, is among the most capable jumpers in the insect world. Males are overall pale brown—the rear of the pronotum grades to a much lighter brown—but with three dark markings across the forewings. The first marking is incomplete; the second two, more distinct.

Females lack this banding and, therefore, can be difficult to distinguish from other solid-coloured leafhoppers. The male pictured here was taken in Logy Bay, Newfoundland and Labrador, by Mardon Erbland in 2009. Erbland's observation may be the first record of this European species on the island of Newfoundland, although the origin of this specimen might be Nova Scotia, where it is more commonly observed.

Giant water bug.

GIANT WATER BUG

Lethocerus americanus
Toe Biter, Electric Light Bug

This huge, dangerous-looking insect is Newfoundland and Labrador's biggest bug (not a beetle) and is frequently brought to Memorial University for identification. Typically, specimens are found in a parking lot, and usually injured. While the giant water bug's forelegs are menacing, its middle and hind legs are broad, flat, and fringed with hairs—adaptations for swimming. Periodically, giant water bugs take night flights in search of a new pond. They can be attracted to street lights (hence the common name "electric light bug") reflecting onto wet parking lots, which may fool them into making a dangerous landing on what they mistook for a pond.

Giant water bugs are ambush predators and can eat vertebrate prey larger than themselves, such as frogs and fish. They grab prey with their strong grasping forelegs,

- Size: 50-60 mm body length
- Habitat detail: ponds and slow creeks
- Distribution: northern US and into southern Canada

Giant water bug.

ram their rostrum (stout beaklike mouthparts) into the prey, and inject digestive enzymes. The bug waits for the enzymes to work, then sucks up the prey's liquefied tissue. The only records of this species biting people are incidents during which the bug was mishandled (if they are really pestered, like poking a finger into their face, their bite will hurt). In some parts of southeast Asia the tables are turned—several species related to *Lethocerus americanus* are fried and sold in food markets.

These bugs are reared by their fathers, that is, they exhibit unilateral postzygotic paternal care. Among insects, parental care is rare; fathers doing all the work is even rarer, observed in only about 150 species (99 per cent of which are species of giant water bugs) out of more than a million described insects. Female *Lethocerus americanus* lay eggs on vegetation that emerges out of the water. The male guards the egg mass and periodically drips water onto it. Without his attention, the eggs would desiccate, or other animals might consume them.

 Giant water bugs are scuba divers in that they capture an air bubble under their wings, prolonging the time they can spend underwater.

Spittle bug.

MEADOW SPITTLE BUG

Philaenus spumarius
Meadow Froghopper

The family Cicadellidae (leafhoppers, of which there are at least 136 species in Newfoundland and Labrador) and family Cercopidae (froghoppers, three species) are similar in appearance: members of each family are small and have back legs modified for jumping. They are also sap suckers, with piercing and sucking mouthparts. Leafhoppers are slenderer than froghoppers and can be distinguished by a row (or rows) of bristles running the length of their hind tibia (see brown-and-white hopper, page 246). Froghoppers have a band of spines at the tip of their hind tibia. The froghopper nymphs do something that the young leafhoppers do not: they live in their own spit—sort of.

Spittle bug nymph.

- Size: 8–10 mm body length
- Habitat detail: meadows, woodland edges, and roadsides
- Distribution: North America, Europe, North Africa, part of Russia, Afghanistan, and Japan

The meadow spittle bug is a froghopper that feeds on the sap of a wide variety of meadow plants, but it appears to prefer nitrogen-fixing plants such as clover. The female lays eggs, up to hundreds in her lifetime, on plants that her offspring can feed on. Nymphs hatch from the eggs and produce a foam made from their anal secretions (*not* spit) that they then cover themselves in. Some have suggested that the foam is a predator deterrent, but the most detailed research shows that its primary function is to reduce the temperature extremes that a nymph experiences—which is good for living on the island of Newfoundland.

Adult meadow spittle bug populations are highly variable in colour and pattern, and some entomologists have proposed that multiple subspecies are present. On the Burin and Avalon Peninsulas, the dominant subspecies is an intermediate between subspecies *spumarius* and *quadrimaculatus*. The remainder of the island of Newfoundland is dominated by a pure line of *spumarius*. This subspecies is also found in Scandinavia, and it has been suggested that the Norse may have introduced them at L'Anse aux Meadows around 998 AD; perhaps eggs were on straw that was being transported by the Norse.

A predatory stink bug, *Podisus serieventris*.

Adult *Perillus exaptus*.

STINK BUGS AND RELATIVES
Superfamily Pentatomoidea

Fifteen families make up the superfamily Pentatomoidea. Five have been identified in Newfoundland and Labrador, including the stink bugs (family Pentatomidae) and the parent bugs (family Acanthosomatidae).

True to their name, stink bugs can produce a foul odour. This odour comes from scent glands in the thorax of the adult or in the abdomen of the nymph. In adults, the chemicals are released through the ostiole, a small pore situated behind the second leg. The odour is released if the bug is disturbed, but it may also be important for communication within its own species.

Some stink bugs are brightly coloured or distinctly marked, making identification of these species relatively easy. The red-cross shield bug, *Elasmostethus cruciatus*, is green with a red to brown cross on its back; the aptly named twice-stabbed stink bug, *Cosmopepla lintneriana*, has two red slashes on its back; *Perillus exaptus* has a prominent transverse black bar across its pronotum, with yellow in front of it and red behind. Other stink bugs and

- Size: 4-20 mm body length
- Habitat detail: variable, depending upon species; many plant-eating species prefer certain grasses or trees
- Distribution: Newfoundland and some species in Labrador

Nymph red-cross shield bug.

Podisus brevispinus (with rostrum extended) feeding on a caterpillar.

Twice-stabbed stink bug.

Female mottled shield bug caring for her nymphs.

Adult red-cross shield bug.

parent bugs are various shades of brown and more difficult to identify in the field.

These bugs have specialized sucking mouthparts contained in the rostrum that fold under the head when not in use. The name Pentatomoidea refers to the five (*penta-*) sections (*-tomo*) of the antennae, a feature of most members of this family; other members of the Hemiptera have four antennal sections or less. These true bugs also have a prominent triangular scutellum extending down their backs, which may be very ornate, as in *Perillus exaptus*.

Females may lay large numbers of eggs, which hatch into nymphs and undergo five instars before reaching adulthood. Most stink bugs feed on plants, although some prey on other insects, in particular caterpillars. Predatory stink bugs may be beneficial to plants by reducing the number of plant-eating insects—this has led to their use as a biological pest control (such as *Podisus serieventris* on the eastern blackheaded budworm). None pose a danger to people.

Brown marmorated stink bug.

 Brown marmorated stink bug, *Halyomorpha halys*, is a significant invasive plant pest. Originally from Asia, this species is now spreading in Canada. It feeds on fruits, vegetables, and ornamental plants. They are recognizable by the two white bands on their antennae. During the writing of this field guide, the authors identified the first incidence of this stink bug in this province. The extent and economic impact of this pest is yet to be determined. If you think that you may have seen one, please collect a sample, or take photos, and contact an entomologist with Agriculture and Agri-Food Canada.

WATER BOATMEN
Family Corixidae

- Size: 1.5–16 mm body length
- Habitat detail: in ponds with vegetation, although some live in slow-moving rivers and streams
- Distribution: worldwide

These small true bugs are common in ponds and resemble backswimmers in appearance. Water boatmen, however, do not swim upside down but rest horizontally under the water surface. The body of a water boatman is slightly flattened and dark yellowish or reddish brown with narrow, dark transverse lines.

Each pair of legs is adapted for a specific purpose: the front pair is scoop-shaped for feeding, the middle legs are used to hold on to plants underwater, and the third pair is fringed with long hairs and used like oars for swimming. At first glance, water boatmen appear to have only four legs, because the front pair is so short.

Water boatmen are most common in slow-moving and still waters like ponds and lakes with aquatic vegetation. They carry an air bubble on their body surface or under their wings, which allows them to breathe while underwater. When the air in the bubble is used up, they come to the water surface to breathe and replenish the layer of air next to their bodies.

Most water boatmen are herbivores, feeding on aquatic plants and algae as well as plant debris at the pond bottom; others are predaceous on small insects. Nymphs resemble adults except they are smaller and their wings are not fully developed. The adults can fly well; if the water level in their pond drops too low or dries up, they fly to a new one.

There are 79 species of water boatmen in Canada, with nine from Labrador and 21 from the island of Newfoundland.

Water boatman.

Water striders.

WATER STRIDERS

Family Gerridae
Pond Skaters, Water Doctors

These slender, dark-coloured insects are commonly observed resting on or running across the surface of slow-flowing or still water, where they live. Their long middle and back legs splay out and help water striders literally walk on water. The feet and underside of the body are covered with water-repellant hairs which help them stay afloat.

Some species of water striders gather in groups and scatter when disturbed. In any single population of water striders, some adults have wings, others do not.

The short front legs are used to grab prey, often small dead or drowning insects on the water surface or just underneath the surface. Because the middle and back legs are long and the front legs are short, water striders appear at first glance to have just four legs. Nymphs resemble the adults in appearance, except they are smaller and wingless. Adults and nymphs live in water.

Twenty-two species of water striders are known in Canada, with four from Labrador and five from Newfoundland.

- Size: 2-25 mm body length
- Habitat detail: on the surfaces of temporary or permanent fresh-water ponds and slow-moving areas of streams, some marine species
- Distribution: worldwide

Water strider.

THYSANOPTERA: THRIPS

Thrips are about the size of a comma.

Western flower thrips on a strawberry plant.

THYSANOPTERA
THRIPS

Thrips and thrums from lupine heaps.
—From *Trilce* (1922), César Vallejo (1892–1938)

I used scissor to cut my pant into short. Doesn't sound right, does it? That's exactly the reaction from someone who studies thrips when the "s" gets dropped in the word thrips. *Thrips* is both a plural and a singular noun. A solitary individual is still a thrips. Are all thrips experts such pedants? Mostly.

Thrips are members of the insect order Thysanoptera, and worldwide there are at least 5,000 species. They are small; in fact, they are typically the size of the comma in this sentence. These slithering punctuation marks do not commonly attract the attention of insect enthusiasts. However, many species of thrips are crop pests, and the gardeners and horticulturalists of Newfoundland and Labrador are all too familiar with them.

Thrips are brown to black, and at only a few millimetres in length they are hard to spot. To find them, look closely in leaf litter or under bark—some species feed on fungus. Many more thrips species feed on pollen, flowers, or leaves. To find these species use a sweep net (a net robust enough to be swept through grasses and bushes). Or you could try "beating": place a white tray under a living plant and then knock the plant with a stick (roughly, but not enough to damage the plant) while watching for comma-sized spots to appear on the tray (keep note of the plant species, it might help with identification). Thrips researchers use a small paintbrush moistened with their spit or ethanol to pick up thrips on the tray and transfer them to a small container usually filled with 60 per cent ethanol. No one has inventoried the thrips in the province, so if beating plants and spitting on paintbrushes turns out to be your thing, the field is wide open.

BANDED GREENHOUSE THRIPS
Hercinothrips femoralis

The banded greenhouse thrips has fringed wings and yellowish bands on the head, and they have a pointed abdomen but lack a tube. The specimen pictured was found by Tim Walsh, greenhouse manager of Memorial University's Botanical Garden, on *Amyrillis* spp. in the Biology greenhouse. This thrips is known to infest a wide variety of ornamental plants grown in greenhouses (begonias, chrysanthemums, hydrangeas). Outside of the tropics, these thrips do not naturally disperse, so infestations are typically moved between greenhouses with plant movements. Thrips can also be brought home from a nursery in soil, on plant bulbs, or on leaves.

These thrips, like all thrips, are difficult to see and only a worry for those that are intolerant of the small blemishes that their feeding behaviour causes. Thrips rasp or puncture a hole in plant cells and inject saliva to start the digestion, which leads to white (or silvery) spots on plant leaves that will darken over time.

Banded greenhouse thrips; actual size 1.5 millimetres.

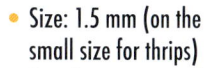

- Size: 1.5 mm (on the small size for thrips)
- Distribution: originally tropical-subtropical; adaptation to greenhouses gives it a worldwide distribution

These thrips have two larval instars: the first is very small; the second, adult sized. Larvae often congregate on the leaf midrib or in dried-up foliage, and they are often covered in a watery globule of their own excrement. They then go through two active pupal stages (prepupa and pupa), during which they look generally like adults, but their wings have not fully formed.

TUBE-TAIL THRIPS
Acanthothrips nodicornis

Tube-tail thrips on 1-millimetre mesh.

The thrips pictured was caught by Mardon Erbland using a sweep net that he swung through the tall grass growing near Outer Cove on the northeastern Avalon Peninsula. This specimen was sitting on the vegetation when it got knocked into the net. Erbland must have sharp eyes to have spotted it in his net; this thrips is walking on a 1-millimetre mesh. Through correspondence with Laurence Mound in Canberra, Australia, the world's foremost thrips taxonomist, the specimen was identified as possibly *Acanthothrips nodicornis*. (Mound was using a photograph for identification, so he advised that, given that the specimen came from Newfoundland and Labrador, it could be confused with another species, *Acanthothrips albivittatus*.)

Both of these thrips species are known to be communal (gather in substantial groups), and one might make such an observation if one searched specifically on recently dead branches on bushes and trees. Look for a tube tail, fringed wings, and cream spots on the margins of the abdomen. These species feed on fungus and are not a known agricultural pest.

- Size: 3 mm (large size for thrips)
- Habitat detail: dead bushes, branches, and trees
- Distribution: Holarctic

FLOWER THRIPS
Thrips validus (possibly)

Flower thrips encompass a diverse group of species. This particular specimen (at right) was collected to the north of St. John's in a field sowthistle, a yellow flower that looks a little like a dandelion.

Identifying thrips specimens to species typically requires a chemical process called clearing as well as the use of a microscope. Clearing removes the dark colouring of the thrips exoskeleton and reveals bristles, glands, and sensory structures that are often important clues to species identification. Supporting this identification is that *Thrips validus* is known to inhabit yellow flowers of plants in the family Compositae, where they consume nectar and pollen. Dandelions are another likely place to find this species. The sowthistles were growing at the edge of a gravel parking lot—this plant likes disturbed sites—an area unlikely to be mowed, which allows the thrips the maximum time on a flower to get through its life cycle.

This species has been studied very little. There is some evidence that the males have glands that emit sex pheromones to attract females. Immature stages, not just adults, have been found in flowers, and it can be surmised that mating and egg laying occur on the flowers. Typically, flower thrips cannot finish their development into the adult stage before the flower wilts. Therefore, adult development usually occurs in the soil.

- Size: 3 mm (large size for thrips)
- Habitat detail: yellow flowers
- Distribution: Holarctic

PSOCODEA: LICE

Book louse.

PSOCODEA
LICE

As with many insect classifications, scientific consensus on the proper classification of book lice, bark lice, and true lice is evolving. Formerly, the wingless, parasitic true lice (including the human head louse) were placed in the order Phthiraptera, while the non-parasitic winged bark lice and wingless book lice were placed within the order Psocoptera. Now all are combined in Psocodea.

The generalist can see the similarities between the book and parasitic lice—lack of wings, body flattened back to front (dorsoventrally), wide head—it is only the specialist who appreciates the genetic analyses that show common ancestries, or the finer points of microscopic anatomy that show similar structures within the entire order. Untangling millions of years of insect evolution can be difficult ... even dinosaurs were infested with parasitic lice.

Nonetheless, within the Psocodea, for practical purposes, lice are still divided into the parasitic true lice, Phthiraptera, and non-parasitic book and bark lice, Psocoptera.

TRUE LICE
Phthiraptera
Booshy, Bully-boo, Graybacks, Saddlebacks, Cooties

The true lice fall into one of two categories: biting/chewing and sucking. As is the case with fleas (page 108), most animals have one or more species of lice particular to them.

Three distinct lice species may infest humans: the head louse, *Pediculus humanus capitis*; the body louse, *Pediculus humanus humanus*; and the pubic or crab louse, *Pthirus pubis*. All three are sucking lice. Although controllable by strict hygienic measures, all three are current in today's society, in particular the head louse and pubic louse. Rare is the school child that has not experienced the head louse, or the parent who has not had to go through a child's hair with a fine-toothed comb to remove eggs, also known as nits.

- Size: 0.5–5 mm body length (adult)
- Habitat detail: on people and animals
- Distribution: worldwide

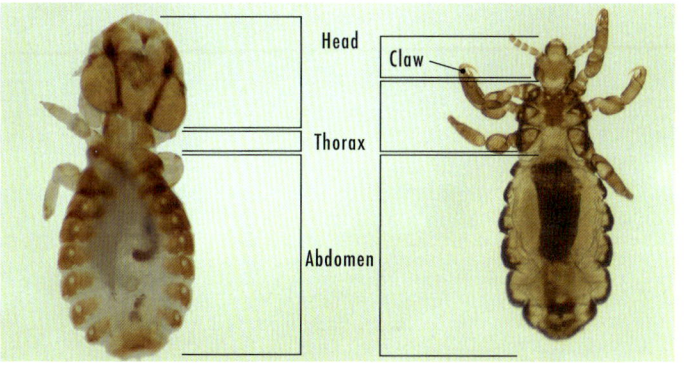

Biting louse from a snowy owl (left) and sucking louse from a human (right), with major body parts identified.

PREVENTION OF LICE AND ITCH

The common custom for prevention of the above was to wear a little bag of brimstone (sulfur) pinned to the inside of your underwear, usually the vest, so it would rest against the skin. I remember having to wear one of these which usually ended with a bright yellow spot on the underwear. My mother used to make me wear this when I was going to school. There were a couple of families in the community that seemed to always have itch or lice so we wore the brimstone bag to prevent us from catching it. —John Dollimount, Francois, NL, 1952

LARKSPUR LOTION

An effective product for destroying head lice and all parasites that infest the hair on any part of the body. —Gerald S. Doyle bulletin

It wasn't the fighting we minded, 'twas the heat and flies and lice. —Howard L. Morry, Royal Newfoundland Regiment

Newfoundland Regiment, Gallipoli Peninsula, 1915. Soldiers reading the Gallipoli Post.

Human head lice.

Human pubic louse.

During periods of disruption in hygiene, lice become a significant problem. This was true for Newfoundland soldiers, and all soldiers, in World War I: it was discovered then that lice could transmit disease, most commonly trench fever, caused by the bacterium *Bartonella quintana*. Lice were called seam squirrels, cooties, chats, graybacks, and, for those in Gallipoli, their removal from infested clothing was called "reading the Gallipoli Post."

Sucking lice are found exclusively on mammals; biting lice, on mammals or birds. They are differentiated by their head shape. Biting lice have a wider head than thorax; sucking lice have a narrower (pointy) head than thorax and commonly have enlarged claws on their legs for grasping hair or feathers (see photos, page 261). Sucking lice feed on body fluids, while biting lice scavenge skin and hair or feather debris on the body surface.

BOOK LOUSE

Psocoptera
***Liposcelis* spp.**

Although resembling parasitic lice, book lice can be easily differentiated by their long antennae (parasitic lice have short antennae) and bulging eyes.

Book louse.

- Size: 1–2 mm body length
- Habitat detail: areas of high humidity in the home or in stored commodities
- Distribution: worldwide

The book lice that may show up in the home are tiny, translucent, almost colourless to light brown, wingless, and harmless. They are primarily grazers on moulds and yeasts that grow well on damp grains or other starchy materials. Book lice are unable to chew holes in smooth paper, so their common name likely came about from the observation of these tiny animals on mouldy books.

Female book lice can live for up to a year and they can reproduce parthenogenetically (without mating). They only produce one or two eggs a day, but the combination of being parthenogenetic and long-lived means that a large population of several thousand book lice can arise after only a few months unchecked. Newfoundlanders and Labradorians are most likely to encounter book lice in basement bathrooms or laundry areas. In case of an infestation, the best remedy is not pesticides but, rather, reducing the humidity of the affected areas. A Government of Canada report suggests that reducing relative humidity to below 58 per cent and sustaining that for more than three weeks will kill book lice. Installing a venting fan or dehumidifier is the best strategy. If you do live with them for a while, do not worry—they are harmless, after all.

BARK LOUSE
Suborder Psocomorpha

This tiny bark louse, from the family affectionately referred to as loving bark lice (Philotarsidae), is about 4 millimetres long. Their wings are usually folded in a tentlike manner. It is also called a barkfly and is commonly found on many tree species, both deciduous and coniferous. They are not considered a pest to trees as they mostly just eat dead material so are scavengers. They can become a minor household pest, consuming any paper- or wood-related product, if moisture and temperature conditions are suitable.

- Size: 4 mm body length
- Habitat detail: in bark, leaf litter, decaying organic material
- Distribution: worldwide

Bark louse.

ORTHOPTERA: CRICKETS - GRASSHOPPERS

Common field grasshopper.

ORTHOPTERA
CRICKETS AND GRASSHOPPERS

Crickets and grasshoppers are not common in Newfoundland and Labrador; only one cricket species is known to be established in the province. At least three other species of crickets are regularly encountered, but they are all thought to be adventitious (repeatedly introduced but have not become established).

About a dozen species of grasshoppers are established, but individual species are not typically seen in large numbers in Newfoundland and Labrador. At least one grasshopper plague has hit Labrador, however.

House cricket.

HOUSE CRICKET
Acheta domesticus

The house cricket is primarily straw coloured with red-brown markings. Males and females have two cerci (male cerci are longer than females'); the female has an additional central spike or ovipositor which is used to deposit eggs on a damp substrate, usually located in a home or garbage dump.

The house cricket is thought to have arrived in French Canada from France in about 1749, and it has probably also been in Newfoundland and Labrador a long time, with likely movements to the area from French Canada and Great Britain. The probable geographic origin of the house cricket is Asia. People in China and Japan have kept house crickets as pets to enjoy their calls, a bright and optimistic sounding series of chirps. If you do not enjoy their calls, many people also praise the nutty taste of dry roasted house crickets.

- Size: 14–21 mm body length
- Habitat detail: in or near homes or buildings
- Distribution: Canada and US (except southern Florida)

MARSH MEADOW GRASSHOPPER
Chorthippus curtipennis

- Size: 15-22 mm body length (females are bigger than males)
- Habitat detail: tall grasses around lakeshores or alpine meadows
- Distribution: most of North America

The marsh meadow grasshopper is highly variable in colour, but typically it is tan on top with green or yellowish sides with a brown stripe. It is a short-horned grasshopper (family Acrididae): it has relatively short antennae compared to other kinds of grasshoppers. It belongs to a subfamily (Gomphocerinae) that is commonly referred to as the stridulating slant-faced grasshoppers.

Males and females have sounding pegs that run along the inner surface of their hind femurs which they rub against the edge of their forewings. They make about 30 leg strokes (hind legs moving in synchrony with each other) of the wings in a five-second song, resulting in a series of high-pitched rasping notes. The sound is generally considered pleasant to human ears. Males sing to females, and females sing back, with the song changing as the male gets closer until mating begins. The female lays five to six eggs in a

Marsh meadow grasshopper.

Marsh meadow grasshopper.

Northern grasshopper. Photographs taken near Happy Valley-Goose Bay by forester Corey Wight during the 2011 "plague."

1-centimetre-deep hole in the soil that she makes with her abdomen and later covers up again with soil. Females have shorter wings than males, but both sexes vary in wing length and they do not typically fly more than a metre or so at a time, at about 30 centimetres above the ground. They are relatively easy to catch.

In the higher latitudes of Newfoundland and Labrador, marsh meadow grasshopper eggs laid in the ground might not hatch for two or three years.

NORTHERN GRASSHOPPER
Melanoplus borealis borealis

The northern grasshopper is generally dark coloured, medium sized, with red hind tibia. Like the marsh meadow grasshopper, the northern grasshopper is a short-horned grasshopper (family Acrididae), but the northern grasshopper falls within a group called the spur-throated grasshoppers—they have a spiny bump between their front legs, near what one might call the throat on a grasshopper. The northern grasshopper is also a stronger flier than the marsh meadow grasshopper. They are often seen basking in the sun.

Forester Basil English reported in *Silviculture Magazine* (2011) that a "plague" of northern grasshoppers had severely damaged black spruce saplings planted a short distance west of Happy Valley-Goose Bay, Labrador. Corey Wight, the forester on site, said, "I just took [pictures] so nobody thought I was crazy." Regional ecosystem forester Paul Whelan said he had not seen anything like the 2011 grasshopper event before or since.

These grasshoppers occur throughout their range in low densities, but infrequently, and for currently unknown reasons, populations explode in number such as experienced in Labrador that year. The northern grasshopper does feed on grasses, but primarily they feed on plants that ecologists call forbs: a herbaceous plant that is not a grass, a grass (for example, the dandelion). Black spruce is an unusual food choice for this grasshopper.

- Size: 19–25 mm body length (females bigger than males)
- Habitat detail: Arctic tundra, bogs, and moist mountain meadows
- Distribution: ranges widely across northern North America

BLATTODEA: COCKROACHES

Unidentified cockroach species.

BLATTODEA
COCKROACHES

Cockroaches have oval-shaped bodies, small heads partially obscured by a distinctive shieldlike pronotum, and long legs which enable fast running. In spite of their reputation as survivors, cockroaches have never permanently established in Newfoundland and Labrador.

Specimens of at least six species are periodically collected in the province; the three most common are the German cockroach, *Blatella germanica* (two black stripes on pronotum); the Oriental cockroach, *Blatta orientalis* (overall dark brown to black); and the American cockroach, *Periplaneta americana* (shiny red brown). The common names of these cockroaches have no connection to their origin. The earliest on record is a German cockroach collected by Joseph Banks in 1766 (read more about his voyage to Newfoundland and Labrador on pages 8 and 9). Banks collected

Asian cockroach.

German cockroach collected in Newfoundland by Joseph Banks in 1766.

one specimen of the German cockroach, which was illustrated by Sydney Parkinson.

German, Oriental, and American cockroaches usually arrive in Newfoundland and Labrador via luggage or imported goods but do not appear to persist or prosper in the province. It is not clear why this is the case, but these species all require a combination of warmth and high humidity that Newfoundland and Labrador rarely provides. As a result, not a single cockroach has been included in several hundred insect collections over a decade by Memorial University undergraduates.

The reproductive tract of females of these three species contains the genital atrium, a chamber into which females deposit a dozen or more eggs surrounded by a foam. The foam hardens into the ootheca, or egg case, to protect the eggs from desiccation. A female will hold the ootheca until she finds a place to safely deposit it—or until the lights come on suddenly and she drops it. The uninitiated may think this cockroach has deposited a fecal pellet, but what is actually being witnessed is an insect mother abandoning her offspring (see page 277 for an example of a more diligent insect mother).

- Size: 12-40 mm body length
- Habitat detail: warm, humid places in homes and buildings
- Distribution: worldwide, approximately 5,000 species

PLECOPTERA: STONEFLIES

American salmonfly, *Pteronarcys dorsata*, a species of giant stonefly, from the Eagle River watershed in Labrador.

Stonefly, *Isoperla transmarina*.

PLECOPTERA
STONEFLIES

Stoneflies are not flies (of the order Diptera) but a separate order, the Plecoptera (*plecto*, pleated; *ptera*, wings), a name which refers to the way the wings fold over the abdomen. Stonefly adults are long and narrow with four membranous wings, although most are poor fliers. The wings sit flat on the body when the insect is at rest. The antennae are long and threadlike, and stoneflies have two distinctive long cerci, or tails, at the end of the abdomen.

Most adult stoneflies do not feed, although some species eat algae or plants. Stoneflies can be divided into summer or winter stoneflies, depending on when the adults emerge. Sometimes winter stoneflies can be observed on snow near the edges of clear streams.

Immature stoneflies, or nymphs, are aquatic and their habit of living under stones and rocks in streams gives them their common name. They have long bodies and long antennae and, like the adults, two cerci at the end of the abdomen. Stonefly nymphs are either predators of other aquatic organisms that actively pursue their prey, or scavengers that feed on decaying plant and animal material. The nymphs of most species live in cold, clean, fast-flowing streams, as they require water containing lots of air in order to breathe. They are sensitive to water pollution, so their presence is often an indicator of good water quality.

About 1,550 species of stoneflies are known throughout the world, with most occurring in the cooler regions.

- Size: 6-60 mm body length
- Habitat detail: stonefly nymphs live in clean, running fresh water; adults occur near the water bodies where they lived as nymphs
- Distribution: worldwide

Stonefly, *Isoperla transmarina*.

DERMAPTERA: EARWIGS

European earwig.

The horny goloch is an awesome beast,
Supple and scaly;
It has twa horns, and a hantle of feet
And a forkie tailie.

A wee bird sat upon a tree,
When the year was done and auld,
And aye it cheepit pitiously,
"My, but it's cald, cald!"
—Scottish children's song

DERMAPTERA
EARWIGS

The word *earwig* suggests that these insects like to crawl into ears—this is likely an apocryphal story. The "-wig" comes from the Old English word *wicga*, meaning insect, but more specifically beetle, and this small insect order of about 2,000 species was initially included in the Coleoptera (beetle) order. Both beetles and earwigs fold their hindwings underneath their forewings. In both cases, the forewings have evolved into protective covers for the hindwing; the beetle's is hard, the earwig's leathery. This gives the earwig order its name: *derma* meaning skin, and *ptera* meaning wing.

The most distinct feature of these insects is their forked tails. These forceps, evolved from the ancestral earwigs' cerci, sensory structures that now function for defence and/or mate competition. Males often have the more robust forceps. Earwigs may use these forceps to pinch, but they are unlikely to break human skin and they have no venom.

It is not as noticeable as the forceps, but some male earwigs also have a pair of penises. Two penises are not necessary—only one is used in a single copulation event. Careful observation of one group of earwig species has shown that the male chooses which penis to use at random. For another group, the choice is biased toward the right penis (used in 90 per cent of matings). A third group uses the right penis 100 per cent of the time because the left does not develop. Two penises, chosen for use randomly, is the ancestral state; behavioural bias toward the right penis evolved next. The atrophying of the left penis is the most recent stage in earwig penis evolution. Newfoundland and Labrador has one species of earwig, and it has one penis.

- Size: adult 12–15 mm body length
- Habitat detail: cool and moist places, including basements and bathrooms
- Distribution: Europe, Asia, and North Africa; introduced to North America in early 20th century

EUROPEAN EARWIG
Forficula auricularia
Forky-tail

Memorial University undergraduate student Rebecca Mattinson (2008) surveyed shoppers at the Avalon Mall in St. John's regarding their attitudes toward arthropods. The overwhelming answer to "What is your least favourite arthropod?" was "Earwigs." Perhaps it is their oily appearance, slithery movements, and pincers—and their false reputation for crawling into ears and nesting in human brains—that turn people off.

But they are not all bad. In fact, earwigs are wonderful mothers. In the fall, European earwigs produce a clutch of 40 or 50 eggs in a crevice or underground nest. The mother stays with the eggs, and as the temperatures drop

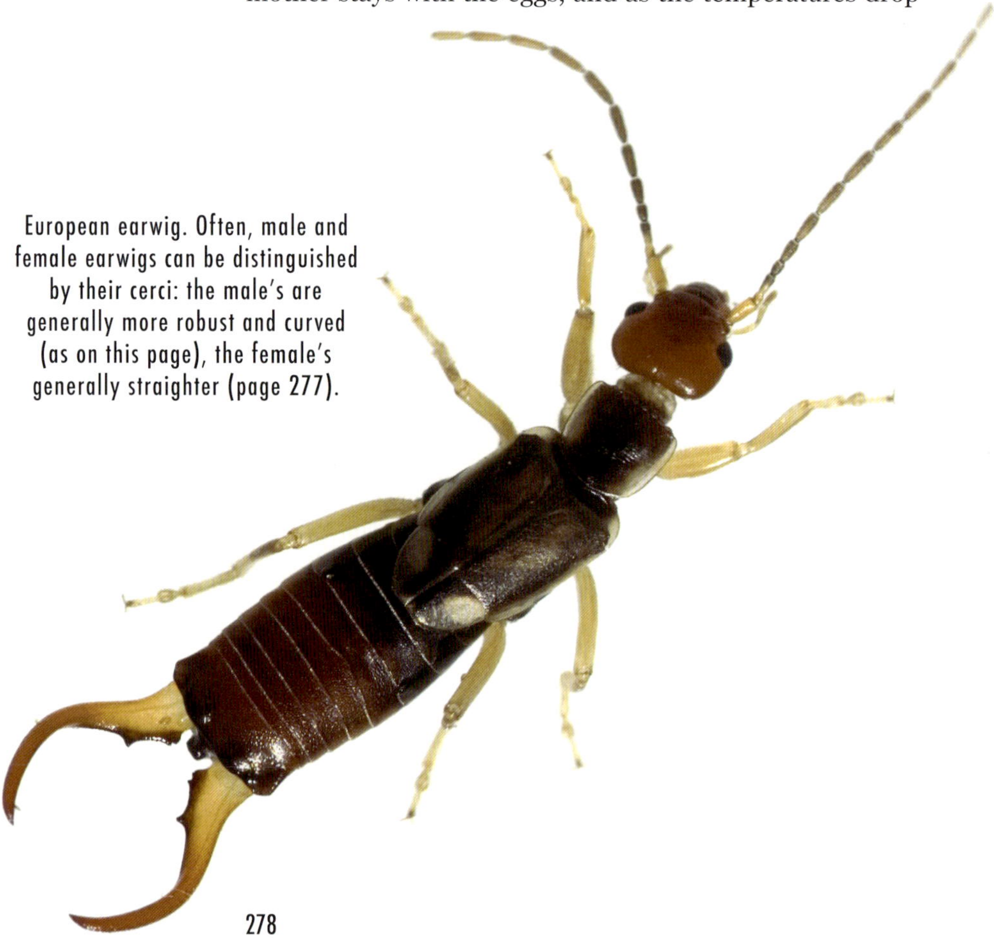

European earwig. Often, male and female earwigs can be distinguished by their cerci: the male's are generally more robust and curved (as on this page), the female's generally straighter (page 277).

she goes into dormancy. The warmth of spring reactivates the mother and she spends her time cleaning and shifting the position of each of the eggs to prevent them from succumbing to a fungal infection. When she senses that the time is right, she moves the eggs into a single layer and watches them hatch. She stays and protects her brood from predators until the brood matures (about a month). There are not a lot of dedicated mothers like that among the insects.

Earwigs like to hide out in damp crevices during the day, and they are more active at night. They are omnivorous, and they do have wings but they rarely fly.

ODONATA: DRAGONFLIES · DAMSELFLIES

Dragonfly.

Damselfly.

ODONATA
DRAGONFLIES AND DAMSELFLIES

Dragonflies and damselflies are not flies (of the order Diptera) but belong to the insect order Odonata. Dragonflies and damselflies are active during the day and easily recognizable due to their large size (Newfoundland and Labrador species range from 27 to 80 millimetres in body length), two pairs of usually transparent, net-veined wings, large bulging eyes, tiny antennae, jewel-like colours, and agile flight. They spend most of their lives as larvae underwater, and only spend a short time (a few days or weeks) as adults.

At last count, in 2018 a total of 41 species have been recorded in Newfoundland and Labrador, 22 from Labrador and 39 from the island of Newfoundland.

Dragonflies can be distinguished from damselflies in the field by careful observation. Adult dragonflies have stouter bodies than damselflies and are stronger fliers, with large eyes that usually meet at the top of the head. Dragonfly hindwings are usually shorter and broader at the base than their forewings, and they often hold their wings straight out at right angles from the body when resting. Some can

Shadow Darner; note the huge eyes.

fly great distances in search of prey. Adult damselflies are slender, usually slower flying insects. Their eyes are widely separated at the top of the head and all of the wings are more or less equal in size and shape. When at rest, they hold those wings closed above the body rather than flat and away from it. Damselflies are usually found flitting about grassy areas and other vegetation close to fresh water.

Dragonflies and damselflies are known colloquially as "devil's darning needles," a name which stemmed from the myth that they could sew your eyelids and lips shut. Dragonflies are sometimes called horse-stingers in Newfoundland and Labrador, possibly because the large species, in particular, often fly around horses in fields, feeding on the flies attracted to the horses.

Adult dragonflies and damselflies do not sting or bite humans, but they are fearsome predators of other flying insects. They are agile fliers and voracious predators, darting about in pursuit of prey such as midges and mosquitoes, butterflies, moths, and other insects, including smaller dragonflies and damselflies. Some of the largest dragonflies can fly up to 60 kilometres per hour, although their average speed is probably about 15 kilometres per hour; damselflies and smaller dragonflies are slower. Both dragonflies and damselflies can move any wing independently of the others, allowing them to hover in mid-air as well as fly backwards.

Dragonflies rely more on their eyesight than they do on touch or smell, so they do not need the large antennae found on many insects; their antennae are tiny and difficult to see. Their eyes, however, are large and they have excellent vision.

Brush-tipped Emerald.

> *The face of the dragonfly*
> *Is practically nothing*
> *but eyes.*
> —Chisoku

Damselfly larva.

Some dragonfly species are highly territorial, each male defending a territory that usually coincides with the ideal habitat for female egg laying. Other species of dragonflies do not defend territories. Most male damselflies are not territorial like dragonflies; rather, they defend no more than the perch they momentarily rest on. Mating in dragonflies and damselflies is unique among insects. While in flight, a male will seize a female, and if she is receptive, sperm is transferred. Most dragonflies drop their eggs directly in water or on nearby mud; some dragonflies and all damselflies have a knifelike ovipositor that the females use to cut holes in, and lay eggs in, plants in or near the water. Other dragonflies place their eggs in mud or waterlogged wood. If a dragonfly is observed dipping her "tail" in the water, she is laying eggs. In many species, the male will keep his grip on his mate even while eggs are laid, protecting her from being bothered by competing males.

Eggs hatch into aquatic larvae (also called nymphs or naiads), which, like the adults, are predaceous. They have a hinged, pincerlike jaw (labium) that shoots out incredibly quickly to catch prey. Prey includes other insects living in the water, worms, snails, leeches, freshwater shrimp, and small fish. It is easy to tell dragonfly and damselfly larvae apart. Dragonfly larvae are stout bodied and the gills, which allow them to breathe, are inside their bodies. Damselfly larvae are slender and their gills take the form of three leaflike structures at the end of their abdomen.

Unlike many other winged insects, dragonflies and damselflies do not have a pupal stage. Instead, larvae leave the water and climb onto nearby vegetation or rocks, where they transform to adults, leaving behind cast skins called exuviae. These exuviae can often be seen on plants surrounding the bodies of water where the larvae live.

Dragonfly larva.

American Emerald.

DRAGONFLIES
AMERICAN EMERALD
Cordulia shurtleffii

Dragonflies in the family Corduliidae are about 45 millimetres in length and usually seen around ponds, lakes, and peatlands. The American Emerald has a dark face with brilliant green eyes which meet at the top of the head. The abdomen is dark and the thorax greenish bronze. The American Emerald is one of the first dragonflies to emerge in the spring. Males aggressively patrol their territories and chase away males of their own as well as other species. Adults will eat almost any flying insect they can catch, including mosquitoes, flies, butterflies, and moths. The larvae live in vegetation and woody debris at the bottom of ponds or bogs and lie in wait for prey.

- Size: 45-46 mm body length
- Habitat detail: ponds, peatlands
- Distribution: North America; common in Newfoundland and Labrador

DARNERS
Family Aeshnidae

Darners are among the largest and fastest of Newfoundland and Labrador dragonflies. Adults are noticeable during the day as they fly quickly, frequently changing direction as they hunt and chase prey over and near ponds and streams. Darners range widely in search of food. Males vigorously defend their territory along the water's edge, and females lay eggs in water plants or floating wood.

At least eight species of darners are in Newfoundland and Labrador, and often have blue, green, or yellow markings. The Azure Darner, the Sedge Darner, and the Shadow Darner are abundant in many areas of northern North America, including both Labrador and the island of Newfoundland. Both are native.

- Size: 57–60 mm body length
- Habitat detail: fens and shallow ponds
- Distribution: northern North America, including Labrador and northern Newfoundland

Azure Darner
Aeshna septentrionalis

The Azure Darner, *Aeshna septentrionalis*, lives near marshes and ponds, especially peatlands with sphagnum moss. Its face and the stripes on its thorax are blue, sometimes with pale green. Males have blue abdominal spots so large that they look like irregular blue stripes; female abdominal spots are blue or yellow green. Azure Darner bodies are 57 to 60 millimetres long.

Azure Darner.

Sedge Darner
Aeshna juncea

The male Sedge Darner, *Aeshna juncea*, has two broad, straight stripes on the sides of the thorax, usually yellow green on the lower surface of the body and blue and bordered with black on the upper surface. The underside of the abdomen has pale spots and the face is yellow or greenish yellow. The female is similarly marked, except the spots on the abdomen are yellow, yellow green, or less commonly blue. Sedge Darners are most abundant in peatland ponds and marshes with acidic waters, especially those with extensive stands of sedges. Body length for both sexes is about 65 to 66 millimetres.

Sedge Darner.

- Size: 65-66 mm body length
- Habitat detail: peatland bogs, marshes with acidic water
- Distribution: northern North America and Eurasia

Shadow Darner
Aeshna umbrosa

The Shadow Darner is a common dragonfly found across much of Canada and the United States. Adults are found at ponds, lakes, and slowly moving streams, where larvae live in aquatic vegetation. The Shadow Darner is a slender, dark darner with light areas which are usually pale green to blue green. Its face does not have a dark line; the lateral thoracic stripes are straight and narrow, yellow to green and edged in black. Abdominal spots are small. Some females have light yellow markings (see photos 282, 288).

- Size: 70-75 mm body length
- Habitat detail: ponds, lakes, streams
- Distribution: North America; not recorded from Labrador

FOUR-SPOTTED SKIMMER
Libellula quadrimaculata

One of the most common dragonfly species throughout Newfoundland and Labrador is the Four-Spotted Skimmer, *Libellula quadrimaculata*. This skimmer gets its name from the distinctive dark spot halfway along the front edge of each

Dragonflies typically rest vertically with their head upwards. By rotating the page you can now see the Four-Spotted Skimmer (left) and Shadow Darner (right) resting in their natural positions.

wing. The scientific name describes the same important feature as the common name: *quadri*, four; *maculata*, spots.

Males and females are brownish black with brown eyes which meet broadly at the top of the head. The Four-Spotted Skimmer is one of the earliest dragonflies to emerge in the spring and can often be observed perched on twigs and rocks near the water. Like many dragonflies, males vigorously patrol their territories.

- Size: 40-45 mm body length
- Habitat detail: bogs, ponds, and lakes
- Distribution: Canada, northern US, northern Europe, and Asia

 Dragonflies in the family Libellulidae are known as skimmers because they often fly low along the surface of ponds and lakes, although they also frequently perch on vegetation near the water's edge. Eight species of skimmers have been documented from Newfoundland, of which four also occur in Labrador.

HUDSONIAN WHITEFACE
Leucorrhinia hudsonica

The Hudsonian Whiteface, a member of the skimmer family, is part of the genus *Leucorrhinia*, the whitefaces. In general, members of this genus are small dragonflies with, as their name suggests, white faces. The Hudsonian Whiteface is common in both Labrador and on the island of Newfoundland. Its common name reflects the fact that it occurs near Hudson Bay.

Apart from their distinctive creamy white faces, the sexes are dimorphic. Males are black with red markings and most females are dark brown with yellow markings; however, some females are similar in colour to the male and have red markings. Adults perch on shoreline vegetation and hunt prey from there. Larvae live in submerged aquatic vegetation and feed on aquatic insects like mosquito larvae as well as freshwater shrimp.

Hudsonian Whiteface.

- Size: ~30 mm body length
- Habitat detail: ponds surrounded by vegetation, lakes, peatlands
- Distribution: throughout Canada, parts of northern US and western US mountains

DAMSELFLIES
BLUET DAMSELFLIES
Family Coenagrionidae

Bluets are small damselflies in the family Coenagrionidae, separated into two genera, *Coenagrion* and *Enallagma*. Most species of *Coenagrion* live in Europe and Asia, but three are North American, and two of these occur across most of northern North America, including Newfoundland and Labrador: the Taiga Bluet, *Coenagrion resolutum*, and the Subarctic Bluet, *Coenagrion interrogatum*. The genus *Enallagma* contains a large number of species, including the Northern Bluet, *Enallagma annexum*, and the Boreal Bluet, *Enallagma boreale*, both of which occur throughout Newfoundland and Labrador.

Identification of bluets can be tricky because the species are similar in appearance. Species identification often requires a hand-held magnifier or even a microscope for close inspection of critical features. Females of most bluet damselfly species lay eggs (using an ovipositor at the end of the abdomen) in living aquatic plants in various habitats. As with other damselflies, both adults

Taiga Bluet.

and larvae are predaceous.

Coenagrion males are blue or blue green marked with black; females have pale areas and are blue, green or pinkish brown. For both sexes, the quickest identification character is the divided blue stripe on top of the thorax in the Subarctic Bluet (looks like an exclamation mark); only very few Taiga Bluets ever have this stripe divided. Both species are usually between 29 and 31 millimetres in length and are found in sedge marshes and peatlands.

Species in the genus *Enallagma* occur in a variety of ponds and lake habitats as well as bodies of water in boggy areas. Males of the common species are blue marked with black. Females of most species have two colour forms, with one blue, resembling the male, and the other brown to slightly greenish. *Enallagma* species range from 26 to 40 millimetres in body length. The males can be distinguished by the shape of the dorsal claspers, or cerci, using a hand-held magnifier and practice. Identification of the females requires examining the structure on the front of the thorax where the males grasp them during mating. This usually requires a microscope.

- Size: 26-40 mm body length
- Habitat detail: ponds, lakes, streams, bogs
- Distribution: worldwide; both Newfoundland and Labrador have several species

Mating pair, *Enallagma* sp.

Eastern Forktail.

- Size: 20-33 mm body length
- Habitat detail: ponds, marshes, slowly moving streams
- Distribution: common in central and eastern Canada and US; widespread across island of Newfoundland but to date no records from Labrador

EASTERN FORKTAIL
Ischnura verticalis

Eastern Forktails are small green damselflies with black markings and blue at the tip of the abdomen. The thorax of the male is green with black markings; the abdomen is largely black with blue at the tip.

Females have two colour forms; one is green like the male; the other, more common one, is orange and black, without the blue tip on the abdomen. As females of both forms age, they become grey, although the black stripes on the thorax show through and the face and eyes remain green. Females may be observed flexing their abdomens and rapidly beating their wings; this behaviour repels other damselflies, including males of their own and other species.

Northern Spreadwing.

NORTHERN SPREADWING
Lestes disjunctus

The spreadwings are damselflies in the family Lestidae. They are called spreadwings for their habit of holding their wings at about 45 degrees to the body when at rest, unlike other damselflies, which hold their wings together above or along the body when resting.

Three species of spreadwings are found on the island of Newfoundland, two of which also occur in Labrador. The male Northern Spreadwing has a dark metallic thorax with pale blue stripes; much of the thorax becomes grey with age. The abdomen is dark with a greenish tinge and a pale blue-grey tip. The eyes of spreadwing males are generally blue. Females are brownish with brown eyes. The Northern Spreadwing is present throughout Newfoundland and Labrador, mostly around ponds, streams, and marshes with abundant aquatic vegetation.

- Size: 35–37 mm body length
- Habitat detail: slow streams, weedy ponds, marshes
- Distribution: Newfoundland and Labrador, widespread and common in much of Canada and northern US

RIVER JEWELWING

Calopteryx aequabilis

These damselflies are widespread in the vicinity of rivers and streams, where they hunt soft-bodied flying insects. Males have iridescent green bodies (they may appear bluish in some lights), females are more bronze coloured. The outer third of their broad, densely veined wings is black, making the River Jewelwings easy to identify.

The adults are slow but graceful fliers, exhibiting a dancing motion resembling the flight of a butterfly. Larvae are predaceous, living in streams where they cling to the roots and stems of aquatic vegetation as they wait for prey to come within range.

- Size: ~47 mm body length
- Habitat detail: small rivers, slow streams
- Distribution: Newfoundland island but no documented records from Labrador, widespread across Canada and much of the US

River Jewelwing (see atypical form, page 26).

EPHEMEROPTERA: MAYFLIES

Mayfly.

EPHEMEROPTERA
MAYFLIES

Mayfly adults are delicate in appearance and extremely short-lived, giving the order its name: *ephemeros*, ephemeral; *ptera*, wings. They are distinguished by their large, heavily veined triangular forewings and much smaller, round hindwings. Mayflies also have two or three long, hairlike "tails" at the end of the abdomen. Many species have large heads and short antennae. Some, especially males, have prominent eyes.

Adult mayflies are common around ponds and lakes. Most of the life of a mayfly is actually spent in fresh water as an immature larva, or nymph. The larvae have gills which are either leaflike or finely divided along the sides of the abdomen. They live in crevices under rocks or logs or in debris and underwater vegetation, as well as on the surface of substrates. Many are active swimmers and climbers;

This Adams fly is an example of an imitation adult mayfly used in fly fishing.

Mayfly larva.

some are burrowers in sand and mud. Depending on the species, they feed on algae or dead plants, or filter-feed on plankton in the water. Mayfly larvae are an important food source for freshwater fish, and as adults for birds and bats.

Adult mayflies do not feed and their mouthparts do not function. Their only purpose is to mate and, for the females, to lay eggs. Mature adult mayflies usually emerge from water en masse in mid-summer, and swarms of males performing mating dances are often seen at this time. The sheer numbers of individuals emerging to mate make them very noticeable at certain times of year—as do the mounds of dead mayflies on the shores of ponds and lakes or under street lights.

Both larvae and adults are used as models for fly fishing flies. Of the 335 species of mayfly in Canada, 29 are in Newfoundland and 63 in Labrador.

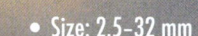

- Size: 2.5–32 mm
- Habitat detail: mayfly nymphs live in actively moving fresh water in rivers, streams, and lakes; adults live in the proximity of fresh water, usually near where they lived as nymphs
- Distribution: worldwide

This adult mayfly has just emerged from its aquatic larval form; its shed skin is visible under the water.

ZYGENTOMA: SILVERFISH·FIREBRATS

Silverfish.

ZYGENTOMA
SILVERFISH AND FIREBRATS

Silverfish (*Lepisma* spp.) and firebrats (*Thermobia* spp.) are commonly found in homes and buildings with some species unable to survive outdoors in Newfoundland and Labrador's climate. These fast-running insects are often glimpsed scurrying out of sight when the lights are turned on, or they are discovered trapped in the bathtub or container into which they accidentally fell. Unlike most insects, they lack wings and are considered primitively wingless, meaning neither they nor their ancestors ever had wings.

Both silverfish and firebrats are scavengers in the home, searching for material high in protein, sugar, or starch. They eat cereals, starch in book bindings, paper with glue or paste behind it, and wallpaper.

Silverfish have a characteristic carrot-shaped tapered body. Adults are silvery in colour and have long antennae and three tail-like appendages on the rear end. Worldwide, most species of silverfish (of which there are about 250) live outside and hide under stones or leaves during the day, coming out at night to feed. In Newfoundland and Labrador, however, the most familiar are those that inhabit moist bathrooms and kitchens, those in the genus *Lepisma*.

Firebrats, *Thermobia domestica*, are similar in shape to silverfish but are mottled grey and brown and have tufts of hair on the back of the abdomen as opposed to the evenly distributed hairs of silverfish. Firebrats, as their name suggests, are common in hot environments and require high temperatures in order to breed and reproduce. They are often encountered in furnace rooms and boiler rooms around radiators or hot water pipes.

- Size: 12-19 mm
- Habitat detail: anywhere in the home, most often in moist bathrooms (silverfish) or warm areas (firebrats)
- Distribution: cosmopolitan

Firebrat.

NON-INSECT ARTHROPODS

Mass of spiderlings, *Araneus* sp.

Scanning electron microscope image of a common dust mite.

Rabbit tick.

Harvestman, *Phalangium opilio* male.

Sowbugs.

NON-INSECT ARTHROPODS, ARACHNIDA, CRUSTACEA, MYRIAPODA

The Arachnida is a class of the Arthropoda. Of the 11 orders of arachnids, four occur in Newfoundland and Labrador and are included in this book: Opiliones (harvestmen), Acari (mites and ticks), Araneae (spiders), and Pseudoscorpiones (pseudoscorpions). Araneae comprises at least 45,000 species worldwide, with at least 400 species recorded in Newfoundland and Labrador.

HARVESTMEN
Order Opiliones
Daddy Longlegs

Harvestmen (order Opiliones) is the third largest order within the Arachnida, with about 6,600 described species worldwide. At least 10 species are found in Newfoundland and Labrador—probably more. *Mitopus morio* and *Phalangium opilio*, both in the family Phalangiidae, are fairly common. Harvestmen are most obvious in the fall, historically during harvest. The common name daddy longlegs is descriptive of the long legs of some species.

Harvestmen are not spiders. Like spiders, they have eight legs and no wings—but harvestmen have a single, usually oval, body section, while spiders have two body sections. As well, harvestmen lack silk glands and therefore cannot create webs. Most spiders have six or eight eyes but harvestmen have just two, which are located on an eye tubercle on the top part of their bodies.

 In Newfoundland and Labrador, the common name daddy longlegs can refer not only to harvestmen but also to crane flies (page 88).

Most harvestmen are brown, grey, or black. Immature harvestmen resemble the adults except they are smaller, soft, and smooth.

Phalangium opilio female.

For the most part, harvestmen are carnivorous predators, mainly feeding at night on earthworms, aphids, springtails, mites, earwigs, and other small organisms. Harvestmen can eat food in chunks and take it into their mouths, unlike other arachnids, which must dissolve their prey before eating. Harvestmen are also scavengers and will, for example, try to steal insects caught in spider webs. The majority live in damp places, including lawns, gardens, roadsides, grasslands, forest floors, litter, and gardens, under rocks, on the surface of trees, and in soil crevices.

- Size: 4-8 mm body length
- Habitat detail: forest litter, gardens, tree trunks, and ground vegetation
- Distribution: Europe, Asia, North America

A noticeable characteristic of many harvestmen is that the second pair of legs is much longer than the others; when the animal is walking, this second pair is stretched out and used to tap the ground ahead. Most species in eastern Canada are characterized by very long legs, although not all harvestmen have this feature. If one of their legs is seized by a predator, most long-legged harvestmen are able to detach that leg, increasing their chances of escape.

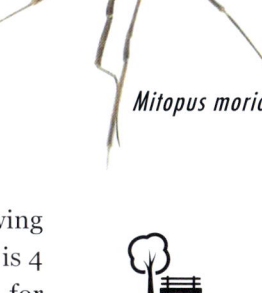

Mitopus morio.

Mitopus morio

Mitopus morio is a widely distributed species in Newfoundland and Labrador in many habitats, including in forest litter and gardens, and on tree trunks and ground vegetation, especially in thick grass growing against the bases of buildings. The usual body length is 4 to 8 millimetres for females and 5 to 6 millimetres for males. The length of the second leg for both sexes is usually between 30 and 40 millimetres. Adults are common between August and October.

- Size: 6-9 mm body length
- Habitat detail: shrubs, wooded areas, long grass, and disturbed areas
- Distribution: worldwide

Phalangium opilio

Phalangium opilio was introduced to North America from Europe and now has a worldwide distribution. It is common and widely distributed in Newfoundland and Labrador. Its usual habitats are wooded areas, long grass,

Nelima elegans.

and shrubs, although it also is frequently found in disturbed areas such as lawns, gardens, and agricultural areas and along roadsides. Female body length is 6 to 9 millimetres, the length of their second legs is an average of 38 millimetres; male body length is 4 to 7 millimetres and their second leg 54 millimetres. Adults are present from July to November.

Other native species are not as common but are fascinating: *Nelima elegans* individuals overwinter in clusters in protected areas like caves and abandoned mines. Individuals are 5.5 to 7.5 millimetres long.

Caddo agilis is a tiny native harvestman (3 millimetre body length) with relatively gigantic eyes. All are female.

Caddo agilis close-up.

MITES
Subclass Acari

Over 50,000 species of mites have been identified worldwide, with some estimates suggesting that there may be 1 million more unidentified. They occupy almost every known habitat, on and in our body, in homes, on plants and animals, on the seashore, in the water, in the trees, and in the soil. Some parasitize plants and animals, and others live free in nature.

Mites are also extremely diverse in habit and appearance—some are visible to the naked eye, while most are too small to be seen without a microscope. *Demodex folliculorum*, a common mite that infests the facial hair follicles (eyebrows and eyelashes) of almost every human, is only 0.33 millimetres long.

Ticks (page 308) are in fact large mites, and the two groups share the same general body shape. In general, adult and nymph mites have eight legs, the larvae only six. Eggs may be laid singly or by the thousands. Generally, the larger the mite, the more eggs laid.

While all tick species are parasitic and require a blood meal during their life cycle, mites survive through different methods, both free-living and parasitic.

Mites have invaded most niches of the animal body: nasal mites, ear mites, tracheal mites, feather or fur mites, and skin mites—just to start.

A few mite species may infest human skin or internal organs, the most well known being scabies, or itch mites (*Sarcoptes scabiei*), and face or eyelash mites (*Demodex folliculorum* in hair follicles; *Demodex brevis* in sebaceous glands). *Demodex* mites rarely cause serious problems, but scabies mites burrow under the skin and usually cause severe itching.

Many animals have similar infestations. Dogs have their own follicular mites (*Demodex canis*) and are susceptible to a subspecies of scabies mites (*Sarcoptes scabiei canis*), which can also infest other animal species.

- Size: generally <1 mm
- Habitat detail: varied, mites can be parasites of plants and animals or free-living
- Distribution: worldwide

Finger mite galls (probably *Eriophyes emarginatae*) on chokecherry leaves.

Bright red bladdermite galls on a maple leaf.

Mite infestations in animals other than humans are commonly referred to as mange (from the same source as the French word *manger*, "to eat"). Mites can cause mange in a variety of domestic and wild animals, including the genera *Cheyletiella*, *Dermanyssus*, *Ornithonyssus*, *Otodectes*, *Chorioptes*, and *Psoroptes*.

Domestic and wild birds may become infested with various species of *Knemidocoptes* mites that often infest the non-feathered areas of the skin and may be called scaly-face or scaly-leg mites.

The Varroa mite (*Varroa destructor*), an external parasite, and the honey bee tracheal mite (*Acarapis woodi*), an internal parasite, are of concern to honey bee populations. Infestations can weaken or kill a

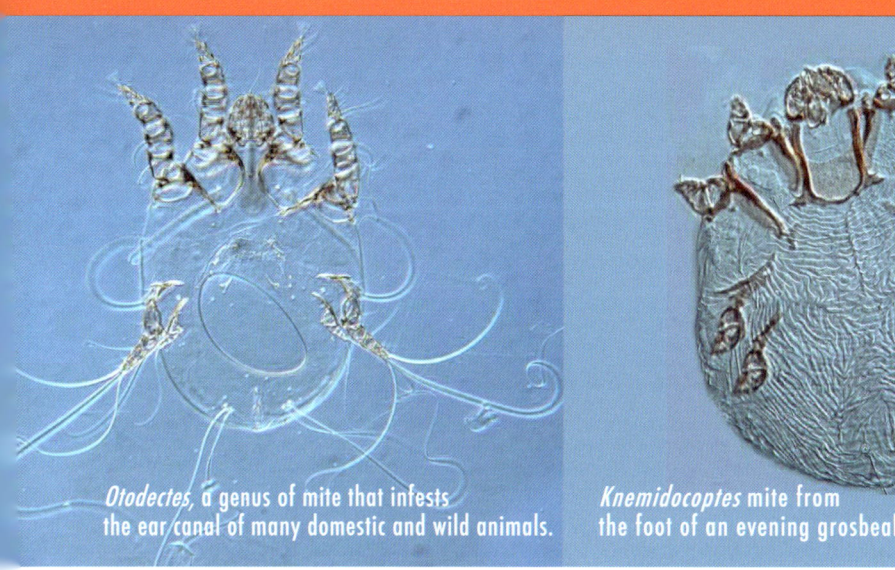

Otodectes, a genus of mite that infests the ear canal of many domestic and wild animals.

Knemidocoptes mite from the foot of an evening grosbeak.

colony. Neither has been reported in Newfoundland and Labrador as of 2019—the absence of such pests, if maintained, could help the economics of the honey bee industry, including the export of mite-free bees to other parts of the world.

Chigger mites (usually Trombiculidae family, such as *Neotrombicula microti*), approximately 0.2 millimetres in diameter and a red-orange colour, live outside in the grass, brush, or woods. As larvae, they feed by creating a small hole in their host's skin and digesting the cells below as food. Once full, they drop off, leaving behind a red spot that can become itchy after 24 to 48 hours. Chigger mites are uncommon but have been reported in Newfoundland and Labrador.

Dust mites live in homes and feed on skin flakes. *Dermatophagoides farinae* (American house dust mite) and *Dermatophagoides pteronyssinus* (European house dust mite) live on the edge of visibility (0.2 to 0.3 millimetres in length) and may cause allergic reactions, such as asthma and eczema, in susceptible individuals. Pseudoscorpions and silverfish are recognized as predators of dust mites.

Sidewalk mite, *Balaustium* sp.

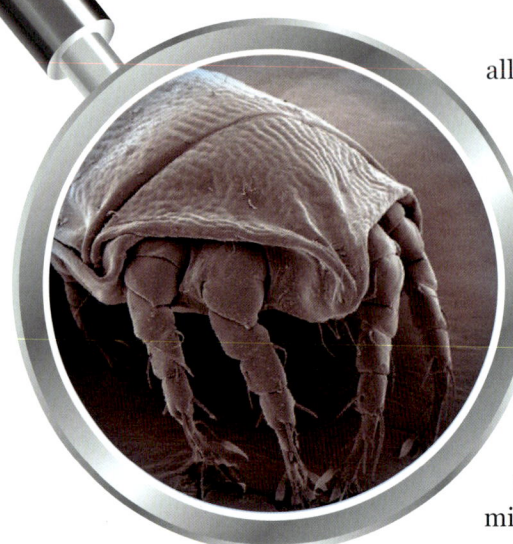

Scanning electron microscope image of a fur mite (Glycyphagidae) from a muskrat.

Mites can infest trees and almost all other plants, often causing a gall or abnormal growth—like a tumour. In some cases, mite galls provide a protective area in which larvae can mature before exiting to the outside world; in others, they may provide all that is required for multiple generations of mites to live in throughout their existence. Gall mites are among the smallest of the known mite species, approximately 0.2 millimetres in length. Larvae have wormlike bodies with only two pairs of legs. Most gall mites are specific to one species of plant. In some cases, gall mites make the plant more susceptible to other diseases.

TICKS
Families Ixodidae, Argasidae

Ticks are blood-feeding parasites that may cause illness through blood loss, lethal if thousands of ticks feed on a single animal; through the spread of Lyme and other diseases; and through tick paralysis, caused by the release of tick proteins into the blood of its host. Ticks can be found on mammals, birds, reptiles, and amphibians and are often named after the animal on which they most commonly feed (rabbit tick, squirrel tick, etc.). Although we commonly classify them separately from the mites (covered elsewhere in this book), they are, in fact, just large, specialized mites.

Almost all ticks encountered in Newfoundland and Labrador are from

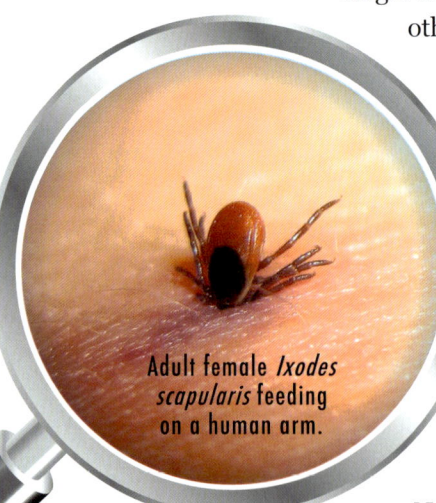

Adult female *Ixodes scapularis* feeding on a human arm.

Engorged adult female rabbit tick.

Snowshoe hare infested with rabbit ticks.

the hard tick family, Ixodidae. Soft ticks, family Argasidae, appear rarely through imports of infected animals or contaminated goods. These ticks are distinguished by the presence (hard ticks) or absence (soft ticks) of a hardened scutum, or external shell.

Hard ticks have four life cycle stages: egg, larvae, nymph, and adult. The adult female lays thousands of eggs that hatch into six-legged larvae. Nymph and adult ticks have eight legs. Larvae, nymph, and adult ticks must seek out a blood meal for survival and reproduction; adults die shortly after laying eggs. The life cycle can take more than a year, depending on the favourability of the weather.

To find a host, most ticks climb grass or low plants and then grab passing prey. This act of waiting for a host is

- Size: unengorged larvae <1 mm body length; engorged adult female up to 10 mm
- Habitat detail: on low plants or on host
- Distribution: worldwide

American dog tick.

called questing. Many ticks feed on a variety of animals—not just their namesake species. The black-legged tick or deer tick, *Ixodes scapularis*, for example, may feed on rodents and birds as a larva or nymph, and then, as an adult, move on to larger mammals such as deer, foxes, dogs, and cats. All stages may feed on humans.

Some ticks are permanent residents of Newfoundland and Labrador, including the rabbit tick, *Haemaphysalis leporispalustris*; the mouse tick, *Ixodes muris*; the vole tick, *Ixodes angustus*; the squirrel tick, *Ixodes marxi*; and the seabird tick, *Ixodes uriae*. Though commonly found on the animal species for which they are named, these ticks may also be found on animals that share the same habitat or which are their predators.

Other species are transient, as the province does not provide the necessary climate or hosts for long-term survival. These ticks may arrive on migratory birds, on (or in) imported goods, or attached to humans or animals which have recently travelled to tick-infested areas. Black-legged ticks, American dog ticks (*Dermacentor variabilis*), brown dog ticks (*Rhipicephalus sanguineus*), and lone star ticks (*Amblyomma americanum*), for example, have been identified in the province, although none have become resident species.

The most well-known tick-borne disease in North America is Lyme disease, caused by the bacteria *Borrelia burgdorferi*. Spread by black-legged ticks, Lyme disease affects humans and dogs. The Canadian range for this tick was limited to southern Ontario until the late 1990s. Due to climate change and the expanded range of a critical host, the white-tailed deer, this tick has become established in most Canadian provinces, including the Maritimes.

Only about 20 per cent of black-legged ticks carry the bacteria that causes Lyme disease. For disease transmission, the tick must be attached to, and feeding

Seabird ticks (foreground) in nesting materials of common murres (background) on Gull Island. Inset: Engorged adult female seabird tick.

Memorial University graduate student Hannah Munro studied seabird ticks (2014) to see if they carry *Borrelia garinii*, a cause of human Lyme disease in Europe.

on, the host for 24 to 36 hours, as it is only at the end of the feeding that it releases the bacteria into the host. As of 2018, black-legged ticks have only been known to enter Newfoundland and Labrador as a transient species.

In Europe, the sheep tick, *Ixodes ricinus*, is an important vector of Lyme disease. In Newfoundland and Labrador, an unrelated external parasite, the sheep ked, *Melophagus ovinus*, a wingless fly, is commonly called a sheep tick but does not transmit Lyme disease.

PREVENTING LYME DISEASE INFECTION
Newfoundland and Labrador has the lowest risk of Lyme disease infection of the Canadian provinces. This does not mean that there is no risk, as veterinarians have diagnosed and treated Lyme disease in dogs that have not travelled outside the province. For up-to-date information on the symptoms and prevention of Lyme disease in humans and pets, contact the provincial public or animal health authorities.

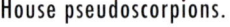
House pseudoscorpions.

PSEUDOSCORPIONS
Pseudoscorpiones
False Scorpions

Pseudoscorpions are rarely seen due to their small size and secretive nature. Depending on species, pseudoscorpions are tan to reddish brown to black, with a pear-shaped, flattened body, four pairs of legs, and no wings. They have two long pincers which resemble the pincers found on a scorpion, hence the common name. False scorpions and scorpions are easy to tell apart, however: false scorpions are tiny and they do not have a stinging tail like true scorpions do—in fact they do not have a tail at all. Their pincers are used for defence and to capture prey.

- Size: generally <5 mm
- Habitat detail: bathrooms and other damp areas in the home, in soil and decaying vegetation
- Distribution: worldwide

Most of the 3,400 species of false scorpions known in the world live in the tropics. About 25 species are found in Canada, and of the three species known from Newfoundland and Labrador, the house pseudoscorpion, *Chelifer cancroides*, is the one most commonly encountered, in bathroom sinks, tubs, showers, and other damp areas.

False scorpions are no cause for alarm. Harmless to humans, they are predators and eat many small arthropods, including dust mites, springtails, caterpillars, and flies. The house pseudoscorpion is cosmopolitan and usually lives in close association with humans; the other species are found in decaying vegetation such as leaf litter and compost piles, under bark, in caves, and even in bird nests.

Microbisium brunneum, a northern species that occurs in acidic soils such as boreal forest litter and bogs, is widespread and common across North America, including in Labrador and Newfoundland.

Microbisium brunneum.

 Some pseudoscorpions are phoretic, which means they hitch a ride on other arthropods such as house flies, holding on to their transportation with their pincers.

SPIDERS

Order Araneae

Spiders have two body sections, the cephalothorax and abdomen (see page 17), unlike insects, which have three (head, thorax, and abdomen). Spiders are also distinguished by having eight legs, no wings, and no antennae. Most spiders have eight eyes, but some have six or fewer. The number of eyes and their arrangement is important in identifying spider families. Despite all of those eyes, spider eyesight is generally poor.

At the tip of the spider's abdomen is a group of structures called spinnerets, which produce silk for making webs and egg sacs and for wrapping prey caught in the webs. Some spiders hide in silk tunnels or retreats attached to their webs, and others make silk safety lines in case they lose their footing or want to retrace their steps. Female spiders can produce hundreds of eggs, usually in an egg sac. Newly hatched spiders are called spiderlings and resemble their parents, except they are smaller. Mothers in some spider families carry their egg sacs and spiderlings on their bodies to guard them. Many spiderlings disperse by "ballooning": the spiderlings release silk threads which, when caught by the wind, carry them away to a new area. Spider silk, weight for weight, is stronger than steel.

All spiders are predators and are either web-builders or hunters, based on how they catch their prey. Spiders can only ingest liquid. After catching prey, they inject digestive fluids into the prey's body and then suck up the contents of the body.

Web designs can be circular, spiral orb webs (families Araneidae or Tetragnathidae), funnel webs (family Agelenidae), horizontal sheet webs (family Linyphiidae), or irregular webs (family Theridiidae). Spiders are rarely aggressive; most bites are defensive and happen when a spider is squeezed inadvertently. More than 400 species are known from the province; below is a small selection.

Closeup of common house spider face.

- Size: female 6–12 mm body length; male 6–9 mm
- Habitat detail: homes, sheds, and barns, and outside in sheltered areas such as woodpiles and under rocks
- Distribution: introduced from Europe; widespread and common in Canada

Common House Spider
Tegenaria domestica
Basement Spider, Barn Funnel Weaver, Bottle-Arse Spider

Like many of Newfoundland and Labrador's insects and spiders, the common house spider was accidentally imported from Europe into the shipping ports of North America, including those of this province.

Common house spiders (family Agelenidae, funnel web spiders) have dark brown or dark greyish brown abdomens, with a series of pale markings resembling chevrons running down the centre. Their dark-coloured legs also have bands or stripes, although these are sometimes quite faint. Males and females are similar in appearance. They use silk to construct a funnel-shaped retreat in, for example, the corners of basement windows, and they sit motionless inside the retreat, rushing out and grabbing prey if it moves within range. Common house spiders will eat just about anything they can subdue. They often are found in bathtubs, where they accidentally slide down the slippery sides of the tub, and cannot escape, or in basements.

A related species, the giant house spider, *Eratigena duellica* (formerly *Tegenaria gigantea*), resembles the common house spider but has solid-coloured legs without stripes and female body length can reach 18 millimetres; males, 14 millimetres. The giant house spider, a European introduction (like the common house spider), lives in houses and in sheltered situations outdoors. There is no documented evidence of it in Newfoundland and Labrador outside the St. John's area, where it was first found in 1995. Despite its size, the giant house spider is harmless.

Common house spider.

Orb Weavers

Orb weaver spiders (family Araneidae) build circular, spiral webs. Some common orb weavers spin webs in vegetation overhanging ponds and lakes to catch insects emerging from the water such as mayflies. These spiders are able to run on the surface of water.

- Size: Adult females 12-20 mm; males 7-9 mm body length
- Habitat detail: near human settlements, including on or near homes, sheds, fences, and gardens
- Distribution: Palearctic; common in Newfoundland and Labrador

Cross Orb Weaver
Araneus diadematus
Cross Spider, Common Garden Orb Weaver

Cross orb weavers are one of the most common and best known of the orb weavers in Newfoundland and Labrador. Individuals vary from light yellow to ginger to dark grey, but all females have white markings on the abdomen which look like a cross, giving it its common name.

After building a web, a cross orb weaver either hangs upside down in the centre of it, or hides in the nearby vegetation with one claw hooked to a line of silk connected to the main web. Vibrations in the web let the spider know prey has been captured; an initial bite paralyzes the prey, which is then wrapped in silk for dinner later.

Cross orb weaver.

The first specimen of this species in North America was reported from Brigus, Newfoundland in 1881.

Long-Jawed Orb Weaver
Tetragnatha extensa
Common Orb Weaver

The body of long-jawed orb weaver spiders (family Tetragnathidae) is very elongate and, when disturbed, they often stretch their front legs forward and their back legs back. This allows them to camouflage their bodies and hide on thin structures such as blades of grass or plant stems.

The colouration of common orb-weavers is variable but usually the abdomen is creamy yellow or greenish, with a pair of undulating stripes, and the head is reddish brown. They have very long legs.

They build loose, circular webs with an open centre called orb webs and eat mosquitoes, midges, and moths, or any insect that becomes entangled in the webs.

- Size: female 11 mm body length; male 9 mm
- Habitat detail: low-growing vegetation, especially around ponds and wet areas
- Distribution: native, occurs across the northern hemisphere, including Newfoundland and probably Labrador

Long-jawed orb weaver, *Tetragnatha* sp.

Long-jawed orb weaver, *Tetragnatha* sp.

Flower Crab Spider
Misumena vatia
Flower Spider

It is easy to see how crab spiders (family Thomisidae) got their name: they hold their legs out to the side, giving them a crablike appearance, and they can walk forward, backward, and sideways, much like a crab can. The flower crab spider does not produce a web. Instead, it is an ambush predator: it will sit and wait on flowers, then pounce on any insect that lands, including bees, flies, and butterflies.

Flower crab spider with prey.

The abdomen of female flower crab spiders ranges from creamy white to yellow or greenish, with pairs of reddish bands. Females have the ability to slowly—over a few days—change their overall colour to match the background, usually the flowers, on which they are sitting. This protective coloration allows them to sit exposed but somewhat camouflaged while they wait to ambush prey. Males are much smaller than females with darker, longer legs and more slender abdomens than their female counterparts. Males are not able to change colour.

Flower crab spider with prey.

- Size: female, up to 10 mm body length; male, up to 5 mm
- Habitat detail: anywhere flowers bloom: gardens, roadsides, parks, meadows, woodland clearings
- Distribution: Holarctic; Newfoundland and likely Labrador

Flower crab spider.

Rabbit Hutch Spider
Steatoda bipunctata

- Size: male 4–5 mm body length; female up to 7 mm
- Habitat detail: homes, sheds, and barns; on old and dead trees and in dry leaf litter
- Distribution: introduced from Europe, where it is a common house spider; widespread in Newfoundland and probably Labrador

Because of their globular shape, rabbit hutch spiders are often mistaken for ticks or the similarly shaped black widow spider. In fact, other common spiders in the genus *Steatoda* are sometimes called "false widows." Rabbit hutch spiders, however, are not dangerous—their fangs cannot puncture human skin. Black widow spiders are occasionally found in Newfoundland and Labrador when they are accidentally imported on produce.

The small, globular rabbit hutch spiders are members of the family Theridiidae, or cobweb spiders. They are dark brown in colour and usually have a pale line down the centre of the abdomen; the female's abdomen is glossier than that of the male. Two dark dimples on the top of the abdomen reflect where the muscles are attached underneath, and give the spider its scientific name (*bipunctata*, two spots). The rabbit hutch spider makes an irregular tangled web of sticky silken fibres for trapping prey, which includes other spiders, carpenters (sowbugs), and small insects.

Rabbit hutch spider.

Wolf Spiders
Family Lycosidae

Lycosidae, or wolf spiders, encompasses approximately 450 species around the world, 50 in Canada, and 25 in Newfoundland and Labrador. Wolf spiders do not spin webs, rather, they live as wandering hunters, using their long legs to run quickly after prey and taking it on the ground. Not surprisingly, this is one of the few spider families with excellent eyesight.

Wolf spiders have a characteristic eye pattern: four in a row at the very front of the head, and a rectangle of four more eyes behind the row. The front two eyes of that rectangle are much larger than the others. Prey includes springtails, small flies, and small spiders of other species (and sometimes their own species). Their eyesight permits wolf spiders to use visual cues in courtship. Male wolf spiders wave their legs in a rhythmic manner to attract a female; she chooses the best dancer. Female wolf spiders carry their egg sacs attached to their spinnerets. When the young spiderlings emerge, they climb onto their mother's abdomen and are carried around for a few days.

BLACK BEACH SPIDER
- Size: 8-9 mm body length
- Habitat detail: boulder beaches; rocky, wave-washed lakeshores
- Distribution: Newfoundland and Labrador

STRIPED WOLF SPIDER
- Size: 5-6 mm body length
- Habitat detail: barrens, clearings in woods and heathlands
- Distribution: Newfoundland and Labrador

Black beach spider with egg sac.

Two species are native and most commonly seen in Newfoundland and Labrador: the black beach spider (*Pardosa groenlandica*) and the striped wolf spider (*Pardosa hyperborea*). Black beach spiders, 8 to 9 millimetres in length, are often seen on rocky beaches along most Newfoundland or Labrador freshwater and marine shorelines—they can be spied scampering to safety under seaweed or beach rocks. The striped wolf spider, slightly smaller at 5 to 6 millimetres long, is found in boggy areas, spruce forests, and rocky hillsides and among lichens in Arctic and alpine tundra.

Striped wolf spider carrying her spiderlings.

Zebra Jumper
Salticus scenicus
Zebra Spider, Zebra Jumping Spider

This distinctive spider (family Salticidae, jumping spiders) is black with accents of gold and brown, and patches of white hairs which look like zebra stripes. Zebra jumpers are wanderers—they do not spin webs, but their large eyes and excellent eyesight make them great hunters. A zebra spider stalks its prey by moving slowly toward it and then jumping on it. Before jumping, the spider will glue a silk thread to the surface it is on so that if it misses its target, it can climb back up. Prey is any insect or other spider that it can catch, including small spiders of any species, even its own.

- Size: 4–7 mm body length
- Habitat detail: in or near homes, sheds, and on fences; around the sites of abandoned communities
- Distribution: widespread globally, present in Newfoundland and Labrador

Zebra spiders can move forward and backward equally well, and then jump on their prey when in the right position. The name *Salticus* is derived from the Latin word for dancing or leaping. In courtship dances, the males wave their striped legs to attract females as they dance in a zigzag pattern.

These spiders often seem to be aware of humans. Staring at a zebra spider may cause it to raise its head and look right back with its two very large and six smaller eyes (see photo, page 13).

Zebra jumper with prey.

Carpenter (*Porcellio scaber*).

CRUSTACEA
SOWBUGS

Order Isopoda
Carpenters, Boat-Builders, Woodlice

- Size: 3-30 mm body length
- Habitat detail: moist, dark places: under rocks or damp logs and wood, in plant debris, leaf litter, gardens, landscape mulch, and compost piles
- Distribution: worldwide

Carpenters, of the order Isopoda, are crustaceans related to lobsters and crabs. Most are dark grey with a flattish, oval, hard shell-like body and seven pairs of short jointed walking legs. Young carpenters resemble adults in every way except size.

Females have a brood pouch, or marsupium, on the underside of their bodies in which eggs are incubated until they hatch. Carpenters have an unusual method of moulting: they shed half their skin at a time. The skin first splits in the middle and the back half is shed; a few days later the front half is shed.

Carpenters do not bite humans, but they are scavengers. They feed on decaying vegetation like dead leaves and play an important role in breaking down plant debris.

In damp conditions they can reach very high numbers. They are commonly found outdoors under stones, wood, and flowerpots where they feed on decaying organic matter, and they frequently find their way inside homes. Carpenters cannot survive when their surroundings are too dry, which is why dead dried-up carpenters are often found in heated, dry areas of homes—but they survive in humid areas like laundry rooms, basements, and crawl spaces.

Carpenters are nocturnal and avoid light, seeking shelter like mulch and leaf litter. Unlike insects, carpenters require calcium carbonate for their external skeletons and may be common near building foundations adjacent to lawns and gardens to which lime has been added. Lime decreases the acidity of the soil and provides calcium carbonate for the carpenters.

All 12 species of carpenters recorded in Newfoundland have been introduced from Europe. Limited anecdotal evidence points to carpenter presence in Labrador; if they are in Labrador, they must be quite localized and rare.

One of the most abundant and widespread species of carpenters in Newfoundland is *Porcellio scaber*, which can reach 17 millimetres in length. Their colour varies from slate grey to mottled grey and orange or grey and white. Another common species, *Oniscus ascellus*, grows to about 16 millimetres and is usually grey with small pale patches. The species often occur together.

Carpenter (*Porcellio scaber*).

Carpenter (*Porcellio scaber*).

Millipede.

MYRIAPODA
CENTIPEDES AND MILLIPEDES

Myriapoda (*myria*, countless) is a group of arthropods that includes the millipedes and centipedes. Myriapods have 40 or 50 or more legs on an elongate body. In general, all are terrestrial and most live in the soil, under stones, and in or under decaying logs and plant litter. They require a humid environment to thrive because, unlike insects, they do not have a waxy cuticle covering their bodies, and thus they can lose water rapidly. With both millipedes and centipedes, the young have fewer legs than their parents. They moult several times on the way to adulthood, adding more pairs of legs each time.

CENTIPEDES
Class Chilopoda

- Size: 5-30 mm body length
- Habitat detail: terrestrial habitats, including forest, prairie, and gardens
- Distribution: worldwide

Centipedes are typically found in soil and leaf litter or under rocks and dead wood. Unlike millipedes, most centipedes have one pair of legs on each body segment, and each leg is clearly visible as it extends out from the sides of the body. Centipedes are carnivorous hunters and can run quickly. They live in a variety of habitats.

The majority of the 2,500 species of centipedes in the world live in the tropics. Of the 12 species known on the island of Newfoundland, nine are of European origin; the Labrador fauna is not well known.

Centipede, *Lithobius* sp.

Geophilus terrae novae is native to Newfoundland and found across the island; it has also been collected in Labrador. The first ever example of this species was found in 1949 at Grand Bruit, Newfoundland. It is yellow to whitish yellow with a slightly darker head, 10 to 17 millimetres long, and has 37 to 41 pairs of legs. It is often found on banks along rivers and streams and along the coast in open locations where the soil is covered with mosses.

The brown centipede, *Lithobius forficatus*, is a European introduction widespread across Canada, including Newfoundland. As of 2019 there are no documented records of it in Labrador, although it is probably present. The brown centipede has a flat body and is brownish red with long antennae at the front and a pair of long legs at the back. It can be difficult to tell which end is which. Individuals are 15 to 30 millimetres long and mature individuals have 15 pairs of legs. The brown centipede is typically found in open areas around human settlements such as gardens, roadsides, and gravel pits. It also found along the seashore, on riverbanks, and in peat bogs.

The red-spotted snake millipede (*Blaniulus guttulatus*) is 8–14 millimetres long but its width is that of a pencil lead.

MILLIPEDES
Class Diplopoda

More than 10,000 species of millipedes are found worldwide, most of which live in tropical regions. Eighteen species are known from Newfoundland; of these, 16 are introduced. The Labrador fauna is not as well known. Millipedes have two pairs of legs on most of their body segments, although a few segments may have no legs or only one pair. The legs extend only a little (or not at all) beyond the sides of the body. Millipedes move relatively slowly and are generally found in dark damp places, often under leaf litter, woodpiles, and rocks, or in the top inch or two of soil, where they eat decaying organic matter.

Millipedes usually live outdoors but at certain times—after excessive rain, for example—they leave the waterlogged soil and occasionally large numbers end up in basements, porches, garages, and cabins, and on walkways and similar concrete structures. Although the numbers may be alarming, millipedes are harmless.

Underwoodia iuloides of the family Caseyidae is a native millipede common throughout Newfoundland and occurring in the Straits area of Labrador. Its body is shiny dark brown and lighter on its underside than on its topside. It has slightly banded antennae. Mature adults average about 10 millimetres in length. Adults and immature individuals are found in damp wooded areas with thick leaf litter or coastal barrens that experience frequent fog and rain, preferring to hide under stones or logs. They feed on decaying leaves.

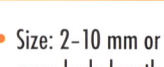

- Size: 2–10 mm or more body length
- Habitat detail: humid locations such as leaf litter, in or under dead wood, on the forest floor, in soil
- Distribution: worldwide

GLOSSARY

G. = Greek s. = singular
L. = Latin pl. = plural
F. = French

Adventitious (L. *adventicius,* foreign): existing outside the area of normal distribution.

Alates (s. alate) (L. *alatus,* wing): the winged form of an insect, where a wingless form also exists, as with ants.

Altruistic (L. *alter,* the other): individual behaviour that is of no benefit to that individual—it may even be fatal—but which is of value to the larger group in which it lives. Occurs in some social insect species.

Ametaboly (G. *a,* without; metamorphosis): the simplest form of development, also called direct development, during which the insect changes only in size. Characteristic of such orders as the Zygentoma (silverfish). See also **metamorphosis**, **complete metamorphosis**, and **incomplete metamorphosis**.

Antenna (pl. antennae) (L. *antenna,* yardarm): also called feelers; long, paired, segmented, sensory appendages extending from the head of some arthropods that may be sensitive to touch, smell, and sound.

Apical (L. *apex,* tip): at or near the apex, or tip, of a structure.

Cauda (L. *cauda,* tail): a tail, or tail-like structure.

Cephalothorax (G. *kephale,* head; *thorax,* chest or breastplate): a fused head and thorax, known as the prosoma in some arthropods; the front part of an arachnid's, or crustacean's, body.

Cerci (s. cercus) (L. *cercus,* tail): paired appendages on the terminal segments of many arthropods that may function in defence, reproduction, sensation—or none at all—such as the large defensive pincers of the earwigs and the finer cerci of the silverfish.

Chrysalis, or **chrysalid** (pl. chrysalides) (G. *chrysos,* gold): the intermediate stage in Lepidoptera (butterflies and moths) between a larva and an adult that is enclosed in a cocoon. Known as a pupa in other insects. May have a distinct metallic coloration.

Cocoon (F. *coque,* shell): a fibrous covering woven by some larvae, particularly of moths, to protect themselves while pupae, or chrysalides.

Commensalism (L. *com,* together; *mensa,* table, to share a table): in nature, organisms of different species may live in a symbiotic relationship. If the relationship benefits both organisms, it is called mutualism; if one benefits and the other neither gains nor loses, it is commensalism (see **phoresy**); and if one benefits but the other loses, it is parasitism.

Complete metamorphosis: the most complex form of insect development, also called holometaboly; it includes four distinct stages: egg, larva, pupa, and adult (or imago). The pupa is a non-feeding, resting stage. Complete metamorphosis is characteristic of many insect orders, including Coleoptera (beetles), Diptera (flies), Hymenoptera (bees, wasps, and ants), Lepidoptera (butterflies and moths), and Siphonaptera (fleas). See also **metamorphosis, ametaboly,** and **incomplete metamorphosis**.

Conspecific (L. *con,* with; *species,* kind): organisms of the same species.

Corbicula (pl. corbiculae) (L. *corbicula,* little basket): a structure on the hind legs of some bees that carries pollen, also called a pollen basket.

Cornicles (s. cornicle) (L. *corniculum,* little horn): tubes extending from the abdomens of aphids through which pheromones or defensive substances are secreted. Although sometimes called honey-tubes, they are not the means by which these insects secrete honeydew.

Cosmopolitan distribution: when an insect, or group of insects, is found around the world, where habitat permits.

Coxa (pl. coxae) (L. *coxa,* hip): the first segment of an insect's leg, which is attached to its thorax.

Cuticle (L. *cuticula,* skin): the outer layer of an insect's exoskeleton.

Defoliation (L. *de,* away from; *folium,* leaf): loss of plant leaves.

Dimorphism (G. *dis,* two; *morphe,* shape): occurring in two different forms, such as colour, size, or shape, within the same species, depending on sex, season, or location.

Elytra (s. elytron) (G. *elutron,* sheath): the hardened forewings of beetles and earwigs that cover the more delicate hindwings.

Eusocial (L. *eu,* good; *socialis,* companionship): a high-level social arrangement within some insect groups, such as bees, ants, and wasps, where reproduction is limited to specific groups, or individuals, such as a queen or queens.

Exoskeleton (G. *exo,* outer; *skeletos,* skeleton): the external covering of arthropods, made of the polysaccharide chitin, that provides structure and protection to the body. As the exoskeleton itself cannot grow, it will moult when the arthropod grows.

Exuvia (pl. exuviae) (L. *exuo,* to take off): skin that is cast off by a moulting insect (larva).

Frass (German *fressen,* to eat): the solid excrement of insect larvae.

Hamulus (pl. hamuli) (L. *hamulus,* little hook): a structure that connects the fore- and hindwing of Lepidopterans.

Haplodiploidy (G. *haplo,* single; *diplous,* double): the genetic system of some insects (e.g., hymenoptera) in which the males result from unfertilized eggs, and therefore carry only a single set of chromosomes (haploid), and the females result from fertilized eggs, thus containing two sets of chromosomes (diploid).

Hibernaculum (pl. hibernacula) (L. *hibernaculum,* winter quarters): a winter shelter that may be natural, as in a crevice (e.g., lady beetles), or made by the insect, as in a spun silk shelter (e.g., eastern spruce budworm).

Holarctic: encompassing most habitats found in the Earth's northern continents.

Honeydew: a sugary waste excreted by aphids after feeding from plants, which attracts other insects, such as ants, which in turn may provide protection to the aphid.

Imago (L. *imago,* image): the final, or adult, stage in an insect's development.

Incomplete metamorphosis: the second level of complexity in insect development, between ametaboly and complete metamorphosis, also called partial metamorphosis or hemimetaboly. In this case, the immature stage (nymph) resembles the adult but may be smaller and have less-developed wings. There is no pupal stage. It is characteristic of such insect orders as Hemiptera (aphids), Odonata (dragonflies and damselflies), Orthoptera (grasshoppers), Blattodea (cockroaches), Phthiraptera (sucking lice), and Ephemeroptera (mayflies). See also **ametaboly**, **metamorphosis**, and c**omplete metamorphosis**.

Instar (L. *instar,* form, or likeness): any development stage between hatching and sexual maturity in an arthropod, including larval or nymphal stages. Instars are usually numbered, with the first instar being the stage immediately after hatching.

Kleptoparasite (G. *klepto,* I steal): animals that steal food or prey from another animal, as in kleptoparasitic bees.

Labium (pl. labia) (L. *labium,* lip): the lower lip of an arthropod.

Larva (pl. larvae) (L. l*arva,* ghost): an immature stage of development for insects that undergo complete metamorphosis. For Lepidoptera (butterflies and moths), the larva is called a caterpillar; for some Diptera (true flies), the larva is a maggot; for Coleoptera (beetles) and Hymenoptera (wasps, bees, and ants), the larva is a grub. See also **nymph**.

Leaf litter: a layer of decomposing leaves on top of the soil.

Mandibles (s. mandible) (L. *mandere,* to chew; *bula,* instrument): paired jaws of most arthropods.

Metamorphosis (G. *meta,* after; *morphe,* form): the development of insects from hatching to adulthood and the relative amount of changing that occurs between the various immature-to-adult stages. Moulting of the exoskeleton usually occurs between each stage. See also **ametaboly, incomplete metamorphosis,** and **complete metamorphosis.**

Moulting (L. *mutare,* transform): or ecdysis, is the process by which an insect sheds its old skin (cuticle) and grows a new one as it moves from one life stage to the next.

Nearctic: encompassing the majority of the habitats of North America and Greenland.

Nectar (G. *nectar,* nourishment of the gods): a sugary fluid secreted by glands called nectaries in flowers and other plant structures, commonly attractive to a variety of insects, which in turn provide pollination to the plant.

Nectaring: when an insect, such as a butterfly, feeds from the nectar of a plant.

Nymph (L. *nympha,* bride): an immature stage of an insect that undergoes incomplete metamorphosis. Also used for the immature stage of acari (mites and ticks), that is, between the larva and the adult. See also **larva**.

Ootheca (pl. oothecae) (L. *oo,* egg; *theca,* case): egg case, a covering over an egg mass, as seen in some insects such as cockroaches.

Osmeterium (pl. osmeteria) (G. *osme,* smell): a defensive organ in the prothorax of butterfly larvae in the papillonidae family (swallowtails). When the larva is startled, the osmeterium extends out of the prothorax to resemble the fangs of a snake, which along with spots resembling eyes, and a foul-smelling secretion, discourage large (bird) and small (other insects) predators.

Ostiole (pl. ostiolae) (L. *ostiolum,* small door): an opening in the thorax of some insects, such as stink bugs, through which a noxious substance is released.

Ovipositor (L. *ovum,* egg; *positor,* to deposit): an organ at the end of an insect's abdomen for egg-laying functions, including the creation of a burrow in which to lay eggs, the actual laying and placement of the eggs, but also the piercing of another insect's body by parasitic insects (e.g., parasitic wasps) so that eggs can be placed into the host's body. See also **stinger**.

Parasitoid (G. *parasitos,* one who eats at the table of another; *oid,* form): an insect that lives in, or on, another organism and eventually kills it; most are in the hymenoptera.

Parthenogenetic reproduction (G. *parthen,* virgin; *genesis,* creation): reproduction in the absence of a male.

Pheromone (G. *phero,* I carry; *hormo,* to set in motion): a chemical released, often during mating, that changes the behaviour of another insect.

Phloem (G. *phloos,* bark): the transport system within a vascular plant that moves nutrients from one part of the plant to another.

Phoresy (G. *phoresis,* the act of bearing): the relationship between two organisms in which one (the phoretic) attaches itself to a second (the host) for the sole purpose of being carried. Examples include certain mites that attach to a bee to be carried from flower to flower, or pseudoscorpions that attach to flies.

Pile: short, fine hairs found on some insects (bumble bees, some flies) that appear like fur.

Proboscis (pl. proboscises or proboscides) (G. *pro,* before; *bosko,* to feed): an elongated feeding tube in the mouth of many insects such as butterflies and mosquitoes.

Prolegs (G. *pro,* before; legs): also called false legs, they appear on the abdomen of many larvae, particularly Lepidopteran, and function as legs, although they have no joints or segments.

Pronotum (G. *pro,* before; *noton,* back): a covering on the dorsal surface of the thorax that is often hardened.

Pupa (pl. pupae) (L. *pupa,* doll): the third stage in complete metamorphosis, where the insect, encased in a protective covering, is relatively immobile.

Rostrum (pl. rostra) (L. *rostrum,* snout): a snoutlike projection from the head of an insect, may be jointed or rigid.

Scopa (pl. scopae) (L. *scopa,* broom): specialized dense brushlike structures on various hymenopterans; in some bees they appear on the hind leg and are involved in transporting pollen.

Scutellum (pl. scutelli) (L. *scutum,* shield): a protective triangular plate on the back (thorax) of many insects, technically the posterior end of the mesonotum. Very prominent in Hemiptera and Coleoptera, present but diminished in Diptera and Hymenoptera.

Scutum (pl. scuta) (L. *scutum,* shield): a protective plate on the back (thorax) of many insects. It is also the shield on hard ticks (Ixodidae) which covers the entire back of the male and only partially on females.

Setae (s. seta) (L. *seta,* bristles): stiff "hairs" that exist on many insect species both on the out- and inside of the body; its functions include camouflage and defence.

Siphuncle (pl. siphuncles or siphunculi) (L. *siphunculus,* little tube): a synonym for cornicle.

Solenophagy (G. *solen,* pipe; *phage,* to eat): blood feeding (e.g., mosquitoes), where the blood is drawn directly from a blood vessel. See **telmophagy** for comparison.

Spinneret: an organ in spiders, the larvae (caterpillars) of certain lepidoptera, and some other insects that produces and deposits silk. Silk may be used for trapping prey (e.g., webs), reproduction (e.g., sperm transfer), movement (e.g., ballooning), and protection (e.g., cocoons).

Spiracle (pl. spiracula) (L. *spirare,* to breathe): breathing pores in insects and arachnids.

Stinger: a modified ovipositor, common in Hymenoptera, that can deliver venom. In most cases, the stinger can no longer lay eggs.

Subdorsal (L. *sub,* under; *dorsalis,* the back): any structure or feature that appears below the back (dorsum), such as the subdorsal line or ridge in some caterpillars.

Subspiracular (L. *sub,* below; spiracle): any structure or feature that appears below the spiracles, such as the subspiracular line in some caterpillars.

Tegmina (s. tegmen) (L. *tego* + *men*; a covering): the thickened forewing of insects such as cockroaches, grasshoppers, and earwigs.

Telmophagy (G. *telmo,* pool; *phage,* to eat): blood feeding (e.g., black flies), where the blood is drawn from a pool caused by tissue laceration. See **solenophagy** for comparison.

Tergum (pl. terga) (L. *tergum,* back): the dorsal surface; may be applied specifically to the head, thorax, or abdomen, or all three.

Thorax (pl. thoraces) (G. *thorax,* chest or breastplate): the middle section of an insect or crustacean body, between the head and abdomen; may be divided into the prothorax, mesothorax, and metathorax.

INDEX

SCIENTIFIC NAME

Acanthothrips albivittatus, 258
Acanthothrips nodicornis, 258
Acarapis woodi, 306
Acari, 305–308
Acheta domesticus, 267
Acleris curvalana, 190, 191
Adalia bipunctata, 138, 139
Aedes aurifer, 103, 104
Aedes canadensis, 107
Aedes impiger, 100–101
Aedes japonicus, 102
Aedes nigripes, 100–101
Aeshna juncea, 287
Aeshna septentrionalis, 286
Aeshna umbrosa, 282, 287, 288
Aeshnidae, 286, 287
Aglais milberti, 215, 218
Agriades glandon, 201–204
Agrotis ipsilon, 178
Aleochara bilineata, 147, 148
Alypia octomaculata, 178, 179
Amara fulva, 121
Amblyomma americanum, 310
Andrena clarkella, 43
Andrena wilkella, 44, 45
Andrenidae, 38, 42–45
Anisosticta bitriangularis, 135
Anoscopus serratulae, 246
Anthrenus museorum, 116, 117
Anthrenus verbasci, 116, 117
Aphidae, 240, 242, 243
Apidae, 38, 45–56

Apis mellifera, 54, 55
Araneae, 313–325
Araneidae, 316–318
Araneus diadematus, 316–318
Araneus sp., 300
Archiearis infans, 172
Arctia opulenta, 163
Arctiinae, 163
Argasidae, 308–311
Atheta pseudovestita, 150
Attagenus unicolor, 116, 117

Bembidion carinula, 122
Bembidion grapii, 122
Bembidion lampros, 122
Bembidion scopulinum, 122
Bembidion spp., 122
Bembidion transversale, 122
Blaniulus guttulatus, 330
Blattodea, 272, 273
Boloria spp., 214
Bombus borealis, 50
Bombus rufocinctus, 18, 51
Bombus spp., 46–53
Bombus ternarius, 52
Bombus terricola, 38, 53
Bombus vagans, 48

Caddo agilis, 304
Callophrys augustinus, 210, 211
Calopteryx aequabilis, 293
Calvia quatuordecimguttata, 14, 141

Camponotus herculeanus, 32, 33
Camponotus pennsylvanicus, 32, 33
Carabidae, 120–130
Carabus meander, 123
Carabus nemoralis, 110, 124
Carterocephalus palaemon, 195
Caseyidae, 330
Catocala relicta, 172
Catocala spp., 169–172
Celastrina lucia, 206–207
Cerambycidae, 142–145
Cerapteryx graminis, 176–178
Chelifer cancroides, 312
Chilopoda, 328, 329
Chironomus plumosus, 94–96
Choristoneura fumiferana, 193
Chorthippus curtipennis, 268, 269, 271
Chrysopidae, 154, 155
Chrysops spp., 85, 86
Cicindela duodecimguttata, 129
Cicindela longilabris, 130
Cicindelinae, 128–130
Cimex adjunctus, 245
Cimex lectularius, 245
Coccinella septempunctata, 110, 139, 140
Coccinella transversoguttata, 137
Coccinella trifasciata, 137
Coccinellidae, 131–142
Coelioxys spp., 69
Coenagrion interrogatum, 290, 291
Coenagrion resolutum, 290, 291
Coenagrionidae, 290, 291
Coenonympha tullia, 229
Coleoptera, 110–153
Colias interior, 239

Colias philodice, 238
Colletes spp., 28, 57–59
Colletidae, 38, 57–59
Cordulia shurtleffii, 285
Corixidae, 254
Cosmopepla lintneriana, 251
Creophilus maxillosus, 149
Crustacea, 301, 326, 327
Ctenocephalides canis, 108, 109
Ctenocephalides felis felis, 108, 109
Ctenucha virginica, 165
Culex pipiens molestus, 104, 105
Culex pipiens pipiens, 104, 105
Culicidae, 99–108
Curculionidae, 150–152

Danaus plexippus, 216–218
Delia radicum, 78, 79
Demodex brevis, 305
Demodex canis, 305
Demodex folliculorum, 305
Dermacentor variabilis, 310
Dermaptera, 276–279
Dermatophagoides farinae, 307
Dermatophagoides pteronyssinus, 307
Dermestes lardarius, 118, 119
Dermestidae, 116, 117
Desmocerus palliates, 142, 143
Diplopoda, 328, 330
Diptera, 63–107
Dolichovespula maculate, 70, 71
Dytiscidae, 145, 146

Elaphrus clairvillei, 125
Elasmostethus cruciatus, 251
Elasmuchas lateralis, 19

Enallagma annexum, 290, 291
Enallagma boreale, 290, 291
Ennomos subsignaria, 173, 174
Ephemeroptera, 294–297
Eratigena duellica, 314
Erebidae, 162–171
Eriophyes emarginatae, 306
Eristalis tenax, 93
Evodinus monticola, 110

Fannia canicularis, 96
Forficula auricularia, 278, 279
Formica glacialis, 28, 35, 36
Formica rubicunda, 36, 37
Formicidae, 30–37

Geometridae, 172–175
Geophilus terrae novae, 328, 329
Geotrupes stercorarius, 119, 120
Gerridae, 241, 255
Glaucopsyche lygdamus, 208
Grapholita libertina, 191, 192
Gyrinidae, 152, 153

Haemaphysalis leporispalustris, 300, 309, 310
Halictus spp., 61
Halictidae, 38, 60–62
Halyomorpha halys, 253
Harmonia axyridis, 135, 136
Harpalus rufipes, 127
Hemaris thysbe, 184–187
Hemerobiidae, 154, 155
Hemiptera, 240–255
Hercinothrips femoralis, 257
Hesperia comma borealis, 197
Hesperiidae, 194–200

Hippodamia tredecimpunctata tibialis, 140, 141
Hylaeus spp., 58, 59
Hymenoptera, 28–62

Icaricia saepiolus, 204
Ischnura verticalis, 292
Isopoda, 301, 326, 327
Ixodes angustus, 310
Ixodes marxi, 310
Ixodes muris, 310
Ixodes ricinus, 311
Ixodes scapularis, 308, 310, 311
Ixodes uriae, 310, 311
Ixodidae, 308–311

Lambdina fiscellaria, 174
Lasioglossum spp., 28, 60, 61
Lepidoptera, 158–239
Lepisma spp., 298, 299
Lestes disjunctus, 292, 293
Lethocerus americanus, 247–248
Leucoma salicis, 167–169
Leucorrhinia hudsonica, 289
Libellula quadrimaculata, 287–289
Liposcelis spp., 263–265
Lithobius forficatus, 328, 329
Lucilia sericata, 76, 81–83
Lycaena epixanthe phaedra, 209, 211
Lycaenidae, 200–211
Lycosidae, 323, 324
Lymantriinae, 166, 167

Megachile frigida, 67
Megachile spp., 38, 39, 63, 66
Megachilidae, 38, 63–69

Melanoplus borealis borealis, 270, 271
Melophagus ovinus, 311
Microbisium brunneum, 312
Misumena vatia, 319–321
Mitopus morio, 301–303
Monochamus scutellatus, 144
Musca domestica, 84
Mycetophilidae, 94
Myriapoda, 328–330
Myrmica rubra, 34, 35
Mythimna unipuncta, 159, 176–180

Nelima elegans, 304
Neotrombicula microti, 307
Neuroptera, 154, 155
Nicrophorus defodiens, 112, 114
Nicrophorus investigator, 112, 113
Noctua pronuba, 172, 179
Noctuidae, 176–180
Nomada cressoni, 56
Nomada spp., 56
Notonectidae, 244
Nymphalidae, 212–230
Nymphalis antiopa, 219, 220

Odonata, 280–293
Oeneis bore, 230
Oeneis jutta, 230
Oeneis melissa, 230
Oeneis polixenes, 230
Oniscus ascellus, 326, 327
Ontholestes cingulatus, 148
Opiliones, 300, 301–304
Orgyia antiqua, 167
Ornithomyia anchineura, 97
Orthoptera, 266–271

Osmia spp., 68
Otiorhynchus sulcatus, 151

Papilio brevicauda, 232, 233
Papilio brevicauda brevicauda, 232, 233
Papilio canadensis, 231, 232
Papilionidae, 231–234
Pardosa groenlandica, 323, 324
Pardosa hyperborea, 323, 324
Pediculus humanus capitis, 261–263
Pediculus humanus humanus, 261–263
Pentatomoidae, 251–253
Perillus exaptus, 251
Phalangium opilio, 300, 301–303
Phanerotoma libertinecida, 192
Philaenus spumarius, 247–248
Phthiraptera, 261–263
Picromerus bidens, 240
Pieridae, 234–239
Pieris oleracea, 237
Pieris rapae, 235–237
Plebejus idas, 205
Plecoptera, 274, 275
Plutellidae, 181, 182
Podisus serieventris, 251, 253
Polites peckius, 200
Polydrusus formosus, 152
Polygonia spp., 212, 213
Porcellio scaber, 326, 327
Prosimulium mixtum, 98, 99
Pseudoscorpiones, 312
Psila rosae, 80, 81
Psocodea, 260–265
Psocomorpha, 265
Psychodidae, 87, 88

Psyllobora vigintimaculata, 142
Pterostichus adstrictus, 126
Pterostichus melanarius, 126
Pthirus pubis, 261–263
Pulex irritans, 108, 109
Pyrgus centaureae, 199
Pyrrhalta viburni, 110

Rheumaptera hastata, 175
Rhipicephalus sanguineus, 310
Rhyssa persuasoria, 28

Salticidae, 325
Salticus scenicus, 13, 325
Sarcophaga spp., 90
Sarcoptes scabiei, 305
Sarcoptes scabiei canis, 305
Sciaridae, 94
Sericomyia militaris, 77
Sericomyia sp., 76
Silphidae, 112–114
Silusa prettyae, 150
Siphonaptera, 108, 109
Siricidae, 73–75
Smerinthus cerisyi, 188, 189
Speyeria atlantis, 214
Sphecodes spp., 62
Sphingidae, 182–189
Sphinx canadensis, 183
Sphinx gordius, 183
Sphinx kalmia, 186
Staphylinidae, 147–150
Steatoda bipunctata, 322
Syrphidae, 90–93
Syrphus ribesii, 90–93

Tachinus rufipes, 149
Tegenaria domestica, 314, 315
Tetragnatha extensa, 317
Tetragnathidae, 317
Thermobia spp., 299
Thomisidae, 319–321
Thrips validus, 259
Thymelicus lineola, 197
Thysanoptera, 256–259
Tipula paludosa, 88, 89
Tortricidae, 190–193
Tribolium confusum, 115
Trichiosoma arcticum, 8, 9
Trichoptera, 156, 157
Trombiculidae, 307
Tyria jacobaeae, 164

Underwoodia iuloides, 330

Vanessa atalanta, 225, 228
Varroa destructor, 306
Vespula maculifrons, 72

Wyeomyia smithii, 106

Zygentoma, 298, 299

COMMON NAME

American dog tick, 310
American Emerald, 285
American house dust mite, 307
American lady, 222–223, 225
American salmonfly, 274
anglewings, 212, 213
antler moth, 176–178
ants, 30–37

aphidlions, 154, 155
aphids, 240, 242, 243
apple sphinx moth caterpillar, 183
Arctic blue, 201–204
Arctic mosquito, 100–101
Arctic skipper, 195
Arctics, 230
armyworm moth, 159, 176–180
Asian bush mosquito, 102
Asian cockroach, 272, 273
Asian lady beetle, 135, 136
Asian rock pool mosquito, 102
Azure Darner, 286

backswimmers, 244
bacon beetle, 118, 119
black carpet beetle, 116, 117
bald-faced hornet, 70, 71
banded greenhouse thrips, 257
banded sexton beetle, 112, 113
bark louse, 265
barn funnel weaver, 314, 315
basement spider, 314, 315
bat bug, 245
bed bug, 245
bees, 38–69
beetles, 110–153
black beach spider, 323, 324
black cutworm, 178
black fly, 98, 99
black-legged tick, 310, 311
black vine weevil, 151
blueberry leaftier moth, 190, 191
Bluet damselflies 290, 291
boat-builder, 326, 327
body louse, 261–263
bog copper, 209, 211

book louse, 263–265
Boreal Bluet, 290, 291
bottle-arse spider, 314, 315
briseis underwing, 170–171, 172
brown-and-white hopper, 246
brown centipede, 328, 329
brown dog ticks, 310
brown elfin, 210, 211
brown lacewing, 154, 155
brown marmorated stink bug, 253
brush-footed butterflies, 212–230
bugs, 240–255
bumble bees, 46–53
burying beetles, 112–114
butterfly, 158–161, 194–239
buzzer midge, 94–96

cabbage maggot, 78, 79
cabbage root maggot, 78, 79
cabbage white, 235–237
caddisflies, 156, 157
Canadian sphinx, 183
Canadian tiger swallowtail, 231, 232
carpenter, 301, 326, 327
carpenter ant, 32, 33
carrion beetles, 112–114
carrot rust fly, 80, 81
cellophane bee, 28, 57
centipede, 328, 329
chigger mite, 307
Clarke's mining bee, 43
clear wing moth, 184–187
clouded sulphur, 238
cockroach, 272, 273
commas, 212, 213
common branded skipper, 197
common garden orb weaver, 316, 317

common green bottle fly, 76, 81–83
common house fly, 84
common house spider, 314, 315
common orb weaver, 317
common ringlet, 229
confused flour beetle, 115
crab louse, 261–263
crab spider, 319–321
crane fly, 76, 88, 89
cricket, 266–267
cross orb weaver, 316–318
cross spider, 316–318
cutworm moth, 176–180

daddy longlegs, 88, 89, 301–304
damselfly, 280–284, 290–293
dark sword-grass moth, 178
darners, 286, 287
deer fly, 85, 86
deer tick, 310, 311
dermestid beetle, 116, 117
diamondback moth, 181, 182
dor beetle, 119, 120
dragonflies, 280–289
drain fly, 87, 88
drone fly, 93
dung beetle, 119, 120
dust mite, 300

earwig, 276–279
Eastern Forktail, 292
eastern yellowjacket, 72
eight-spotted forester, 178, 179
elderberry borer, 142, 143
elm spanworm, 158, 173, 174
erebid moths, 162–171

European crane fly, 88, 89
European earwig, 278, 279
European fire ant, 34, 35
European ground beetle, 110, 124
European honey bee, 54, 55
European house dust mite, 307
European skipper, 196–198
European wool-carder bee, 65, 66
eye-spotted lady beetle, 134

false scorpion, 312
finger mite, 306
firebrat, 299
fleas, 108, 109
flesh fly, 90
flies, 63–107
flower crab spider, 319–321
flower flies, 90–93
flower spider, 319–321
flower thrips, 259
Four-Spotted Skimmer, 287–289
fourteen-spotted lady beetle, 14, 141
frigid leafcutter bee, 67
fritillaries, 214
froghopper, 247–248
fungus gnat, 94

gall mite, 308
geometer moths, 172–175
German cockroach, 272, 273
giant house spider, 314
giant water bug, 247–248
gold-and-brown rove beetle, 148
golden bog mosquito, 103, 104
gossamer-winged butterflies, 200–211
grasshopper, 266, 268–271

green lacewing, 154, 155
green immigrant weevil, 152
greenish blue, 204
grizzled skipper, 199
ground beetles, 120–130

hairy rove beetle, 149
half-black bumble bee, 48
halloween lady beetle, 135, 136
harlequin lady beetle, 135, 136
harvestmen, 300, 301–304
hawk moth, 182–189
head louse, 261–263
hemlock looper, 174
honey bee tracheal mite, 306
horntails (hawk moth larvae), 182–189
horntails (timberflies), 73–75
horse fly, 85, 86
horse stinger, 283 *see also* dragonfly
house cricket, 267
house fly, 77, 84
house pseudoscorpion, 312
hover fly, 76, 77, 90–93
Hudsonian Whiteface, 289
hummingbird moth, 184–187

icy ant, 28, 35, 36
imported cabbage worm, 235–237
inchworm, 172–175
infant moth, 172
ipsilon dart moth, 178
itch mites, 305

jumping spider, 325
jutta Arctic, 230

Labrador skipper, 197
lacewing, 154, 155
lady beetles, 131–142
ladybug, 131–142
lake midge, 94–96
larder beetle, 18, 119
large yellow underwing, 179
laurel sphinx, 186
leafcutter bee, 38, 39, 63, 66
leafroller moth, 190–193
leatherjacket, 88, 89
lemon cuckoo bumble bee, 28, 48, 49
lesser house fly, 96
lice, 260–265
ligated furrow bee, 40–41
lingonberry fruitworm, 191, 192
lone star tick, 310
long-horned beetles, 142–145
long-horned flower beetle, 110
long-jawed orb weaver, 317
long-lipped tiger beetle, 130
loopers, 172–175
louse fly, 97
lousy watchman, 119, 120

marsh lady beetle, 135
marsh meadow grasshopper, 268, 269, 271
masked bees, 58, 59
mason bee, 68
mayflies, 294–297
meadow spittle bug, 247–248
Melissa Arctic, 230
Milbert's tortoiseshell, 215, 218
millipede, 328, 330
mining bees, 38, 42–45

mites, 305–308
mixed-up black fly, 98, 99
monarch, 216–218
mosquitoes, 99–108
moth fly, 87, 88
moths, 158–193
mottled stink bug, 19
mourning cloak butterfly, 19, 219, 220
mouse tick, 310
multicoloured Asian lady beetle, 135, 136
museum beetle, 116, 117
mustard white, 237

nippers, 99–108
nomad bees, 56
northern amber bumble bee, 50
northern blue, 205
Northern Bluet, 290, 291
northern grasshopper, 270, 271
northern house mosquito, 104, 105
Northern Spreadwing, 292, 293
northern spring azure, 206–207

one-eyed sphinx moth, 188, 189
opulent moth, 163
orb weaver spiders, 316–318
owlet moth, 176–180

painted lady butterfly, 14, 221, 224, 225
parasitic wasps, 192
Peck's skipper, 200
phantom crane fly, 76
pink-edged sulphur, 239
pitcher plant mosquito, 106
polixenes Arctic, 230

pond skater, 255
predaceous diving beetle, 145, 146
pseudoscorpion, 312
pubic louse, 261–263

rabbit hutch spider, 322
rabbit tick, 300, 309, 310
red admiral, 225, 228
red-belted bumble bee, 18, 51
red-cross shield bug, 251
red-shouldered pine borer, 111
red-spotted purple, 226–228
red-spotted snake millipede, 330
River Jewelwing, 293
root maggot, 78, 79
rove beetles, 147–150
ruddy slave-making ant, 36, 37
rusty tussock moth, 167

satin moth, 167–169
sawfly, 8, 9
scabies mite, 305
seabird tick, 310
Sedge Darner, 287
seven-spotted lady beetle, 110, 139–140
Shadow Darner, 282, 287, 288
sheep ked, 311
sheep tick, 311
shield bug, 251–253
short-tailed swallowtail butterfly, 232, 233
silverfish, 298, 299
silvery blue butterfly, 208
skin beetle, 116, 117
skippers, 194–200
snout beetle, 150–152

345

sowbug, 301, 326, 327
spanworm, 172–175
spear-marked black moth, 175
sphinx moth, 182–189
spiders, 313–325
spiked shield bug, 240
spittle bug, 240, 247–248
spotted tussock moth, 164
spring azure, 206–207
spruce budworm, 193
squirrel tick, 310
stink bugs, 251–253
stoneflies, 274, 275
stout, 85, 86
strawberry seed beetle, 127
striped wolf spider, 323, 324
Subarctic Bluet, 290, 291
sulphurs, 234, 238, 239
swallowtail butterflies, 231–234
sweat bee, 28, 60–62

Taiga Bluet, 290, 291
thirteen-spotted lady beetle, 140, 141
three corner fly, 85, 86
three-banded lady beetle, 137
thrips, 256–259
ticks, 308–311
tiger beetles, 128–130
tiger moth, 163
timberflies, 73–75
tortricid moth, 190–193
transverse lady beetle, 137
tricoloured bumble bee, 52
true bugs, 240–255
true lice, 261–263
tube-tail thrips, 258

tussock moth, 166, 167
twelve-spotted tiger beetle, 129
twenty-spotted lady beetle, 142
twice-stabbed stink bug, 251
two-spotted lady beetle, 138, 139
underwings, 169–172
varied carpet beetle, 116, 117
Varroa mite, 306
viburnum leaf beetle, 110
Virginia ctenucha, 165
vole tick, 310

wasp, 29, 70–73
water boatman, 254
water doctor, 255
water strider, 241, 255
weevil, 150–152
western honey bee, 54, 55
whirligig beetle, 152, 153
white admiral, 226–228
white underwing, 172
white-spotted sawyer, 144
white-veined Arctic, 230
whites, 234–237
Wilke's mining bee, 44, 45
wolf spider, 323, 324
woodland pool mosquito, 107
woodlouse, 326, 327
wool-carder bee, 64, 65
woolly bear, 163

yellow-and-white hopper, 240, 246
yellow-banded bumble bee, 38, 53
yellow underwing, 172
yellow woolly bear, 164

zebra jumper spider, 13, 325

PHOTO CREDITS

Aiwok (licensed under CC BY-SA 3.0): *Andrena clarkella* m5, f2, 43.

Seth Ausubel: brown marmorated stink bug, 253.

Richard Ballard: *Podisus brevispinus,* 252.

Scott Bauer (USDA): fourteen-spotted lady beetle, 14.

Frederic Beaulieu, Agriculture and Agri-Food Canada: scanning electron microscope image of *Dermatophagoides farinae,* 300.

Todd Boland: lemon cuckoo bee, 28, 49; wasp, 29; ants, 30; leafcutter bee, 38; yellow-banded bumble bee, 38, 53; male *Andrena* sp. resting on a flower, 42; tricoloured bumble bee, 47; northern amber bumble bee, 50; red-belted bumble bee worker (red form), 51; tricoloured bumble bee, 52; honey bee worker, 55; sweat bee, 60; eastern yellowjacket, 72; hover fly, 76, 77, 91, 93; common green bottle fly, 76, 81, 82, 83; European crane fly, 89; drone fly, 92; long-horned flower beetle, 110; viburnum leaf beetle, 110; seven-spotted lady beetle, 110; red-shouldered pine borer, 111; elderberry borer, 143; white-spotted sawyer, 144; caddisflies, 156; Virginian tiger moth caterpillar, 162; white underwing (bottom), 169; geometrid moth, 172; hemlock looper, 174; antler moth, 176; laurel sphinx caterpillar, 186; clearwing moth, 187; European skipper, 196, 197, 198; underside view of a grizzled skipper, 199; northern spring azure (form lucia) underside, 207; silvery blue, 208; green comma, 212, 213; Milbert's tortoiseshell, 215; mourning cloack butterfly, 220; American lady butterfly, 222–223; red admiral butterfly, 225; Canadian tiger swallowtail butterfly, 231; Canadian tiger swallowtail caterpillar, 232; short-tailed swallowtail butterfly, 233; cabbage white butterflies, 235, 236; pink-edged sulphur, 239; yellow-and-black leafhopper, 246; *Podisus serieventris,* 251; dragonfly, 280; damselfly, 281.

> Todd Boland, horticulturalist at the Memorial University of Newfoundland Botanical Garden in St. John's, is a founding member of the Newfoundland and Labrador Wildflower Society and an active volunteer with the North American Rock Garden Society. He is the author of several books published by Boulder Books, including *Trees & Shrubs of Newfoundland and Labrador, Wildflowers and Ferns of Newfoundland and Labrador,* and *Favourite Perennials for Atlantic Canada.* He is an avid gardener, photographer, and bird watcher.

Marnix Bos (http://www.arachophoto.com): rabbit hutch spider, 17, 322.

Joseph Bowden: spotted tussock moth, 164; striped wolf spider, 324.

Andrea Brauner: diamondback moth adult, larvae, 181.

Joe Brazil: orange-legged furrow bee, 61; dirt-covered *Sphecodes* sp., 62; opulent moth in Labrador, 163; Virginia ctenucha moth sipping nectar, 165; flower crab spider with prey, 319.

Chris Buddle: *Microbisium brunneum,* 312.

Erica Burke: tricoloured bumble bee, 52; long-lipped tiger beetle, 26; gold-and-brown rove beetle, 148; white underwings, 169; northern spring azure (form *marginata*), 207; house pseudoscorpion, 312.

Rob Cannings: Azure Darner, 286; Sedge Darner, 287.

Zeynel Cebeci (licensed under CC BY-SA 4.0): grizzled skipper (top), 199.

Tom Chapman: flesh fly, 90; louse fly, 97; mixed-up black fly, 98; golden bog mosquito, 103; northern house mosquito, 105; pitcher plants and pitcher plant mosquitoes, 106; spittle bug, 240; thrips 256, 257, 259; engorged rabbit tick, 309.

Andrew Chaulk: female wool-carder bee, 66; Virginia ctenucha moth and caterpillar, 165.

Jared Clarke, www.birdtherock.com: eight-spotted forester, 179; Arctic skipper, 195; jutta Arctic, 230; mustard white butterfly, 237.

Patrick Clement (licensed under CC BY 2.0): *Orgyia antiqua,* mating, 166.

Murray Colbo: caddisfly larva and case, 156; mayfly larva, 295.

CSIRO Science Image: silverfish, 298.

> Mardon Erbland was trained as an electrical engineer. When he retired in 2003 from the electric utility business, he quickly renewed his childhood fascination with insects. That fascination, combined with a life-long interest in photography, led to his current interest in close-up photography of arthropods. He is an avid contributor to BugGuide.net, iNaturalist.org, and NLNature.com. His free, self-published ebook, *Island Insects,* is available at www.JustPhotos.ca/book. Mardon lives in Logy Bay, Newfoundland and Labrador.

Lauren Culler, researcher at Dartmouth College: Arctic mosquitoes, 101.
Cupids Legacy Centre: Larkspur Lotion, 262.

Emily Denief: yellow underwing moth, 180.

Didier Descouens (Projet Phoebus, Muséum de Toulouse): varied carpet beetle adult, 116

Peggy Dixon: caddisfly necklace, 156; Shadow Darner, 282, 288; sowbugs, 301.

André-Philippe Drapeau Picard (licensed under CC0 1.0 universal public domain): *Lycaena epixanthe,* bog copper, 211.

Lynette Elliott: nymph red-cross shield bug, twice-stabbed stink bug, 252.

Mardon Erbland: zebra jumper, 13; common field grasshopper, 17, 266; mourning cloak butterfly caterpillar, 19, 219; icy ants, 28, 35, 36; ants, 30; carpenter ant, 32, 33; European fire ant, 34; ruddy slave-maker ant, 36, 37; Wilke's mining bee, 45; deer fly, 85, 86; drain fly, 87; Asian bush mosquito, 102; ground beetle larva, 120; lady beetle pupa, 133; eye-spotted lady beetles, 134; two-spotted lady beetle, 138; water tiger, 145; weevil, *Rhinoncus* sp., 150; brown lacewing, 154; green lacewing, 155; caddisflies, 157; satin moth, 168; antler moth, 177; blueberry leaftier moth, 190; backswimmers, 244; brown-and-white leafhopper, 246; spittle bug, 249, 250; water boatman, 254; water strider, 255; tube-tail thrips, 258; marsh meadow grasshopper, 268, 269; earwig, 279; damselfly larva, 284; dragonfly larva, 284; stonefly, 274, 275; mass of spiderlings, 300; *Phalangium opilio* female, 302; *Mitopus morio,* 303; *Nelima elegans,* 304; sidewalk mite, 307; common house spider, 314, 315; cross orb weaver, 316; flower crab spider, 320–321; zebra jumper with prey, 325; carpenters (*Oniscus ascellus* and *Porcellio scaber*), 326, 327; millipede, 328; centipede, 329.

Melinda Fawver, Adobe Stock: bald-faced hornet, 70.

Barry Fitzgerald, USDA: Asian cockroach, 273.

Heidi Fry: elm spanworm moth, 158; centipede attacking elm spanworm, elm spanworm mess on car, elm spanworm caterpillar, 173.

Caitlin Fudge: northern amber bumble bee, 50.

Craig Goudie: snowshoe hare infested with rabbit ticks, 309.

Henri Goulet: *Rhyssa persuasoria,* 28; black horntail, 73; blue horntail female, male, 75; *Amara fulva,* 121; *Bembidion* spp., 122; *Carabus meander,* 123; European ground beetle, 124; *Elaphrus clairvillei,* 125; *Pterostichus adstrictus, Pterostichus melanarius,* 126; strawberry seed beetle, 127; twelve-spotted tiger beetle, 129; seven-spotted lady beetles, 139; *Phanerotoma libertinecida,* 192.

Peggy Greb, USDA: red flour beetle feeding, 115.

Patrick Hacala: Arctic blue, 201, 202–203.

Gene Herzberg: painted lady butterfly, 14, 224; phantom crane flies, 76; rusty tussock moth caterpillar, 166; Arctic skipper upperside, 194; Atlantis fritillary, 214; painted lady butterfly, 221; American lady underside, 223; white admiral butterfly, 226–227; common ringlet butterfly, 229; clouded sulphur, 238; Four-Spotted Skimmer, 288; mating pair, *Enallagma* sp., 291; Northern Spreadwing, 292.

Kirk Hillier: lingonberry fruitworm, 191.

Philip Hiscock: red-cross shield bug, 252.

Douglas Hnatiuk: Adams fly, 295.

Ryan Hodnett (licensed under CC BY-SA 4.0): multicoloured Asian lady beetle, 136.

Terrance Hounsell: wool-carder bees, 64, 65; larder beetle, 118.

Robbin Lindsay, Public Health Agency of Canada: adult female *Ixodes scapularis*, 308; American dog tick, 310.

Stephen Luk: black carpet beetle larva, pupal case, and adult, 117.

Laurent Jackman: apple sphinx moth caterpillar, 183; northern blues, 205; bog copper 209; monarch butterfly, 216–217.

Molly Jacobsen: house cricket, 267.

Jan Klimaszewski: *Aleochara bilineata*, 147; hairy rove beetle, 149; *Tachinis rufipes*, 149, *Atheta pseudovestita, Silusa prettyae*, 150.

Wayne Knee, Agriculture and Agri-Food Canada: mites, 307, 308.

Dave Larson: *Dytiscus dauricus*, 146; whirligig beetles, 152, 153.

Albert Legge: red-spotted snake millipede, 330.

Beatrice Lewis: short-tailed swallowtail caterpillar, 234.

Leah Madore: carrot rust fly larvae, 81; leatherjackets, 88; lady beetle larvae, 132; transverse lady beetle, 137; fourteen-spotted lady beetle, 141; green lacewing eggs, 155.

Katie March: yellow woolly bear caterpillar, 164.

Steve Marshall: carrot rust fly, 80; marsh lady beetle, 135; twenty-spotted lady beetle, 142; River Jewelwing, 293.

Darryl Martin: lingonberries, 191.

Stephen C. McKenzie: water striders, 27, 241, 255.

Mid-Island Veterinary Clinic: female rabbit tick, 300.

Hannah Munro: seabird ticks / common murres, 311.

Deborah Moreau: aphid colony, 242; aphid live birth, 243.

Tom Murray: book louse, 260.

National Maritime Museum, Greenwich, UK: barges collecting ballast, 80.

Maciej Olszewski, Adobe Stock: European earwig, 276.

Ryan Oram: andrenid bee scopa, 42; *Nomada cressoni,* 56; compact cellophane bee, 58; masked bee, *Hylaeus* sp., 58; *Specodes* sp., 62; *Osmia bucephela* female, 68; *Coelioxys* sp., 69.

Orkin Canada: bed bug, bat bug, 245; human head lice, 263.

Emily Papagiannis: spruce budworm moth, underside, 193.

Carolyn Parsons: bumble bee colony, 18; mourning cloak butterfly underside, 19, 220, cellophane bee, 28; sweat bee, 28; bee branched hair, 39; leafcutter bee nest, 39; mining bee nest entrance, 43; bumble bee corbicula, 45; male bumble bee sleeping, 46; half-black bumble bee worker, 48; male red-belted bumble bee (black form), 51; yellow toadflax flower, 54; cellophane bee, 57; leafcutter bee, 63; frigid leafcutter bee, 67; leafcutter bee circles, 67; cabbage maggot fly, 79; cabbage maggot larvae, 79; syrphid larva, 93; fungus gnat, 94; lake midge antennae, 95; lake midges on window screen, 95; European ground beetle, 110; museum pests, 117; larder beetle larva, 118; tiger beetle, 128; elderberry shrub damage, 143; black vine weevil, 151; green lacewing on cabbage leaf, 154; green lacewing pupa, 155; moth expanding its wings, 158; moth wing, 158; armyworm moth, 159; butterfly antennae, 160; feathery moth antennae, 161; satin moth caterpillar, 168; briseis underwing, 170–171; spear-marked black moth, 175; cutworm moth, 178; clear wing moth, 184–185; one-eyed sphinx moth wing, 188; twin-spotted sphinx moth, 189; tortricid moth, 190; spruce budworm moth, 193; Peck's skipper, 200; Peck's skipper underside, 200; northern spring azure, 206; Atlantis fritillary underside, 214; mud-puddling Canadian tiger swallowtail butterflies, 232; aphids, 240; winged aphid, 243; house pseudoscorpion, 312; flower crab spider with prey, 319.

Dennis Paulson: American Emerald, 285; Hudsonian Whiteface, 289.

Lee Peddle: American salmonfly, 274.

Claude Pilon: mottled stink bug, 19; mottled stink bug and nymphs, 252.

Andy Reago and Chrissy McClarren (licensed under CC BY 2.0): Canadian sphinx moth, 183.

Lucie Royer: *Aleochara bilineata* larva, 147.

Gilles San Martin (licensed by CC BY-SA 3.0): thirteen-spotted lady beetle, 140.

Sarefo (licensed under CC BY-SA 2.5): *Tribolium.confusum*, 115.

Udo Schmidt (licensed under CC BY-SA 2.0): *Trilobium castaneum*, red flour beetle, 115.

Alan Schmierer (licensed under CC0 1.0): greenish blue, 204.

Manfred Schulenburg (licensed under CC BY SA-4.0): seven-spotted lady beetle, 131.

Jeffrey W. Schultz: harvestman, *Phalangium opilio* male, 300.

Katja Schultz (licensed by CC BY 2.0): aphidlion, 154.

Walter Siegmund (licensed by CC BY-SA 3.0): *Calophrys augustinus*, brown elphin, 210.

Netta Smith: Taiga Bluet, 290.

Susan Leach Snyder, volunteer with the Environmental Science Division of the Conservancy of Southwest Florida: book louse, 264.

Judie Squires: black beach spider, 323.

Susan Squires: limestone barrens, 182.

Lt. James R. Steele, Steele Family Collection, Accession 07-115, Archives and Special Collections, Memorial University: Newfoundland Regiment, Gallipoli Peninsula 1915, 262.

Syrio (licensed under CC BY-SA 4.0): *Thermobia domestica*, firebrat, 299.

TheBookDetective (licensed under CC BY-SA 3.0): three-banded lady beetle, 137.

Terry Thormin: long-lipped tiger beetle, 130.

Clyde Thornhill: River Jewelwing, atypical form, 24; brush-tipped Emerald, 283.

US Center for Disease Prevention and Control: human pubic louse, 263.

USGS Bee Monitoring and Inventory Lab: ligated furrow bee, 40–41; Wilke's mining bee, 44; male modest masked bee, 59.

Joe Warfel: *Caddo agilis*, 304.

Hugh Whitney: trilobites, 16; fleas (from the collections of Ted Miller, Memorial University, and Peter Daley, Eastern Health), 108; spiked shield bug, 240; biting louse, sucking louse (collections of Ted Miller and Peter Daley), 261; finger mite galls, bladdermite galls, 306.

Corey Wight: northern grasshopper, 270.

Margie Wilkes: *Osmia inermis* nest, 68.

Philip Winters: mayfly, 294, 296–297; long-jawed orb weaver, 317, 318.

Brandon Woo: adult *Perillus exaptus*, 251.

Diane Young: bark louse, 265.

FURTHER READING/SELECTED REFERENCES

Acorn, J. 2007. *Ladybugs of Alberta. Finding the Spots and Connecting the Dots.* Edmonton, AB: University of Alberta Press.

Bitam, I., K. Dittmar, P. Parola, M.F. Whiting, and D. Raoult. 2010. "Fleas and Flea-borne Diseases." *International Journal of Infectious Diseases* 14: e667–e676.

Bousquet, Y., P. Bouchard, A.E. Davies, and D.S. Sikes. 2013. *Checklist of Beetles (Coleoptera) of Canada and Alaska.* 2nd edition. Sofia, Bulgaria: Pensoft Publ.

Brock, J.B., and K. Kaufman. 2003. *Kaufman Field Guide to Butterflies of North America.* New York, NY: Houghton Mifflin Company.

Cannings, R.A. 2002. *Introducing the Dragonflies of British Columbia and the Yukon.* Victoria, BC: Royal British Columbia Museum.

Erbland, M. 2008. *Island Insects. A Photographic Potpourri of Newfoundland "Bugs."* Logy Bay, NL: JustPhotos.ca Publ.

Fraser, H., and T. Baute. 2013. "Brown Marmorated Stink Bug." Ontario Ministry of Agriculture, Food and Rural Affairs. http://www.omafra.gov.on.ca/english/crops/facts/info_bmstinkbug.htm.

Goulson, D. 2010. *Bumblebees: Behaviour, Ecology and Conservation.* Oxford, UK: Oxford University Press.

Kirk, W.D.J. 1996. *Thrips.* Naturalists' Handbooks 25. Slough, UK: The Richmond Publishing Company.

Klimaszewski, J., D. Langor, D. Pelletier, C. Bourdon, and L. Perdereau. 2011. *The Aleocharine Beetles (Coleoptera, Staphylinidae) of the Province of Newfoundland and Labrador, Canada.* Sofia, Bulgaria: Pensoft Publ.

Larson, D.J., and M.H. Colbo. 1983. "The Aquatic Insects: Some Biogeographical Considerations." In *Biogeography and Ecology of the Island of Newfoundland*, edited by G.R. South. The Hague-Boston-London: Dr. W. Junk Publishers.

Layberry, R., P. Hall, and D. Lafontaine. 1998. *The Butterflies of Canada.* Toronto, ON: University of Toronto Press, Scholarly Publishing Division.

Lindberg, H. 1958. "Hemiptera Heteroptera from Newfoundland, Collected by the Swedish-Finnish Expedition of 1949 and 1951." *Acta Zoologica Fennica* 96. Zoological Institute Helsingfors University. http://research.amnh.org/pbi/library/0539.pdf.

Lindquist, E.E., T.D. Galloway, H. Artsob, L.R. Lindsay, M. Drebot, H. Wood, and R.G. Robbins. 2016. *A Handbook to the Ticks of Canada*

(Ixodida: Ixodidae, Argasidae). Biological Survey of Canada Monograph Series No. 7. http://biologicalsurvey.ca/public/Bsc/Controller/Page/AGR-001-Ticks-Monograph.pdf.

Mallory, C. 2012. *Common Insects of Nunavut*. Iqaluit, NU: Inhabit Media Inc. http://nbes.ca/wp-content/uploads/2014/03/Common-Insects-of-Nunavut-low-res.pdf.

Marshall, S.A. 2012. *Flies. The Natural History and Diversity of Diptera*. Richmond Hill, ON: Firefly Books Ltd.

Marshall, S.A. 2017. *Insects. Their Natural History and Diversity*. 2nd edition. Richmond Hill, ON: Firefly Books Ltd.

Marshall, S.A. 2018. Beetles. *The Natural History and Diversity of Coleoptera*. Richmond Hill, ON: Firefly Books Ltd.

McAlister, E. 2017. *The Secret Life of Flies*. Richmond Hill, ON: Firefly Books Ltd.

Morris, R.F. 1980. *Butterflies and Moths of Newfoundland and Labrador. The Macrolepidoptera*. Publication 1691, Minister of Supply and Services, Canada.

Paiero, S.M., S.A. Marshall, J.E. McPherson, and M.-S. Ma. 2013. "Stink Bugs (Pentatomidae) and Parent Bugs (Acanthosomatidae) of Ontario and Adjacent Areas: A Key to Species and a Review of the Fauna." *Canadian Journal of Arthropod Identification* 24. doi:10.3752/cjai.2013.24. https://cjai.biologicalsurvey.ca/pmmm_24/pmmm_24.html.

Paulson, D. 2011. *Dragonflies and Damselflies of the East*. Princeton, NJ: Princeton University Press

Pohl, G.R., J.-F. Landry, B.C. Schmidt, J.D. Lafontaine, J.T. Troubridge, A.D. Macaulay, E.J. Van Nieukerken, J.R. DeWaard, J.J. Dombroskie, J. Klymko, V. Nazari, and K. Stead. 2018. *Annotated Checklist of the Moths and Butterflies (Lepidoptera) of Canada and Alaska*. Sofia, Bulgaria: Pensoft Publ.

Schiff, N.M., H. Goulet, D.R. Smith, C. Boudreault, A.D. Wilson, and B.E. Scheffler. 2012. "Siricidae (Hymenoptera: Symphyta: Siricoidea) of the Western Hemisphere." *Canadian Journal of Arthropod Identification* 21. doi:10.3752/cjai.2012.21.

Walter, D.E., and H.C. Proctor. 2013. *Mites: Ecology, Evolution & Behaviour: Life at a Microscale*. 2nd edition. New York: Springer Science.

Williams, P., R. Thorp, L. Richardson, and S. Colla. 2014. *Bumble Bees of North America: An Identification Guide*. Princeton, NJ: Princeton University Press.

Wilson, J.S., and O.J. Messinger Carril. 2016. *The Bees in Your Backyard: A Guide to North America's Bees*. Princeton, NJ: Princeton University Press.

ACKNOWLEDGEMENTS

We appreciate all those who contributed photos, which are such an integral part of this book. We also sincerely thank colleagues and friends who provided information or kindly reviewed previous drafts of the text, including Frederic Beaulieu, Jeremy Bono, Pat Bouchard, Chris Buddle, Robert Cannings, Kate Carson, Murray Colbo, Peter Daley, Henri Goulet, Barry Hicks, Ian Jones, Wayne Knee, David Langor, David Larson, Robbin Lindsay, John Maunder, Eric Maw, Ted Miller, Laurence Mound, NL Veterinary Medical Association, Ryan Oram, Dennis Paulson, Roger Pickavance, Greg Pohl, Sean Rollo, Jeffrey Schultz, Cory Sheffield, Jeff Skevington, and Jim Woodrow.

Special thanks to the Facebook group "Insects of Newfoundland" for their shared interest in this part of the natural world and for the various contributions they have made, and to bugguide.net for providing access to many interested professional and amateur entomologists.

Finally, we would like to thank Boulder Books for their Field Guide series and agreeing to produce this entry in it, and our editor, Stephanie Porter, for her patient approach to managing four different authors, all with different interests and writing styles.

Carolyn, Hugh, Peggy, and Tom

ABOUT THE AUTHORS

TOM CHAPMAN, a behavioural and evolutionary ecologist whose taxonomic focus is insects, has studied ants, bees, mosquitoes, thrips, ticks, and wasps. Tom has been part of the Faculty of Science at Memorial University since 2007; his duties have included teaching Introduction to Entomology, a third-year undergraduate course, with the primary ambition of inspiring an appreciation for insects among Memorial's biology students.

PEGGY DIXON, an entomologist with Agriculture and Agri-Food Canada in St. John's since 1992, is an adjunct professor at Memorial University. Her fascination with insects and their relatives started with her first insect collection at age 10. Although Peggy has a particular fondness for beetles and aphids, she has worked with many different arthropod groups. Peggy is an avid reader and traveller and is involved with dragonboating, weightlifting, and science fiction conventions.

CAROLYN PARSONS, part of the entomology laboratory at Agriculture and Agri-Food Canada since 2000, has an interest in sustainable agriculture and the role of diversity in creating balanced agroecosystems. Insect identification is not only a job but a hobby for Carolyn; she is keen on documenting and sharing the diversity of insects in Newfoundland and Labrador. Carolyn loves travel and outdoor activities, including fishing, snowshoeing, and hiking.

HUGH WHITNEY worked for 30 years as this province's chief veterinary officer (1985–2015). In the latter half of that time he was also, and continues to be, an adjunct professor at Memorial University. This brought him into the realities of surveillance, research, and public education for arthropod-borne diseases of interest to the public, such as Lyme disease and West Nile virus infection. He has also published three children's books in the series *The Adventures of Uapikun*.

D is for dows'y poll,
Moth of the night;
He sloos at my window
In search of the light;
Some call him a miller,
But where is his mill?
He seems far from home
When he lands on my sill.

—Tom Dawe, *Alley-Coosh, Bibby, and Cark*